## More Praise for *Infinite Vision*

"In an increasingly complex world where making money and doing good are dichotomized, this thought-provoking story of Dr. V and the Aravind Eye Care System should be required reading for current and future business and charity leaders. Only by breaking down the false separation between business practices and community needs will our societies prosper."

**—Dr. Pamela Hartigan, Director, Skoll Centre for Social Entrepreneurship, University of Oxford, and coauthor of *The Power of Unreasonable People***

"Most business books completely fail to communicate the human and intuitive side of organizational and business success. This book explores both very effectively while describing practical achievements as well. If you aspire to combine entrepreneurship and innovation with higher life purpose, then there can be no better guide than *Infinite Vision* and the life of Dr. V. But beware. Once you are ensnared, it will be impossible to escape!"

**—Tim Brown, CEO, IDEO, and author of *Change by Design***

"A deftly crafted book that relates how Aravind triumphed in business by focusing on compassion. It is rich with lessons that come to life through the vivid personalities of Aravind's torchbearers—their insights on leadership and management forge a path forward for the social as well as corporate sectors. An important and compelling read."

**—V. Kasturi Rangan, Malcolm P. McNair Professor of Marketing, Harvard Business School, and cofounder of the HBS Social Enterprise Initiative**

"A stirring account of how one man's faith and pragmatism healed millions. *Infinite Vision* is a powerful reminder that any of us can overcome the most severe of obstacles and rise to unparalleled heights of spiritual and practical achievement."

**—Huston Smith, Professor of Religion and Distinguished Adjunct Professor of Philosophy, Emeritus, Syracuse University, and author of *The World's Religions***

"*Infinite Vision* offers a lucid and moving account of the Aravind story while detailing its greatest lesson to the world: compassion, when focused with clear goals, thoughtful strategies, and sound management practices, can yield incredible results."
—**Steve Hilton, President and CEO, Conrad N. Hilton Foundation**

"Those seeking inspiration from a spiritual journey or insight into innovative business practices—attributes not normally found in the same story—will benefit from this narration of a profoundly impactful adventure."
—**Dr. Alfred Sommer, MHS, Dean Emeritus, Johns Hopkins Bloomberg School of Public Health**

"This is that rare book that informs you on how to put your compassion to work. Through the accessible genius of the Aravind model of business, you will find a gateway with a road map for you to find your own personal brand of compassion in your work and in your life."
—**Dr. Mark S. Albion, cofounder, Net Impact, and author of *True to Yourself* and *Making a Life, Making a Living***

"A story about an organizational marvel, this book is somehow internally illuminated. It has plot, poetry, and emotion—things you don't expect from a business title. The writing pierces through management abstractions, and what remains is the rootedness of a family, the crazy-beautiful daring, the labor and the thrift, the sense of 'what else is there to do?'"
—**Amulya Gopalakrishnan, columnist, *Indian Express***

"Surgery, service, soul, and sustainability weave together in this inspiring true story. The messages of this book transcend health care and business—they speak to the potential that lives within each of us."
—**Dr. William Stewart, cofounder, Institute for Health & Healing, California Pacific Medical Center, and author of *Deep Medicine***

"Expertly weaves through the challenges and opportunities encountered in transforming a small eye clinic into the largest eye hospital in the world. This story is a gift to aspiring change makers and leaders everywhere. Its visionary protagonist is one of the real heroes of our times."
—**Dr. Suzanne Gilbert, founding member, Seva Foundation, and Director, Center for Innovation in Eye Care**

# INFINITE VISION

# INFINITE VISION

## How Aravind Became the World's Greatest
## Business Case for Compassion

◇◇◇◇◇◇◇◇◇◇◇◇◇◇◇◇◇◇◇◇

Pavithra K. Mehta

Suchitra Shenoy

Berrett–Koehler Publishers, Inc.
San Francisco
*a BK Business book*

Berrett-Koehler Publishers, Inc.
235 Montgomery Street, Suite 650
San Francisco, CA 94104-2916
Tel: (415) 288-0260     Fax: (415) 362-2512     www.bkconnection.com

ORDERING INFORMATION
*Quantity sales.* Special discounts are available on quantity purchases by corporations, associations, and others. For details, contact the "Special Sales Department" at the Berrett-Koehler address above.
*Individual sales.* Berrett-Koehler publications are available through most bookstores. They can also be ordered directly from Berrett-Koehler: Tel: (800) 929-2929; Fax: (802) 864-7626; www.bkconnection.com
*Orders for college textbook/course adoption use.* Please contact Berrett-Koehler: Tel: (800) 929-2929; Fax: (802) 864-7626.
*Orders by U.S. trade bookstores and wholesalers.* Please contact Ingram Publisher Services, Tel: (800) 509-4887; Fax: (800) 838-1149; E-mail: customer .service@ingrampublisherservices.com; or visit www.ingrampublisherservices .com/Ordering for details about electronic ordering.

Berrett-Koehler and the BK logo are registered trademarks of Berrett-Koehler Publishers, Inc.

PRINTED IN THE UNITED STATES OF AMERICA
Berrett-Koehler books are printed on long-lasting acid-free paper. When it is available, we choose paper that has been manufactured by environmentally responsible processes. These may include using trees grown in sustainable forests, incorporating recycled paper, minimizing chlorine in bleaching, or recycling the energy produced at the paper mill.

LIBRARY OF CONGRESS CATALOGING-IN-PUBLICATION DATA
Mehta, Pavithra K.
Infinite vision : how Aravind became the world's greatest business case for compassion / Pavithra K. Mehta, Suchitra Shenoy. -- 1st ed.
    p. ; cm.
Includes bibliographical references and index.
ISBN 978-1-60509-979-8 (pbk. : alk. paper)
I. Shenoy, Suchitra. II. Title.
[DNLM: 1. Aravind Eye Hospital (Madurai, India) 2. Hospitals, Special--history--India. 3. Ophthalmology--history--India. 4. Eye Diseases--therapy--India. 5. Health Services Accessibility--history--India. 6. History, 20th Century--India. 7. History, 21st Century--India. 8. Quality Assurance, Health Care--history--India. WW 28 JI4]

FIRST EDITION
18  17  16  15  14  13  12  11          10  9  8  7  6  5  4  3  2  1

INTERIOR DESIGN: Laura Lind Design          COPYEDITOR: Elissa Rabellino
PROOFREADER: Henrietta Bensussen          COVER DESIGN: The Book
BOOK PRODUCER: Linda Jupiter Productions          Designers/Ian Shimkoviak

*To Dr. Thatha, who lit our world.*

*The banyan tree you planted is well and strong.*

# CONTENTS

◇◇◇◇◇◇◇◇◇◇◇◇◇◇◇◇◇

# THE ARAVIND FAMILY TREE
### (ABRIDGED VERSION)

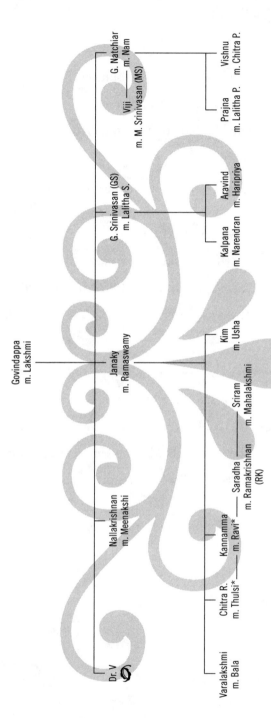

Govindappa
m. Lakshmi

Janaky
m. Ramaswamy

Nallakrishnan
m. Meenakshi

G. Srinivasan (GS)
m. Lalitha S.

G. Natchiar
m. Nam

Viji
m. M. Srinivasan (MS)

Dr. V

Varalakshmi
m. Bala

Chitra R.
m. Thulsi*

Kannamma
— m. Ravi* —

Saradha
m. Ramakrishnan
(RK)

Sriram
m. Mahalakshmi

Kim
m. Usha

Kalpana
m. Narendran

Aravind
m. Haripriya

Prajna
m. Lalitha P.

Vishnu
m. Chitra P.

People are listed by their first name.
Nam is Viji's elder brother.

*Two sisters, Kannamma and Chitra R., married two brothers, Ravi and Thulsi. Sriram and Saradha are siblings of Ravi and Thulsi; their parents are R. Duraisamy and Chellamma (not shown here).

# MEET THE FAMILY

The names of Dr. V's family members are scattered through the book, some more frequently than others. The relationships are multitudinous, the polysyllabic names somewhat daunting, and the usage of monikers common. As you read *Infinite Vision*, if you lose track of who's who in this very extended family, you can look people up in "Meet the Family" (the final listing in the Resource section at the back of the book).

# THE POWER AND PARADOX
# OF ARAVIND

His journal entries from the 1980s read as electrifying notes to self:

*Attachment to your village, your hospital, your state or country—that must go. You must live in your soul and face the universal consciousness. To see all as one.*

*To have this vision and work with strength and wisdom all over the world.*

Perhaps the white-haired man with curiously gnarled fingers paused here for a moment before scrawling the next line.

*To give sight for all.*

❧

THE IMPOSSIBLE RARELY deterred Dr. Govindappa Venkataswamy. As a young surgeon, he watched a crippling disease permanently twist and freeze his fingers out of shape. Those fingers went on to delicately perform more than 100,000 sight-restoring surgeries, but Dr. V, as he came to be known, would not stop there. In 1976, he founded Aravind, an eye clinic operating out of a family home in South India. He was 58 years old. Aravind was his post-retirement project, created with no money, business plan, or safety net. What it did have was 11 beds—and an oversized mission. Its mission was to eliminate curable blindness.

At Aravind, if you could not pay for surgery, you did not have to. If you could not reach the clinic, its doctors would come to you. At first glance, it seemed a venture far too quixotic to be effective. But when intuitive goodness is pitted against unthinkable odds, it stirs the imagination and awakens possibility.

Dr. V integrated a heart of service and deep spiritual aspiration with the best practices of business. In this way, he forged a high-volume, high-quality, and affordable approach to service delivery that would expand to put a serious dent in a problem of global proportions. Today, the Aravind Eye Care System is the largest and most productive blindness-prevention organization on the planet. During the last 35 years, its network of five eye hospitals in South India have treated more than 32 million patients and performed more than 4 million surgeries, the majority either ultrasubsidized or free.[1]

Think David and Goliath: a man stands up in all his devastating frailty, fights the good fight, and wins a victory for humanity. Aravind is luminous proof of what is possible in our world. Dr. V's compassionate vision and the work of his 3,200-person team (including 21 ophthalmologists across three generations of his family) have captured the attention of individuals as diverse as Bill Clinton, England's Princess Alexandra, and management icon Peter Drucker. The organization consults for Nobel laureate Muhammad Yunus and was visited by Google's celebrity cofounder Larry Page; and a case study on Aravind's work is mandatory reading for every MBA student at the Harvard Business School. In 2008 Aravind won the Gates Award for Global Health, the Hilton Humanitarian Prize followed in 2010, and in that same year Aravind's chief executive officer made it to *Time* magazine's list of the 100 most influential people in the world.

None of this means that Aravind is a perfect organization. Its leaders are regular people who struggle, make mistakes, and chafe against their limitations. They are fallible like the rest of us, with only this difference: together, these ordinary individuals made a series of uncommon decisions and commitments that resulted in something extraordinary.

In a country of 12 million blind, where the majority lives on less than $2 a day, Aravind ripped the price tag off of sight-restoring surgery, treating more than a third of its patients at no charge. Simultaneously, it insisted on financial self-reliance, resolving not to depend on government aid, private donations, or foreign funding. Even more curiously, in a move to preserve its patients' dignity and self-esteem, Aravind allowed them to decide for themselves whether or not they would pay. In its self-selecting system, there are no eligibility criteria to be met, no income assessments done. A barefoot farmer can choose to pay for surgery, while the man destined to be president of India can opt to receive high-quality treatment for free (true story). It is a generous arrangement, all the more intriguing for being vigorously profitable. Aravind is a nonprofit organization that consistently runs a substantial operating surplus. Its patient services and major expansion projects are entirely self-funded.

In another paradoxical twist, Aravind's marketing strategies target those least able to pay. The organization invests tremendous energy in bringing eye care to villagers too poor to seek out its services. Its policies ensure that *all* patients get the same high standard of care. The same doctors work across both free and paid services, and patient outcomes hold their own in comparisons with those of the best hospitals in the world. In a recent like-for-like assessment of its surgical performance against the United Kingdom's Royal College of Ophthalmologists, Aravind's overall complication rates were found to be less than those of its British counterpart.[2]

Defying the assumption that high-quality surgery cannot be performed at high volumes, its doctors are among the most productive in the world. Aravind surgeons average 2,000 cataract surgeries a year, against the Indian average of 400 surgeries and the United States' average of under 200.[3] The efficiencies that enable this achievement help make Aravind one of the lowest-cost, highest-quality eye care systems in the world.

Its focus on the penniless does not preclude a breadth or sophistication of services. Aravind's hospitals attract not just the poor but also hundreds of thousands of individuals with the financial means to pick and choose between service providers across the country. It offers a comprehensive range of specialty care, covering everything from corneal ulcers to cancer of the eye. The organization also runs a global research foundation and a postgraduate teaching institute that has trained 15 percent of all ophthalmologists in India.[4] Its short-term fellowships continue to attract residents from leading medical schools around the world (including the Johns Hopkins School of Medicine and the Massachusetts Eye and Ear teaching hospital of Harvard Medical School).

Taking on a goal that far exceeds your capacity has a powerful side effect. It primes you to find allies everywhere. At Aravind, a global mission led to a counterintuitive commitment to training its competition. The organization works with other hospitals, many in its own backyard, helping them to replicate the Aravind model. Not only does it permit others to copy the very systems that give it a competitive advantage—it encourages them to do so. Aravind runs a training and consulting service that has worked with more than 270 hospitals and trained thousands of health care professionals from 69 different countries.[5]

This is a spirited organization that followed the dictates of mission into perilous territory—and lived to tell the tale. When the intraocular lens implant that revolutionized cataract surgery in the West proved too expensive to import for all of Aravind's patients, the organization took a brave step. Against informed opinion and global pressure, it set up its own internationally certified manufacturing facility. Its high-quality implants dropped the price from $150 to $10, making the lenses affordable not just for its own patients but also for the rest of India and other developing countries as well. Today, its ophthalmic exports are indirectly responsible for improving surgical outcomes for millions of patients in more than 120 countries.

These individual actions, amazing in themselves, collectively speak to something more. They are uplifting evidence that an organization with a social mission does not have to depend on external funding; or run at a loss; or make compromises in efficiency, scale, quality, or scope. In all these ways, Aravind is a glowing exception to the usual rules.

Over the decades, numerous case studies and magazine articles have attempted to explain its success. Most of them seek to answer the same implicit question: How has Aravind reached its current scale and prosperity despite giving away specialized, high-quality services for free?

The framing of that question tends to limit the scope of the answer. Aravind is an unconventional model that came into being not despite but *because of* the deep-seated compassion at its core. This is a model that demonstrates the power of integrating innovation with empathy, business principles with service, and outer transformation with inner change.

From this perspective, a new line of inquiry emerges. How did Aravind design a model such that wealthy patients and those in greatest need benefit from each other? What values, experiences, and insights spurred its leaders to make the unexpected choices that they did? How did these choices influence the organization's efficiency, sustainability, and scale? And, at a time when Western health care systems are in crisis and social enterprises are proliferating across multiple sectors, is Aravind an inspiring singularity or a repeatable miracle?

These are some of the puzzles examined in this book. And at its core is a simple riddle that entwines them all: If Aravind is the extraordinary answer, what were Dr. V's questions?

To understand the Aravind model—what made it work and what continues to fuel its expansion and impact—one must look into the heart and mind of the visionary surgeon who set it all into motion. In that sense, this book is an invitation to walk a while with Dr. V, see the world as he saw it, meet the people who would join him, and catch a glimpse of the lives they touch. In the end, it is an invitation to experience a spark of that which drives our deepest intentions to action.

*To see all as one. To give sight for all.* Ultimately, Dr. V's vision and Aravind's work draw an arc between the practical and the profound. This story lives on that arc. It is the tale of a revolutionary business model set in the developing world, focused on the sustainable delivery of eyesight. But it is also the journey of an unlikely hero with an impossible dream, whose story (not without its share of snarls and unresolved dilemmas) transcends its own specificity to speak of universal truths: To be of service to others is to serve ourselves. Our limitations do not define us. And embedded in the human spirit is a wisdom and strength that can rise to meet our greatest challenges. Together we can light the eyes of millions.

# CLIMBING EVEREST

In an interview with Aravind's founder, questions shoot out like impatient arrows from Justin Huggler, Asia correspondent for the British newspaper *The Independent*: "How? How did you do it all? How do you keep on keeping on the way you do? How do you persuade so many others to do the same?"[6]

Dr. V, who can sometimes be very somber during interviews, is at his sunniest. He smiles and says nothing. "How did you manage to do it all, Dr. V?" Huggler persists, and Dr. V chortles. "You know, there are people who have climbed Mount Everest," he says in his strongly accented English. When you spend some time with Dr. V, you eventually begin to understand his seemingly irrelevant answers to questions that refer too closely to the grandeur of his achievements. But this is Huggler's first meeting with Dr. V, so he tries again.

"Yes, but it takes people four weeks to climb Everest, and then they go home and holiday. You've been doing this work day after day after day—how do you do it?"

"People are good at heart; they help you."

"Maybe, but they're also lazy. How did you make this to work?"

Huggler is determined to get somewhere. And after a few more digressions on Everest, unexpectedly he does.

"You see, when people need help, you can't simply run away, no?" says Dr. V. "You say, I will help you, and then you do what you can.

Even when we started, we did good-quality work, so the rich people came and paid us, and we could treat the poor people with the money saved. The poor people brought more poor people; the rich people brought more rich people. So now, here we are."

The man has fit his entire life's work and the evolution of the largest eye care system in the world into five sentences.

Huggler laughs, and his face relaxes for the first time. "Amazing," he says, "this is just amazing." His wonder is still laced with a journalist's curiosity. "But what motivates people to stay and work so hard here when they could have things so much easier somewhere else?"

"What motivates people to climb mountains?" asks Dr. V in return. "It isn't easy to climb Everest, but people do it anyway—isn't it?"

In somewhat more than five sentences, here is a study of that climb.

PART I

# THE 5-MINUTE, $15 CURE
## On Efficiency and Compassion

*My goal is to spread the Aravind model to every*

*nook and corner of India, Asia, and Africa; wherever there*

*is blindness, we want to offer hope. Tell me, what is this*

*concept of franchising? Can't we do what McDonald's and*

*Burger King have done?*

—Dr. V, in an interview from "Aravind Eye Hospital,
Madurai, India: In Service for Sight" (Harvard Business School
case study), by V. Kasturi Rangan, 1993

# OF BURGERS AND BLINDNESS

**B**uilt in the shape of a lotus, Madurai is one of the oldest cities of South India. Home to a million people, it is a dense cultural center, famed for its lofty poetry, heady jasmine, and legendary goddess ruler, Meenakshi. At the heart of Madurai lies the massive complex of the Meenakshi Amman temple, whose origins are believed to trace back as far as 6 BC. The temperamental river Vaigai, which alternates between trickle and monsoon flood, divides the city in two. On one side rise the distant towers of the temple, and on the other is a street that has gradually been taken over by an expanding empire for eye care.

On this spring morning the banana man's cart, festooned with garlands of his yellow fruit, is parked in its customary place. A woman slaps laundry against a stone block on the sidewalk, and clotheslines slung from crowded balconies flutter in the breeze. A beanpole of a man weaves through traffic on a bicycle, holding a cell phone to his ear. Straight ahead, a bus has been held up by a herd of buffalos. Road dividers and traffic lights make a stab at order, but there are cheerful violations everywhere.

This is not an easy country to regulate, not its streets and certainly not its health care. Lawsuits have not deeply permeated India's medical profession, and the kind of stringent mandates and regulations that govern Western medicine are often absent or ill enforced. It is the dawn of the 21st century, and health insurance for the masses is only beginning to emerge here. The vast majority of patients pay out of pocket for private care or seek subsidized service in government hospitals that are overcrowded, understaffed, and rife with serious performance issues. The road to care can be hazardous in such an environment. But there are exceptions.

Up ahead, a frail, elderly woman sits sidesaddle on a scooter behind her son. A green post-surgery patch over her left eye gives her an unexpected rakish air. On this street, such pirate-patients are common—they are evidence that a small miracle of sight has recently occurred. The scooter turns the corner at 1 Anna Nagar, where a pale blue five-story building rises behind a stone wall. Brass letters on black granite announce "Aravind Eye Hospital." The wrought iron gates bearing a flowerlike symbol are open, and the scooter carrying the woman with the green eye patch drives in. Today she will be one of the 7,500 patients that Aravind's network of care examines on a daily basis.

According to the World Health Organization's estimates, 39 million people in the world are blind, 80 percent of them needlessly so.[1] "Needless blindness" is a curious turn of phrase you can't escape at Aravind. It refers to the urgent fact that some forms of blindness are entirely within our power to treat or prevent. Cataract is a prime example. A word whose origins lie in the Greek word for "waterfall," it refers to the clouding of the eye's lens. Painless but progressive, if left untreated, cataract leads from blurred vision to total blindness. A simple one-time operation can restore sight, but the sobering fact is that cataract still accounts for more than 60 percent of blindness in India.[2]

〇

DR. V STANDS in the hallway, quietly observing the registration queue. Patients take no notice of the elderly man with the close-cropped white hair and walking stick. The founder of Aravind is easily overlooked in a crowd. He is a man of unremarkable height and weight, with stooped shoulders and a serious face. Today he is wearing a wrinkled white shirt and no doctor's coat or badge. But those gnarled fingers are unmistakable. On his right hand is a ring that bears the same symbol as the one on the hospital gates. All the founding members of Aravind wear this ring; it is a reminder of a particular spiritual inspiration.

Dr. V bends down slowly, and with difficulty. Two nurses rush forward but are too late. He picks up a discarded candy wrapper (a vintage practice of his), scans the now-spotless floor, and then heads back toward his office.

Aravind was founded by a small band of siblings. Dr. Govindappa Venkataswamy, known to much of the world as Dr. V, was the eldest of five children, and after the early death of their father, he took on the responsibility of educating the others, guiding their careers, and arranging their marriages (as is still the custom in much of India). He himself chose to live a life of celibacy, devoting everything to his family and to the service of the sightless.

In 1976, he asked his siblings (and their spouses) to join him in running a tiny eye clinic *and* to treat patients who could not afford to pay them for free. There was no graceful way to refuse. To say it grew from there is an understatement. The Aravind Eye Care System is now the largest provider of eye surgeries in the world. By 2010, it was seeing more than 2.5 million patients and performing 300,000 surgeries a year.[3] The family's involvement spiraled out, and the employee roster at Aravind now resembles the guest list of a typical Indian wedding.

In the office next door to Dr. V's sits one of his nephews, a man whose grade school report cards Dr. V inspected three decades ago. "If somebody is blind, that's our problem," says Dr. Aravind Srinivasan. "It doesn't matter whether they have money or not. The problem is ours." This charismatic 30-something man is the sole surgeon-MBA in the organization he shares a name with. "Our view of the world is very different because of Dr. V," he continues. "Over time, he has built a conviction in us that serving the poor is good. That giving most of your services away for free is good." He breaks into a boyish grin. "Basically, he has corrupted our view of the world."[4]

Dr. Aravind heads out the door of his office. He is the administrator of the hospital but still operates three mornings a week and cannot be late; punctuality is a religion here. It is 7:30 a.m., and the corridors, waiting rooms, and registration counters are alive with ordered activity. Thirty-three operating theaters across Aravind's five hospitals (each located in different cities and small towns of Tamil Nadu) are already in full swing. By this afternoon, a thousand patients, rich and poor, will have received surgery across the system. "Our focus is on human welfare," says Dr. V. "If a man can't pay me, it doesn't matter. He will give later if he can."[5]

In the early 1990s, a visitor with floppy gray hair walked into Aravind. At the counter he took out a checkbook, but was politely informed that checks were not accepted and he would need to pay in cash. Having no cash on him, he inquired whether it was possible to be treated in Aravind's free section. Yes, it was. Minutes later, the director of Aravind received a frantic phone call. It was from the visitor's security team, who had lost track of him in the corridors. As the story goes, Dr. Abdul Kalam was located in the free division of the hospital, thrilled with the quality of care he had just received. Kalam went on to become the president of India and a dear friend of the organization. And this episode became one of Aravind's legends. It illustrates the unusual degree of choice—and universal high-quality treatment—accorded to patients here.

Thulsi Ravilla, a nephew of Dr. V's by marriage and the organization's very first managerial hire, presents another startling facet of the organization. "The National Health Service for the United Kingdom does a little over half a million eye surgeries annually; Aravind does roughly 300,000," he says.[6] That a single organization in a developing country does about 50 percent of the ophthalmic surgical volume of one of the world's most advanced nations is a compelling fact, but not the punch line. Thulsi's next data point typically drops jaws: Aravind does this *at less than 1 percent* of Britain's costs. The latter's National Health Service spends 1.6 billion pounds annually on eye care delivery against Aravind's modest 13.8 million pounds.[7] "The reasons go beyond a simplistic 'Britain isn't India,' explanation," says Thulsi. While external factors like regional economies, regulations, and cultural expectations are valid differences between East and West, Thulsi maintains that myriad other aspects feed into the numbers and must be taken into account. Things like efficiency, clinical processes, and cost-control measures. "Decoding all this can bring answers to most developed countries," he says.[8]

"High volume, high quality, and affordable cost" is the tri-part mantra of the Aravind model. It can seem disappointingly simplistic in the beginning. Provide good service to enough people, and you can keep your prices low and still make a profit. But the real genius of the Aravind model lies in the mindset behind it, the well-crafted processes and all the built-in interdependencies.

How do you create a system that thrives on generosity, one that actually benefits from serving those most in need? How do you engineer an organization that demonstrates repeatedly that high-quality surgical outcomes can be fostered, not threatened, by high volume; and how do you, in the developing-world context, link high quality with affordability—or more radically still, with "free"? The answers to these questions weave together as inextricable threads in the fabric of Aravind. Each influences, and is affected by, the others. "Fundamentally, it's not just numbers that we are chasing. There is a synergy between quality, cost, and the demand for services," says Thulsi.

The first glimpse of that synergy came from a very unlikely place.

❧

No one knows when Dr. V first came up with the delicious non sequitur that linked eye care service delivery with hamburgers, but his fascination with the golden arches of McDonald's is part of Aravind lore now. Sidestepping the notoriety of the world's most successful fast-food chain and the controversies over its public health impact, Dr. V saw in McDonald's the power of standardization, product recognition, accessibility, and scale. "Just as fast food is affordable to many lower-middle-class families in the West, in developing countries we can organize to provide affordable cataract operations," he declared in an interview in the late 1980s.[9] Even close colleagues found his "hamburger talk" a little absurd. But Dr. V's outlandish references were vindicated in the late '90s by Regina Herzlinger, one of America's leading advocates for health care reform. In her book *Market-Driven Health Care*, Herzlinger analyzed the McDonald's Corporation's service system. Why McDonald's? "Because week after week, year after year, it demonstrates how to attain exactly the qualities that the health-care system needs—consistency, reliability, clear standards, and low costs—in each of its 20,000 restaurants all around the world."[10]

Following the 11-bed clinic Dr. V opened in 1976 came a hospital with 600 beds in 1981. Aravind's second and third hospitals were opened in 1984 and 1988. By the first decade of the new millennium, there were three more Aravind Eye Hospitals across the state of Tamil Nadu, totaling more than 3,200 beds. Dr. V launched all of this starting with a grand total of just five ophthalmologists by his side.

In order to amplify each surgeon's impact and reach the most people in need, he brought in assembly-line techniques and engineered hospital systems that eventually allowed his doctors to perform close to five times more surgeries than the national average. An intensively trained cadre of paraprofessionals, or midlevel ophthalmic personnel (Aravind's designation for them) was also key to making this possible. The two-year training program they undergo has been accredited by the Joint Commission on Allied Health Personnel in Ophthalmology in the United States (JCAHPO).

A routine eye checkup at Aravind entails registration, basic vision testing, a preliminary doctor's examination, measurement of ocular pressure, pupil dilation, and a final examination. If surgery is recommended, detailed counseling takes place to ensure that the patient fully understands the process. Typically an ophthalmologist would perform the bulk of these duties. But at Aravind the entire stream of patient-centric activities, from entry to discharge, is broken up into sets of discrete tasks. Aravind's army of paraprofessionals performs most of these tasks (except for the preliminary exam and the final diagnosis, which are done by doctors). This group includes nurses, counselors, refractionists, and ophthalmic technicians, among a dozen different subcadres, each specialized in a clearly defined set of recurring duties.[11]

A similar role designation is seen in Aravind's operating rooms and postoperative wards. The result is a system that powerfully maximizes the time and skill of Aravind's surgeons. Everything is geared to allow these doctors to focus almost exclusively on diagnosing patients and performing operations. In this way, with less than 1 percent of the country's ophthalmic power, Aravind is able to perform 5 percent of all eye care procedures in India.[12]

A mindset geared toward constant process innovation also contributes to this record-breaking efficiency. From Aravind's earliest years, Dr. V urged his team to reexamine their systems for unnecessary delays and avoidable irregularities, and to find key leverage points in their process where small shifts could yield a significant impact. His journal entries across the decades reflect these preoccupations.

Dr. V has accumulated close to 100 journals over his lifetime. Their yellowing pages carry the forgettable details of various conferences, research papers, projects, hospital inventory, and meticulous accounts. But among these prosaic notes are meditations on life's purpose, frank self-assessments, and questions—copious questions. Inquiry is a deep part of his nature, and Dr. V's private catechism embraces both abiding mysteries and transient practical concerns. In a founding-year entry from 1976, he wrote: *How to train nurses for post-op dressing. How many tables do we need to operate 30 patients a week. Do we have enough operating sets. Can we start operating earlier in the day. What if we had another facility.*[13]

It is striking that in the tens of thousands of journal entries Dr. V has penned over the decades, he almost never uses question marks—as if to him, framing the right question is in itself an answer of sorts.

❧

THE HOSPITAL-AS-FACTORY MINDSET can raise logical objections in the uninitiated, but the reality is that Aravind's approach serves patient interests in multiple ways. The streamlined workflow increases efficiency, which means less waiting time. Task repetition creates competence, which means better clinical outcomes. And employing skilled paraprofessionals for steps that do not require a doctor's expertise not only facilitates individualized attention but also reduces prices. All three factors working in conjunction contribute to scale and affordability while improving patient experience and the quality of care.

It is early 2004, and Dr. V is talking with two guests from the Schwab Foundation for Social Entrepreneurship. One of the visitors remarks that in the United Kingdom, until recently, the wait time for cataract surgery was often as long as two years. "How long do patients have to wait here?" she asks. Dr. V's response is gleeful: "Here we don't give them a chance to wait." When a patient at Aravind is advised to have surgery, the system is prepared to admit him or her the same day and operate the very next.

Aravind deliberately keeps the fees for its paid services low. For those who elect to pay, the consultation fee is roughly $1, and the various surgery prices are capped at local market rates. In this some-thing-for-everyone approach, patients who decide to pay for cataract surgery choose from a tiered range of packages. Midrange prices start at about $110, while high-end packages can go up to $1,000. Service differentiation occurs primarily in terms of accommodation add-ons (air conditioning, attached bath, an extra bed for a family member, etc.) and choice from a range of surgical techniques and ophthalmic implants. Patients who opt for free or minimal-payment surgery pay between $0 and $17. They are housed in dormitories and receive standard surgery and ophthalmic implants. Clinical outcomes are similar whether or not a patient pays.

In Aravind's free department, a young nurse bends to address a woman sitting on a bench. "Grandmother, please cover your left eye with your hand," she says. Her face is serious, and she is intent on the task at hand. Now she waves two fingers inches away from the patient's nose. "How many fingers?" she asks. "Two," says Rukmini, peering between the fingers of her cupped palm. "No, no, you must keep the eye closed!" says the nurse, and Rukmini promptly screws shut both her eyes.

For a villager who has never been to a hospital, much less under-gone an eye exam before, the instructions to close first one eye and then the other, count fingers, and stare at a black-and-white illumi-nated cube covered with strange line drawings can be mystifying.

For actual refraction testing and eyeglass prescription, Aravind's trained refractionists use trial lenses for fine-tuned results. But for ini-tial rapid assessments, nurses use the finger test and then alphabet-based or number-based Snellen charts (the standardized vision charts employed the world over). For patients like Rukmini who are illiterate, the nurses use the Tumbling E chart, with rows of the letter E in different orientations, diminishing in size from top to bottom. Patients are asked to sequentially indicate with their fingers the direction in which the prongs of the letter are pointing.

After a more successful go-around, Rukmini uncovers her eye and blinks a few times. She is wearing a faded red cotton sari and no jewelry. Her face is sun worn, wrinkled, and wears an ancient expression. There's something in her right eye that catches attention—a milky opacity. "Cataract," says the nurse briefly, before helping the woman to her feet. "Grandmother, walk this way; we're going to see the doctor now."

By tomorrow, Rukmini will have a green post-surgery patch covering her eye.

❧

THERE IS A palpable, almost oceanic, quality of calm in Aravind's operating theaters; gowned and masked doctors and nurses flit through the shining hallways, as tranquil patients wait on stretchers or in wheelchairs. Considering that they are about to go under the knife, there is a curious absence of anxiety or tension in the air. *From Here to Nirvana*, a whimsically titled guidebook for spiritual destinations in India, includes an entry on the Aravind Eye Care System. A fitting inclusion, considering that visitors often refer to the organization as a temple for sight.

The nurses have been at work since 6:30 a.m., setting up the theaters and prepping the patients. Each theater has four operating tables lined up parallel to each other, two tables to a surgeon. The chief of cataract services, Dr. Haripriya Aravind, sits on a stool, her gaze locked into a surgical microscope trained on the patient on her operating table. Above the blue surgical mask, only her eyes, with finely arched eyebrows and the tear-shaped *bindi* between them, are visible. Another surgeon is similarly positioned at the far end of the room. In a few minutes, Haripriya looks up. The operation is done, a nurse helps the patient off the table, and the long arm of the surgical microscope is swung over to the next patient, already prepped and waiting on the second operating table.

Purusottam Lal Bhudo is a 75-year-old man who chose to pay $200 (a midrange price) for his treatment. Cataract surgery takes place under local anesthesia—in this case, topical drops that have been administered by an assisting nurse. Draped in a green surgical cloth, Bhudo is silent but awake. Before the surgery, a circulating nurse reads out details of his case to the doctor.

At Aravind, nurses handle 70 percent of all the activities that take place in the operating room.[14] A team of four nurses supports each surgeon; two assist the surgeon directly, while two circulating nurses (shared with an adjacent surgeon) are responsible for bringing in fresh sets of sterile instruments.

The surgery that Haripriya is performing is phacoemulsification (phaco), an elegant technique with excellent visual outcomes. This minimally invasive, high-tech approach delivers ultrasound through a microscopic surgical handpiece controlled by the surgeon via sophisticated software to emulsify the large, hard cataract core. It enables the entire cataract to be suctioned out through a tiny incision less than 3 millimeters long. Phaco is a convenient, same-day procedure with rapid recovery rates. It is the gold standard for cataract treatment in the West.

Haripriya deftly makes an incision and inserts the needlelike ultrasonic device to pulverize the hardened cataract. She aspirates the shattered pieces, suctioning them out. One of the assisting nurses leans in to irrigate the ocular surface. Using a series of delicate sterile instruments, Haripriya folds and inserts a synthetic intraocular lens through the incision and adjusts it for a perfect fit. No sutures are required; the tiny incision is self-sealing. Through all of this, the assisting nurses have handed instruments to the surgeon in rhythmic sequence, anticipatory motions so smooth that the surgeon's eyes don't lift from the microscope. A choreographed exchange between gloved hands. Barely a word is exchanged.

"It's very hot," mumbles a freshly operated-on Bhudo from under the white glare of the overhead lamp. "Don't worry, we're almost done," Haripriya says softly. Within moments, Bhudo is helped off the table and led to his room by a reassuring nurse.

Time taken for entire operation: less than six minutes.

Haripriya swings the microscope over to the table on her right, where her next patient is ready. At Aravind assembly-line processes have reduced lag time between a surgeon's operations to just 1 to 3 minutes, versus an average of 15 minutes at other hospitals in India.[15] Through experience and constant tweaking, Aravind has identified key factors that boost surgical productivity and standardized its processes accordingly. The systems in place aim to reduce the surgeon's wait time—whether for case details, a surgical instrument, or the next patient—to zero.[16] All resources are optimally employed. Aravind knows, for instance, that if a team of one surgeon and two nurses is equipped with two sets of instruments instead of one, they can double the number of surgeries done per hour. With an additional nurse and four more instrument sets, they can quadruple their output. They have also discovered that pre-grouping cases by degree of complexity boosts surgical productivity.

"When I was a resident here, every day Dr. V would want to know how many surgeries I had done," says Haripriya, who is married to his nephew, Dr. Aravind.[17] "To be able to face Chief [Dr. V], I would try and do more and do better—just to hear him say, on rare occasions, 'Very good, Very good.'" Rarely, and only with stringent qualifications, are surgeons from the developing world granted permission to operate in the West. In October 2010, Haripriya was one of four surgeons from around the world (and the only woman) invited to Chicago to demonstrate live surgery at the annual gathering of the American Academy of Ophthalmology.

Cataract surgery comprises 67 percent of all operations performed at Aravind.[18] "All our surgeons help tackle the workload by doing cataract surgeries during the first part of the day, before moving on to cases in their specialty," says Haripriya, who typically handles the more complicated cataract cases. "It's part of the culture here. Everyone does cataracts." While Aravind offers a full range of eye care services, including specialties like cornea, uvea, pediatrics, and neuro-ophthalmology, the system ensures that all of its surgeons (with the exception of its retina specialists, whose surgeries are particularly time intensive) play their part in eliminating the world's leading cause of needless blindness.

"What I do here I can't imagine accomplishing at other hospitals," says the other surgeon operating in the theater with Haripriya. "The numbers we do are only possible because of the efficient systems in place—and the amazing work of our nurses." A doctor at Aravind performs over 2,000 surgeries a year, compared with an all-India average of 400.

"*Amma*, your operation is over; it went well," says Haripriya to the woman on her table. The clock overhead reads 9:20 a.m.; she has been operating since 8 a.m. and is already 15 cases deep. This pace is not unusual at Aravind, but by the standards of the rest of the world, it is nothing short of extraordinary.

✑

IN THE UNITED STATES, Dr. David F. Chang is to cataract surgery what Michael Jordan is to basketball. His surgical speed, technique, research, and teaching skills have made him a household name in the field. Having also chaired the panel that developed the practice guidelines for cataract surgery, now used worldwide, Chang is a voice of considerable authority.

"Many eye surgeons in the United States perform 200 to 300 cases a year, averaging 30 to 45 minutes per case, including turnaround time in the operating room," says Chang, who is a clinical professor of ophthalmology at the University of California, San Francisco (UCSF).[19] "Some, of course, are faster or slower, and the case volumes certainly vary, but these numbers wouldn't be atypical." By contrast, Chang averages 30 cataract surgeries a day, four surgeries an hour. "When Dr. Venkatesh Rengaraj, one of Aravind's top surgeons, visited us in San Francisco and wanted to watch a top cataract surgeon operate, he was pointed to me," explains Chang. He pauses for a moment and then adds matter-of-factly, "In the U.S., I am considered very, very high volume."

In 2003, on his first trip to India, roles were reversed when Chang visited Aravind's hospital in the seaside town of Pondicherry and watched Venkatesh operate. "And of course, my own concept of high-volume surgery was laughable in comparison," he concludes wryly.

Because there is no universal definition for "high volume" in the context of cataract surgery, Aravind formulated its own; in its system, doctors who consistently perform more than 80 surgeries per day in six operating hours are "high-volume surgeons." Venkatesh is one of the faster high-volume surgeons at Aravind. For him, performing 100 operations in the span of a single day is not uncommon. He averages 3.5 minutes a case.[20]

"I've been involved with every aspect of cataract surgery as it is performed in the U.S. and in the Western world," says Chang, "and I really did not expect to see the efficiency, speed, skill, and stamina with which surgery is performed at Aravind. I watched their surgical teams with amazement."

And more than anything, it is the model itself that David Chang believes has tremendous implications. "Aravind is not just about what one ophthalmologist or one eye hospital can do," he says firmly. "This model provides hope that we can solve the huge problem of cataract in the developing world. Unlike other seemingly hopeless challenges, here is a very tangible, affordable, and proven solution. Aravind is one of the greatest success stories in all of medicine."

It is a story that Chang tells as often and as widely as he can. In 2005, he published an article provocatively titled, "A 5-Minute, $15 Cure for Blindness," which describes and validates the quality of M-SICS, a special type of cataract surgery that doctors at Aravind routinely perform on their nonpaying patients.[21]

By 2010, 75 percent of Aravind's paying patients were opting for phaco as their cataract surgery procedure of choice.[22] But phaco machines are expensive to purchase and maintain, the cost of disposable supplies per case is substantial, and the tiny incision requires using high-cost foldable lenses to replace the natural clouded lens that is extracted. For these reasons, scaling the technique to *all* of Aravind's patients posed several challenges. But compromising on outcome quality by using an inferior surgical technique on nonpaying patients was not an option.

In the early 1990s, Aravind addressed the high-cost challenge posed by the phaco method by adapting an alternative surgical technique for its free and deeply subsidized patients. The manual, sutureless, small-incision cataract surgery (M-SICS) that surgeons at Aravind perfected uses relatively inexpensive equipment and supplies, including nonfoldable lens implants (costing a fraction of their foldable counterparts). Like phaco, the modified M-SICS technique adapts the shape and size of the incision, removing the need for sutures, and ensures a self-sealing recovery.

Postoperative vision recovery for the patient is typically faster with phaco surgery, and it is considered a more sophisticated technique (which is often why paying patients choose it). But experts like Chang deem M-SICS comparable in terms of both recovery speed and clinical outcomes. Interestingly, the M-SICS technique has also proved less prone to complications on mature cataracts (an advanced stage of cataract rare in the West but common among the poor in the developing world).[23] Additional benefits are that M-SICS is easier to learn and faster to perform—qualities well suited to Aravind's high-volume setting. Having this technique in its repertoire definitively supports Aravind's broader model and its mission to provide equitable, high-quality care to all its patients.

But there is more to the Aravind story that impresses Chang. He recalls meeting Dr. V during his first visit to Aravind. "He has an amazing aura. It was like being in the presence of a living legend. He brings a lot of energy and purpose to everyone he comes in contact with." Then the man who is arguably one of America's best-known eye surgeons throws in a rather anomalous observation. "I really think Dr. V's spirituality is an important driving force at Aravind."

Spirituality. It is an unusual element to surface in a discussion of comparative surgical techniques. But Chang is not the only person to pick up on this undercurrent to Aravind's work.

# WHEN FREE IS NOT ENOUGH

Dr. V named the Aravind Eye Care System after the freedom-fighter-turned-mystic Sri Aurobindo. Sri Aurobindo's progressive teachings and those of his collaborator, a woman widely known as the Mother (whose flowerlike symbol is wrought in Aravind's gates and on the rings worn by the founding team), have deeply informed Dr. V's own life and vision. *Aravind* (pronounced UH-ruh-vind) is the South Indian variation of *Aurobindo*. The name means "lotus," a flower that, across many Eastern traditions, signifies spiritual consciousness.

In 1980, Dr. V wrote in his journal, *To some of us bringing divine consciousness to our daily activities is the Goal. The Hospital work gives an opportunity for this spiritual growth. In your growth you widen your consciousness and you feel the suffering of others in you.* He frequently referred to the concept of divinity and approaching the divine through work.

Jacqueline Novogratz, the dynamic founder of the Acumen Fund, once asked Dr. V about his idea of God. "He told me that for him, God existed in the place where all beings were interconnected," she shares. "He was able to fuse the power of an unsentimental approach to treating poor people in the most effective way, with the moral imagination to see people, really see them, and listen to their needs and dreams. In this way, I think he saw godliness and beauty in all people and all things."[1] Dr. V's quest to eliminate blindness is fueled by this view of humanity and by his deep empathy for the suffering that blindness inflicts on people—particularly the poor.

◯

CATARACT INCIDENCE IN India is higher than in the developed world.[2] The jury is still out on whether the reasons for this are related to malnutrition, high exposure to UV rays, genetic factors, or other causes. A significant percentage of India's cataract occurs in people under 60 (compared with the average incidence age of 70 in the West).[3] Left untreated, cataract often incapacitates the sole breadwinner of the family; a tailor finds it impossible to thread her needle, a farmer can no longer sort his grain, and a carpenter's hammer does not connect with his nail. The global cost of blindness in terms of lost productivity is a staggering $47 billion per year.[4]

Dr. V knows all the numbers and quotes them with ease, but he always moves quickly from abstract statistics to personal stories: the village woman whose husband abandoned her for a second wife when she lost her sight; the man whose sons refused to take care of him; the five-year-old girl forced to cook in place of a mother who was blind; or the sightless grandfather who, when asked if he had eaten, replied that he had "washed" his stomach, meaning that he had swallowed the watery gruel that was his daily sustenance. There is a cruel phrase in India that refers to a person who is blind as someone who is "a mouth with no hands."

Sundari, a woman in her 50s, lives in a small village at the foothills of the Western Ghats of Tamil Nadu. She has a beautiful face—sharp features, high cheekbones, and wide eyes that look into yours with blue, sightless intensity. A daily-wage field laborer, she could not afford time off from work to undergo surgery. Ironically, when Sundari lost her sight, she lost her job with it and was forced to move in with her daughter. The guilt of being a drain on her family's resources was enormous. Sundari resorted to long periods of fasting, so as not to be a burden to them. Cataract left untreated for too long can lead to irreversible complications. Sundari's condition is now incurable. Hers is the kind of story that haunts Dr. V. He has seen far too many people devastated by the triple loss of eyesight, livelihood, and a sense of self-worth. He knows that these things can lead to even graver losses. Blindness, as one public health expert pointed out, can be a fatal disease in India.[5] Loss of sight and its attendant trials can strip the already poverty-stricken of the will and means to live. Once blindness sets in, life expectancy can reduce to just a few years.

The situation is exacerbated by the fact that 70 percent of India's population is rural, while 80 percent of the country's medical services are situated in urban areas.[6, 7] The problem of service delivery is framed by this drastic imbalance, along with several other challenges. In this scenario, the overarching question Dr. V posed was: How do we sustainably serve, with limited money and personnel, a large population that is poor and difficult to access?

In an Aravind classroom, Thulsi Ravilla, Dr. V's nephew by marriage, and the executive director of the organization's training and consulting division, is addressing a group of international eye care providers. Projected on the screen is a picture of a young African girl in traditional attire. "What do you see?" Thulsi asks the audience of administrators and ophthalmologists in front of him. "A young female with mature cataract," comes the immediate answer. "Look closer—what do you see?" he asks again. Someone from the group offers up a detailed clinical diagnosis of the girl's condition. "Is it treatable?" Thulsi inquires. "Of course, sir!" comes the surprised response. "What else do you see?" Thulsi presses. But no matter how hard they peer at the screen, no one picks up on what he's looking for. Eventually he uses a laser pointer to highlight it—the unusual earring that dangles from the girl's right ear. There is no mistaking that familiar shape. It is the metal tab off the top of a can of Coca-Cola. "What are you looking at?" he asks one final time. The room is intrigued and silent. "You're looking at our collective failure," says Thulsi, his clear voice ringing in every corner of the room. "We have the knowledge and the skills to help this girl. But we didn't. Coke got to her—why couldn't we?"[8]

∽

"If there was anyone in the world who really understood the core necessity of social marketing, I think even before the term was invented, it was Dr. V," declares Dr. Fred Munson, a longtime Aravind volunteer.[9] "He placed a strong focus on the noncustomer," elaborates Thulsi, "the people who need care but who are not in the service loop. Dr. V wanted to design our systems to bring them in. So our energy and marketing focus, if you want to call it that, was directed at them."

Early in Aravind's existence, Dr. V began making weekend trips to the villages surrounding Madurai. He plowed the organization's meager earnings into free cataract operations for the rural poor. Over the decades, those Sunday excursions evolved into a massive outreach operation that now regularly dispatches teams of doctors and nurses to far-flung communities to screen patients. Those requiring cataract surgery receive it at no charge. By 2011, Aravind was conducting roughly 2,100 such screening camps across the states of Tamil Nadu and Kerala every year, averaging 40 camps each week.[10]

The significance of these arterial efforts within the model is far from trivial. About 35 percent of the four million surgeries Aravind has carried out since inception have been performed on patients brought in through its outreach camps.[11] These camps currently ferry in approximately 76,000 patients a year.[12] "Our systems depend on high volume," says Thulsi. When patient numbers go up, even if it's on the nonpaying side, Aravind becomes more effective as a whole. While this seems counterintuitive from a financial perspective, in reality everything at Aravind, from the marketing of its services and the hands-on training of its medical personnel, to the steady workflow in its operating rooms and its data-driven quality improvement systems, benefits from, and in many ways hinges on, Aravind's high influx of nonpaying patients. "It doesn't happen by accident," says Thulsi. "We design for it."

They certainly do. The split between different classes of accommodation bears the imprint of Aravind's bias toward serving the poor. Aravind–Madurai has a total of 1,204 inpatient beds, of which only 284 are reserved for regular paying patients. The remaining 920 are dedicated to its free and steeply subsidized patients.

While giving away free services might appear easy, Aravind's experience proved to the contrary. "In the early days, we didn't know better," says Thulsi, laughing. "We would go to the villages, screen patients, and tell those who needed surgery to come to the hospital for free treatment. Some showed up, but a lot of them did not. It was really puzzling to us. Why would someone turn down the chance to see again?" Fear, superstition, and cultural indifference can all be very real barriers to accessing medical care, but Aravind's leaders were convinced that there was more to it than that. After a few more years and several ineffective pilots of door-to-door counseling, they arrived at the crux of the issue. "Enlightenment came when we talked to a blind beggar," says Thulsi. When pressed on why he had not shown up to have his sight restored, the man replied, "You told me to come to the hospital. To do that, I would have to pay bus fare then find money for food and medicines. Your 'free' surgery costs me 100 rupees."

Following that revelatory conversation, Dr. V initiated a study to determine the real barriers to cataract surgery.[13] The research found that transport and sustenance costs, along with lost wages for oneself and an accompanying family member, were daunting considerations for the rural patient. Aravind learned a valuable lesson: just because people need something you are offering for free, it does not mean they will take you up on it. You have to make it viable for them to access your service in the context of their realities.

So Aravind retrofitted its outreach services to address the chief barriers. In addition to the free screening at the eye camps, patients were given a ride to one of its base hospitals, where they received surgery, accommodation, food, postoperative medication, return transport, and a follow-up visit in their village, all free of charge. "Once we did that, of course, our expenses went up," says Thulsi. "But more importantly, our acceptance rate for surgery went up from roughly 5 percent to about 80 percent." For an organization aspiring to rid the world of needless blindness, this was tremendously significant. It helped achieve the critical, high-volume aspect of the model. And the approach Aravind took to get there is one that Thulsi believes is relevant for any kind of development work. "In hindsight, we found two things are critical," he says crisply. "You have to focus on the nonuser, and you have to passionately own the problem. You can address the barriers only when you own, not shift, the problems." Paradoxically, that mindset led to what is perhaps the most collaborative outreach system the world of eye care has ever seen.

Aravind's outreach model converts grassroots leaders into active partners and turns local hubs of community life—elementary schools, movie theaters, wedding halls, and factory workrooms—into screening sites. Vision-testing and spectacle-dispensing units are set up under trees; high school volunteers, alongside local Rotary or Lions Club members, are recruited to oversee crowd management and registration. Creating ownership in the community takes time but pays off enormously in terms of a program's credibility, sustainability, and scale. Today, Aravind's outreach program boasts a 500-member-strong network of camp sponsors that spans a diverse group of nonprofits, industrial companies, religious bodies, universities, families, and individuals. These sponsors shoulder several support functions that are crucial to the success and smooth functioning of these camps, including publicity campaigns, venue selection, and boarding and lodging for the medical teams.

"It is a fundamental rule that every camp, even our very smallest, is done with active leadership from within the community," says Thulsi. Each Aravind camp has a community sponsor with whom Aravind shares branding and a small percentage of costs. This practice creates deep local ties, builds trust, facilitates onsite planning and trouble-shooting, and helps ensure maximal community attendance.

Today, at least 40 other eye hospitals run outreach initiatives in Tamil Nadu, but Aravind's numbers regularly eclipse all the rest. For instance, one of India's other premier eye institutes is headquartered in Tamil Nadu and, like Aravind, runs outreach camps and offers free cataract surgery for the poor. In 2009, this institute performed about 16,000 free surgeries.[14] That same year, Aravind performed over 76,000 free surgeries (not even counting the more than 74,600 operations done for an ultrasubsidized fee).[15]

As Thulsi is quick to point out, various eye hospitals have different focus areas, but they all contribute toward the mission of ending needless blindness. In some, the development of crucial specialty care services or eye care research may take precedence over community outreach. Given the magnitude of need, he maintains that *all* these efforts, regardless of their scale, are critical. Even so, what undergirds Aravind's own system and puts its scale in a league of its own merits closer examination.

Unusual practices around ownership, funding, and accountability enable the volume of Aravind's outreach work. The organization splits ownership and operational costs with the community. A large camp that screens 500 or more people typically will cost the community sponsor around $400 and Aravind a little over $1,000. Smaller camps that see a couple of hundred patients work out to around $130 for both Aravind and the sponsor.[16]

Vigorous tracking systems at Aravind work to ensure that all outreach costs are optimally utilized. While fixed costs for the organization remain the same regardless of a camp's performance, Aravind's mission to eliminate curable blindness demands that it pay special attention to the lost-opportunity cost at each of its camps—that is, the number of poor patients in need of its services whom it could have reached but did not.

Volume targets are set for each camp, depending on the location, profile, and size of the population being served, along with other factors. Aravind's laserlike focus on the *full use* of resources facilitates its cost-efficiency. The cost to the organization of admitting a patient from Aravind's eye camps for surgery typically works out to roughly Rs. 270 ($6). This "case-finding cost" per patient is tracked for every screening camp it conducts. If camps are inefficient and bring in too few patients, the case-finding cost can skyrocket to as high as Rs. 500 ($11) per patient—cutting in half the number of patients who could have been served.[17]

For well over a decade, Aravind's founding team was heavily involved in outreach and refining the systems that drive these numbers. Hailing from villages themselves, they viewed the community as an extension of the organization. They stress how the success of these camps hinges on the empowerment, and not the dependence, of leadership in the community. "When you first start working with the community, it is very important to make sure that you are the one holding their hand—and not the other way around," says Dr. G. Natchiar briskly. She is Dr. V's youngest sister and one of the founding members of Aravind. "If you hold their hand, then you can let go once they are on their feet. If they hold your hand, then it is harder for them to let go."[18]

Natchiar holds camp activities close to her heart and has an endearing bias for Aravind's rural patients. "Rich people don't bless us," she says squarely, "they just demand our expertise. The poor take it as a gift." She flashes the trademark smile that wins people over despite her bluntness. "It's the love of the common people that has helped us to grow," she says.

As dawn turns gold on the horizon, the Aravind van drives down a narrow street in the small town of Kallupatti and pulls up next to a fluorescent-green building. Already more than 50 people are waiting outside today's screening site, a sizable wedding hall with plastic garlands of marigolds and roses decorating the entrance. Two doctors and half a dozen nurses pile out of the Aravind van, assess the layout of the building, and begin to set up. Wire frames canopied with black canvas serve as refraction cubicles, and a desk to one side is used for patient counseling. A corner of the wedding hall is designated for grinding and fitting spectacle lenses, and up front, black-and-white charts are mounted for preliminary vision tests. There is a table for the doctor examinations and a long bench for glaucoma screening.

The first patient enters at 9 a.m. Within ten minutes, all stations are engaged, and the mood of the crew is upbeat as local volunteers help guide the patients from one stage to the next. Today, this well-lit wedding hall has, for the 154th time, been converted into a highly functional screening eye camp. The owner is a staunch follower of Mahatma Gandhi's teachings. As a teenager, he had volunteered with Dr. V's early rural efforts. Now in his 70s, he heads a 50-member community group that sponsors these camps on a monthly basis.

The young doctor examining patients is kind, firm, and efficient. When someone shows up with an advanced condition, his face grows serious. "Grandmother, why didn't you come earlier?" he scolds gently. "Look how bad your eyes have become." A cup of hot tea cools in front of him, unnoticed. Patients sit to each side, and he swivels from one to the other, in a manner reminiscent of the operating table setup at Aravind. He takes his time with each person and yet manages to keep the flow moving swiftly. The patient stream is steady and the stories endless. They come from the 30-odd villages in the area, people of bare feet and leathery brown skin, the women in bright saris, and several of the men leaning on long wooden staffs.

Pechiamma has four children. She also has diabetes and advanced cataract in both eyes. Karuppanan once had two cows but now has cataract-impaired vision and no means of an independent livelihood. Like three birds on a perch sit Ponnamma, Yelamma, and Muthulakshmi, dressed identically in white widow saris without blouses, thin blue tattoos running the breadth of their foreheads and the length of their arms. All three have mature cataracts and the incongruous air of schoolgirls on an outing. On the other side of the room, among the post-operation review cases, is Kuzhanthiammal, an old lady with a beautiful smile and no teeth. When asked her age, she hazards a good-natured guess: "I must be around 40 or 50, no?" A glance at her case sheet says otherwise. "Grandmother, it says here you're 80," says the nurse. To which Kuzhanthiammal gives an agreeable nod. "That could be true," she affirms. This indifference to mortal years is a common phenomenon in the villages, where time is marked not by the calendar but by the cyclical seasons of sowing and harvest. Next in line is 60-year-old Muthu, who after his operation the previous month was able to return to his work in the fields. The doctor has just told him that all is well, and he is smiling broadly.

A patient survey conducted at Aravind–Madurai revealed that 85 percent of the men and 58 percent of the women who lost their livelihoods as a result of cataract had successfully reentered the workforce after surgery.[19] Dr. V underscores the implications of this reality, urging his team members time and again to understand the system of sight delivery as a whole. He pushes them to view surgery not as an isolated end point but as a vital step in a much larger chain of interconnection. When a doctor restores sight to a woman who is able to work in the fields again, her child has a better chance of going to school and then a better shot at finding a job that will break the cycle of poverty their family has lived in for generations. When a doctor, working with a team, gives sight to not just one or ten but a thousand or tens of thousands of such men and women, then not one family but an entire village, district, state, eventually perhaps an entire country will, in a small but significant way, be helped toward a better future. One of Dr. V's gifts is the ability to see the transformation of a nation, one patient at a time.

By Aravind standards, this is a small camp. It will, with whirlwind efficiency, wrap up before noon, and over half of the 207 patients screened will be advised to undergo cataract surgery. They will be sent by Aravind transport back to the Madurai hospital for free treatment. The leadership's grasp of the complex logistics involved and the precision they have built up over the years allow these events to scale. At Aravind's largest camps, teams screen up to a thousand patients at a single venue in the space of a few hours.

At 3:25 P.M. the following Monday, seven camp organizers file into the conference room on the ground floor of Aravind–Madurai for their weekly performance meeting. Each one holds a spiral-bound book that is a veritable encyclopedia of community-based information: maps of territories, district populations, villages within each district, number of households per village, potential camp sites, suggested frequencies for camps in various locations, statistics of past camps (number of patients screened, number of cataract surgeries performed, number of spectacles ordered), and much more. Camps at Aravind are not treated as casual philanthropic exercises. Senior management monitors their performance every week across an exhaustive set of parameters.

"We built our system based on problems and experience," says R. Meenakshi Sundaram (called RMS), Aravind's energetic director of camp services.[20] He joined the organization just out of his teens, and after close to 30 years in the field, he knows the contours of this work like the back of his hand. RMS oversees a team of 25 camp organizers across Aravind's five base hospitals. Each of the coordinators is assigned an area that covers a population of one million to three million.

A camp organizer's job is a blend of art, sweat, and science that involves hitting rigorous targets, building rapport in the community, coaching new sponsors, organizing transport logistics, monitoring camp flow, and ensuring patient satisfaction. Organizers carry details of temple festival dates, school exam schedules, harvest periods, and election days at their fingertips, and are careful not to schedule an eye camp at the same time as competing community events. "Using GIS [a geographic information system], we can pull up detailed and layered maps—whether it's Kadamalaikundu, Tiruppatur, or Oddanchatram," says RMS, reeling off a list of quintessential small towns in Tamil Nadu. With this new technology, camp organizers can look up a region's population density, ease of access, centrality, and most efficient transport routes at a glance.

Dr. Ilango Krishnamoorthy runs the camp review meeting. His manner is relaxed, but it is clear that nothing escapes him. Looking at numbers for one camp, he notices that 30 of the patients advised to undergo surgery were unwilling to come in. "That's a high number," he says, and proceeds to look into the staff postings for that particular camp.[21] "There weren't enough senior nurses on this team—what happened here?" A quick investigation reveals that they had been shuffled out due to a last-minute event planned by the HR department. "Make sure the next team we send to this village is really strong—we need to do better for the people there," says Ilango.

One of the coordinators reports on a camp where 351 patients showed up for a forecasted turnout of 350, and 104 were advised to have cataract surgery, with a 92 percent acceptance rate. Sixty-eight ended up needing eyeglasses; 100 percent of these patients ordered and received spectacles on the spot. In addition, 13 specialty cases were identified and advised to visit Aravind for follow-up.

Aravind's eye camps involve comprehensive screening not only for cataract and vision testing but also for other eye diseases, like glaucoma and diabetic retinopathy. "Not enough specialty cases identified at this camp," Ilango says to another coordinator. "For the volume of patients screened, there should have been at least one glaucoma case. It means the doctors may not have been working right. Let's watch their trend and correct that if we need to."

The array of information is astounding, as is the determined wading through of minute details. "Hey, what happened here?" he asks the next coordinator. In a camp meant to cover 70 villages, people from only 47 villages had turned up. "What kind of advertising did you have the sponsor carry out?" "Newspaper ads, sir," says the coordinator. He is a new recruit. Ilango shakes his head. "Newspaper ads don't reach remote villages. Those people aren't going to be sitting in the morning and reading the paper—they're working in the fields. You need to call up the village heads, print wall posters, do vocal announcements and that sort of thing." Marketing for Aravind camps is a far cry from high-gloss advertising campaigns, but it works. One of the most popular, effective, and cost-efficient forms of publicity is the hiring of an auto-rickshaw to drive through hamlets and villages, blaring news of an upcoming eye camp over a loudspeaker.

That is how Ponni heard about the eye camp she attended.

SHE IS SITTING in one of Aravind's dormitory-style wards reserved for camp patients, a cheerful, skeletal woman who has all the makings of a ringleader. "I wanted to come to Aravind because I've heard the quality is good here," says Ponni, smiling behind her patch.[22] "Plus I get to come with people I know." Around her, seated on colorful woven mats, are several other women from her area, including her cousin Thenmozhi. That kind of familiar presence is immensely reassuring and part of the genius of these camps. What is it like being away from home in a strange eye hospital? Thenmozhi laughs. She is not yet 40 but had to be operated on for cataract in both eyes. "We like it here," she says. "We have to work so hard back home. Being here is restful for us." That she considers the experience of eye surgery restful is strange, until you look at her regular life.

For most of these women, life begins before sunrise. Water must be hand-pumped and carried home, meals cooked over firewood, and children tended to, all before a full day of backbreaking labor in the fields. Considering the fact that women account for two-thirds of the world's blindness, it is clear that what this group has regained at Aravind cannot be taken for granted.[23] Ponni stands up with an air of touching gravity. "Mark my words," she says, "I, Ponni, hereby declare that every single camp Aravind holds in our villages will be a great success. Many people are scared to come for eye surgery, but we'll tell them what a fine job is being done at Aravind and how well they will be taken care of. Now you go ahead and write that down if you want and put the date on it." The impromptu testimony underscores the roles that compassion and quality play in the equation of delivering care. These things are important because regardless of whether a service is free or paid for, so much in the world of health care depends on trust.

At Aravind, the most impoverished villagers who receive free treatment are often its fiercest advocates.

SAMBALINGAM IS BAREFOOT and wears a threadbare *dhoti*, a shirt, and a pair of crooked glasses. His deeply sunken cheeks give him the endearing look of someone just about to whistle. This man's association with the founders of Aravind goes back a long way.

"I was practically blind; then they operated on me for free," he says in colloquial Tamil. "I could see again, and so I could work again."[24] The grateful patient had promised Aravind's founders that he would bring more patients to them. This was in 1978, and every year since then, Sambalingam has been faithful to his promise. He brings in patients from his own and surrounding villages, sometimes in groups of five or ten, sometimes individually. But he never turns away anyone who asks for help. "People trust me," he says, "because they know that when I came to Aravind, I had lost everything and was ready to start begging for a living. They saw me come back with my eyesight restored, and they saw the difference." With his sight restored, Sambalingam was able to return to working in the fields. He has embraced his self-appointed role as Aravind ambassador and is proud of it. A clip-on badge attached to his front pocket reads, "P. Sambalingam, Village Awareness Program Volunteer." Aravind started the program in the 1990s to train rural volunteers in patient identification and referral. It was discontinued after Aravind's screening camps gained traction, but several volunteers, Sambalingam included, have refused to call it quits.

Sambalingam says that personally escorting patients to Aravind helps immensely. "What do they know about this hospital and how it works and where they have to go? I know everyone here, right from the watchman at the gate to Dr. Venkataswamy and Dr. Natchiar—and they all know me," he says, beaming. Sambalingam unconsciously captures Aravind's own evolution when he says, "In the beginning, I used to go around from house to house and village to village to find patients. But then the Big Doctor [Dr. V] said to me, 'You don't have to look for them, Sambalingam. They will come looking for you.' And that is exactly what has happened. Patients come looking for me. Whenever they have a problem with their eyes, I'm the one they come to."

This man is in his 80s and, despite his age, full of energy and the conviction that he is a part of something greater than his everyday existence. When asked how long he thinks he will continue to serve in this way, Sambalingam peers intently through his lopsided glasses. "I can't tell you that I'll do it after I'm dead and gone," he says firmly. "But as long as I live, I will keep bringing more patients to Aravind."

❧

WITH PATIENTS FROM hundreds of villages regaining sight by the busload, Aravind's reputation for community focus and service excellence rapidly grew. The camps reduced the level of fear and uncertainty around accessing eye care, and prompted many rural patients to proactively seek out Aravind's services. It was a phenomenon that the renowned Northwestern University marketing professor Philip Kotler dubbed as the shift from a market-driven to a market-driving approach. He named Dr. V, along with Richard Branson of Virgin Group and Anita Roddick of The Body Shop, as one of the rare visionaries "who saw the world differently, and whose vision addressed some deep-seated, latent, or emerging need of the customer. Rather than focusing on obtaining market share in existing markets, these market drivers created new markets."[25]

Dr. V looked into the heart of needless blindness, evolved a nuanced understanding of those affected, and stepped forward to own the problem of service delivery for sight. Aravind's trademark effort to meet people wherever they are comes from this ethos. As a result, its systems acknowledge that the price of a surgery does not sum up the cost to the patient, that there are gradations of poverty just as there are gradations of wealth, that affordability is subjective, and that options bestow dignity. Its model is built around a belief that everyone has something to contribute, whether they pay you or not.

# THREE

# THIS CASE WON'T FLY

"We're not a schizophrenic organization," says Thulsi. "We don't reserve a certain quality of care for our paying patients and offer another thing altogether for our free patients." The conventional paradigm operates on the premise that you get what you pay for. But Aravind's founders called for a different framework, where high quality is a given across paid, free, or subsidized care. They also went a step further, making a choice not to brand the services separately, and to house free and paid services under the same roof.[1] "If you set up separate institutions for pure paying or pure free, then you split the culture. Doctors might want to work only in one place or the other. If we had distinctly separate hospitals, it would be a lot harder to circulate staff between the two," says founding member Dr. Perumalsamy Namperumalsamy (known to many simply as Nam).[2] The mandate on equitable care means that no doctors within the organization are "reserved" for paying clientele. All of Aravind's ophthalmologists rotate between its free and paying sections.

Fundamental to this model is a conviction that providing high-quality care is cost-efficient because it minimizes complications and the need for repeat visits, while maximizing patient satisfaction and building trust. "Quality is how we sustain the demand," says Thulsi. "With our kind of volumes, you can ruin your reputation very easily if you don't do good work." Dr. Aravind offers a vivid illustration of this: "When you break it down, one out of three people who has had eye surgery in this state [Tamil Nadu] had it at an Aravind hospital. That's a lot of people we need to keep satisfied!"

In many settings, quality and quantity are assumed to have an inverse relationship. But several research studies in the medical field, and specifically in cataract surgery, validate what most surgeons know to be true: the more you do, the better you get.[3] Aravind's own work consistently demonstrates that high-quality medical care can be fostered, and not undermined, by an enormous patient load.

In *The Fortune at the Bottom of the Pyramid*, C. K. Prahalad published the results of a like-for-like assessment of surgical data from Aravind, and a 2001 national survey in the UK by the Royal College of Ophthalmologists.[4] The comparison was for adverse events during and within 48 hours of surgery, across nearly 20 different complication types. In all but three instances, Aravind demonstrated a lower complication rate than its Western counterpart.[5]

The sheer scale of Aravind's work could have prompted it toward defensive practices. But instead its leadership chose to design systems that take responsibility for anticipated risks to the patient. Here, if patients have critical health conditions that increase the chance of complications in surgery, if they have only one good eye, or if they for any reason require re-surgery, then they are automatically assigned to one of the organization's most experienced surgeons. This proactive approach to quality followed the dictates of compassion but also proved to make sound business sense. Thulsi says that one of Aravind's most effective forms of marketing is simply word-of-mouth praise from Aravind's satisfied patients.

❧

IN HIS BOOK *Quality Is Free*, Philip Crosby discusses the common organizational error of viewing quality as a shimmering intangible that defies measurement. He argues that it is "a conformance to requirements" that demands "unblinking dedication, patience, and time."[6] Aravind's founding team took that approach to quality. In the context of India's largely unregulated health care system, they created their own quality benchmarks, implemented stringent protocols and systems, and soon developed a fierce reputation for being sticklers for perfection. As Dr. Fred Munson, professor emeritus of hospital administration at the University of Michigan, recalls, "Starting with Dr. V, the whole family has developed this passion for quality. Young residents actually have churning stomachs when they know Dr. Natchiar will be visiting the surgical room to observe their work."

For roughly 20 years, Natchiar was a one-woman quality assurance team, making biennial inspection visits to all of Aravind's different hospitals and scrutinizing each of their 23 departments. She looked at everything, including surgical complication rates, research data for clinical studies, employee turnover statistics, camp transportation costs, linen-washing expenditures, and the nutritional value of food at the nurses' hostel. "Then I realized I was getting old and needed to delegate," she says, laughing.

In a move to rely less on churning stomachs and more on systematic data collection and review, Aravind's Parameters Program was born in 2006. Through this initiative, handpicked teams of three senior staff members are appointed to audit each of Aravind's hospitals over a period of three to five days. Each hospital gets an individual feedback report and best practices are shared from hospitals that score the highest points in specific categories.

"Mandatory measurement and reporting of results is perhaps the single most important step in reforming the health care system," write Michael Porter and Elizabeth Teisberg in their book *Redefining Health Care*.[7] It is a perspective that has long been met with suspicion, if not downright outrage, in the medical world. Efficiency expert Charles Kenney traces this reactivity to a problem of culture: "Once you get out of medical school and you go into practice, the culture is that the doctor doesn't report to anybody, that the doctor is an entity unto him- or herself, and that's clearly not conducive to systems thinking."[8] At Aravind, a deeply patient-centric approach led to unconventionally transparent systems for measurement and standardization. The content of its weekly cataract meetings highlights this facet of the model.

The cataract department at Aravind–Madurai handles 67 percent of the hospital's patient volume.[9] Its ward and operating-theater nurses meet with Dr. Haripriya (chief of Aravind's cataract services) on a weekly basis to review performance data. Quality in both the free and paying divisions is measured and scrutinized across the same rigorous set of parameters. Spreadsheets break down the overall totals and percentages of surgeries, complications, re-surgery rates, and infection rates in and across the various theaters and wards. They are backed by a drill-down into the specifics of each case, including the names of the surgeon and assisting nurses, the stage at which the complication occurred, how it was handled and by whom, and postoperative outcome.

There is an element of sleuthing to the whole process. Patient records are produced as evidence, nurses are called on for firsthand accounts, and a gentle but incisive interrogation from the department head ensues. At which step of the surgery did a complication arise? Was it in the surgeon's third or 30th case of the day? Probing these details allows the managers to spot occasional cases of surgeon fatigue and adjust caseloads accordingly. It also alerts them to surgeons who might be faltering repeatedly at a particular step, in which case arrangements are made for targeted retraining.

While it is not mandatory for Aravind surgeons to attend these weekly meetings, they are required to read and sign all case records relating to their complications. The records are available to everyone, from the most senior medical officers to the residents and trainees. "The idea really is to show relative performance and to make it transparent and accessible," says Haripriya. Her husband, Dr. Aravind, also a high-volume cataract surgeon, adds context: "At Aravind–Madurai, a little more than 100 doctors, 80 to 90 operating nurses, and 40 refractionists—basically more than 200 people—access this data regularly. So the focus on quality really gets into your subconscious. People compete in a positive way to do better surgeries and bring the best to the patient."

"My sense is that what's really unusual is the level of transparency," says Thulsi. "Typically, that isn't comfortable for doctors. But the idea is really to use the data to look for patterns. It's about fixing the system, not the individual." Thulsi talks about the use of data to identify patterns and how this translates into systemic change. He provides a telling example from the late '80s, at a time when sutureless surgery was not yet the standard practice at Aravind. Data on postoperative repeat visits triggered a concern that patients were being asked to come back to the hospital more often than necessary. "Some hospitals take pride in saying that they see a patient ten times postsurgery," Thulsi says. That approach, he argues, can actually mean inconvenience and more expense to the patient.

Aravind conducted an in-depth examination of all its post-op repeat-visit data. The records showed that a majority of visits were due to suture-related problems. "So we went back and looked at the monthly data linked to sutures," says Thulsi. It showed that applying fewer than five sutures resulted in problems. "In a thousand cases, we're talking about ten complications, so obviously this wasn't a pattern visible at the surgeon level. It is the data that showed it," he points out. Upon discussion, senior surgeons maintained that suturing quality was a matter of skill and experience. As an initial intervention, the application of a five-suture minimum was mandated for all junior surgeons, while senior doctors were permitted to continue with three. The following month's data yielded unambiguous results. "It turned out seniority didn't matter. All the complications we saw occurred in three-suture cases," says Thulsi. The findings resulted in a five-suture minimum requirement across the board at Aravind—a powerful example of data-driven decision making. And as Thulsi laughingly puts it, "It really helps cut through ego in the organization."

☙

IN *The Best Practice*, which traces the story of the quality movement in Western medicine, Charles Kenney points out one of the greatest barriers to improvement: "As long as doctors and hospitals are paid for volume of procedures rather than for quality of outcomes they have little incentive to change."[10] In the interest of protecting quality outcomes in a high-volume setting, Aravind does one very important thing differently from most other hospitals: it intentionally de-links a surgeon's salary from patient load.

Year by year, complication and infection rates at Aravind have consistently decreased. By 2009, across a total of over 180,000 cataract surgeries in 2009, Aravind's infection rate was down to 0.3 percent. In the same year, its specialty surgeries numbered more than 51,000, with an infection rate of 0.025 percent.[11]

Investing in the patient experience is also fundamental to Aravind's view of quality. Thulsi points out that while patients may not be able to judge clinical quality, they can certainly tell you if the sheets in their room were clean, if the nurse who assisted them was courteous, and if their doctor was on time. Hospitality, in a hospital, is a big part of the picture. Aravind exudes an air of ultracleanliness, despite the level of activity and high patient volume. Visitors accustomed to the dusty clamor of the streets outside are often surprised by the sense of space and graciousness that its hospitals hold. "Patient satisfaction is one of the strongest measures of nonclinical quality that we have," says Thulsi, "and that is where the concept of quality becomes important at every level within the organization."

Outpatient volumes, processing times, and bottlenecks are monitored just as closely as surgical and clinical outcomes. From registration to final examination, a typical outpatient at Aravind will go through a process comprising up to seven different stages. Time estimates for each stage are provided up front, and patients are informed that the duration of their visit (depending on the number of tests required) may be up to two hours.[12] In a country accustomed to opaque systems, interminable queues, and unpredictable waiting times (whether making a bank deposit, posting a letter, or renewing a passport), the efficiency and transparency of Aravind's systems come as a pleasant surprise.

On Chief of Cataract Services Dr. Haripriya's desk, a flat-screen monitor displays a live camera feed of the waiting rooms. At a glance she can assess the situation. A clinical management software tool gives her access to dynamic patient registration numbers; it lets her compare these against the previous day's total or the same day of the previous year. If a patient has been waiting for more than an hour, his or her record onscreen changes to yellow; at two hours it turns red—an immediate flag. To facilitate efficient case distribution, the program also tracks how many patients each doctor has screened. Like many of the systems in place at Aravind, this custom software facilitates speed of responsiveness and allows for data to drive continual improvement.

THE HIGH PATIENT VOLUME plays multiple roles in Aravind's model. It drives up the importance of standardized care in maintaining patient satisfaction. It facilitates cost-efficiency, surgical training, and proficiency; and it helps Aravind's data-driven process-improvement systems to rapidly identify deviant trends. But above all, Aravind's high patient volumes are fundamental to its mission of eliminating needless blindness and delivering compassionate, high-quality eye care services to anyone who needs them.

"Most organizations exist for a purpose but operationally chase a bottom line that is different from that purpose," says Thulsi. "One big lesson we have learned is that you must chase your purpose. Make that the core of your energy, and build your systems to be sustainable from all dimensions. Then the bottom line takes care of itself."

Whenever the bottom line "takes care of itself," the business world cannot help but be intrigued. This might explain why in 1993 a curious visitor from Cambridge, Massachusetts, showed up on Aravind's doorstep.

꩜

THE PROFESSOR HAD OPENED the gate of the Aravind Guest House in Madurai as quietly as possible. It was only 10 p.m., but people went to bed early here and were often up before sunrise. On a whim, he had followed a friend's lead to Aravind. At the end of his first day there, his mind was churning with assorted images —Aravind's gleaming operation theaters, the swift efficiency of the sari-clad nurses, the long queues of patients, and of course his first meeting with Dr. V. The professor had started the day early to get a sense of the patient flow. At 7 a.m. more than 100 people had been in line for registration. The elderly man who hobbled among them, helping a patient here, answering a question there, was the organization's founder. What a man!

Shaking his head, the visitor walked into the living room of the guesthouse, wondering why the lights were on. "Good evening, good evening, Professor!" The newly familiar voice stopped him dead in his tracks. A little jet-lagged from his travels, a little tired from the long day, and more than a little startled by the unexpectedness of the greeting, Harvard Business School's Malcolm P. McNair Professor of Marketing, V. Kasturi Rangan, known to friends, students, and colleagues as Kash, stared uncomprehendingly at the gray-haired figure seated on the sofa, smiling up at him with impish merriment. He cleared his throat slowly. Then, "Good evening, Dr. V," Kash said.

꩜

FOURTEEN YEARS LATER, sitting in his large, book-filled office at Harvard, Kash Rangan looks back at that moment and laughs. "I couldn't understand why he was there," he says. "I knew it had to be way past his bedtime, but there he was, sitting up waiting for me, and wanting to talk."

What Dr. V wanted to talk about also came as something of a surprise. "Spirituality wasn't what I was there to study," Kash says bluntly. "I needed to know about the finances, the number of surgeries, and so on. But when I steered things in that direction, he'd tell me to ask his nephew, Thulsi, about those things. Dr. V wanted to talk about Sri Aurobindo and the evolution of consciousness, things that had absolutely no relation to why I was there. Or he would talk about the poor, how we had to get to them earlier. He never seemed to worry about how that would happen," he says. "Every night, for the three nights I was there, Dr. V would come by after dinner. What was a puzzle initially gave way to admiration. Why would this amazing human being want to lose sleep sharing all this with me—a business professor who wasn't exactly in the same spiritual league as him?"

Kash spent time observing Aravind's systems and processes. He watched surgeries, went out into the villages for eye camps, talked to patients, and interviewed senior staff members to build up the repository of data he would need to design a case study. After that first visit to Aravind, he returned to Cambridge and proceeded to write one that was 26 pages long. Somehow the nocturnal discussions with Dr. V worked themselves into his writing. Kash had not planned on this. When it came down to it, he felt a twinge of guilt at the thought of leaving those discussions out. Meditations on spirituality, Gandhi, family, and service were interspersed with the "business" part of the text. When completed, he shared it with colleagues for feedback. "It's excellent," they told him, "but nobody likes long cases. Just take out all the stuff about spirituality. It's not central and will cut the length by about five pages."

Kash went back to his desk to make the cuts and found that he could not bring himself to ax any of it. "A 74-year-old man stayed up late to drill these things into me. I may not get his logic, but I want to honor it," he thought. Kash left it all in. The first time he wanted to include the case as part of a mandatory first-year marketing course at the Harvard Business School, the faculty voted 7–2 against it, saying, "No—this case won't fly." But Kash was not ready to drop it. "I was too close to it; the Aravind story resonated with my notions of what social entrepreneurs could do for society," he says. He had the latitude to determine his own teaching curriculum. "So I taught the Aravind case in my class—unedited. The students loved it," he recalls. Within the next three years, his colleagues lost their reservations. Suddenly, everyone was teaching the Aravind case.

For well over a decade now, each of the 900 or so students who pass through Harvard's MBA program every year have been handed *In Service for Sight*. Since its publication in 1993, the Harvard Business School has distributed more than 150,000 copies to the top 20 business schools in the United States.[13] When the school started a management course for entrepreneurs, the case study was required reading. From there, its popularity caught on, in Kash's words, "like wildfire." The normal lifespan of a case study, he estimates, is 3, maybe 4 years. This one has lasted 17 and is still going strong. "It has longevity," says Kash. "Dr. V's passion and vision make it timeless."

But that was not all. The first time the case study went live in a classroom, it all started to make sense. "Everything revolved around the things Dr. V was talking about. When we started trying to piece it together, it became more and more evident. This man's spirituality wasn't incidental to the story. It was what everything else hinged on," Kash said.

IN *The Fortune at the Bottom of the Pyramid*, C. K. Prahalad makes a case for models that target the poor and cites Aravind as a powerful example. "Businesses can gain three important advantages by serving the poor," he writes, "a new source of revenue growth, greater efficiency, and access to innovation."[14] Prahalad has framed the argument here according to typical business objectives and a line of inquiry that demands to know, "How much can we get for what we give?"

From the perspective of a social enterprise, the animating question flips from that to, "How much can we give for what we get?" The Aravind model arose, in part, from this potent question. In seeking a sustainable answer to rid the world of one form of suffering, Dr. V and his team formulated a high-volume, high-quality, low-cost approach to eye care delivery—a model that overturned typical assumptions of what it means to provide free services. He focused on reaching the unreached and removed barriers to accessing care wherever possible. He shaped eye camps to tap latent community resources and converted the *need* for eye care into an active *demand*. To treat such masses of people efficiently, he brought in assembly-line systems, skill-based task delineation, and a constant quest for refinement. With this came an insistence on measuring and monitoring and making systems transparent in unprecedented ways. These processes together drove up quality, trust, and service demand. Underlying all this relentless activity was an awareness of how the work fits into the broader framework of society; how restoring sight restores people to meaningful places in their families and communities.

The questions you ask shape the answers you find. "How much can we give?" was not the end of Dr. V's querying. A journal entry from the 1980s, written in a series of eclectic questions (and with his trademark absence of question marks), illustrates how intertwined matters of service delivery, leadership, and spirituality are to Dr. V.

It opens with the magnificent obsession he is known for: *How to organize and build more hospitals like McDonalds*. And then with no warning, it shifts to, *How was Buddha able to organize in those days a religion that millions follow.* This question dramatically changes the plane of inquiry. Other searching questions swiftly follow: *Who were the leaders. How were they shaped. How did the disciples of Christ spread their mission around the world.*

And then a final question that he would ask in a thousand different ways:

*How do I become a perfect instrument.*

THE HIGH-VOLUME, HIGH-QUALITY, low-cost mantra works well as an elevator pitch for the Aravind model, but the reality is far more nuanced. It takes a deeper exploration to understand the context in which Aravind arose: how the culture of a family and its roots and values nourished the ethos of this organization. A radical framework and one man's spiritual conviction guided its formative years. Aravind's founding members put everything on the line for a cause they believed in. "We were activists," says Dr. V's sister Natchiar, "filled with that sort of do-or-die fighting spirit."

PART II

# Do the Work and Money Will Follow

## On Sustainability and Selflessness

*Dr. V, before this trip I used to give things away to others sometimes, but only things that I didn't need very much. After meeting you and seeing what you have done, now I want to give my whole life to serve others—the way you do.*

—Olivier de Cherisey, age ten,
in a 2005 interview with Dr. V

# AN EYE DOCTOR BY
# SHEER ACCIDENT

D r. V wears thick-soled black sandals. His toes, like his fingers, have been twisted permanently out of shape by rheumatoid arthritis, so something as simple as slipping in and out of his footwear proves no small feat. Using the end of his walking stick, he spearholds the top of each sandal in place to ease his foot in. A bright green rubber band has been snapped, twisted, and tied around the toe-hold. He alternates this pair of footwear with a nearly identical one that sports a red rubber band. Dr. V is careful not to wear out either pair too soon, hence the rubber-band ID tags—a trivial detail loaded with his distinct personality: his utter lack of vanity, his frugality, his passion for order and discipline in the smallest details. He has built those qualities into his family and into Aravind. One morning, not long after he had minor surgery, a grandniece knelt to help him ease the bandaged foot into the familiar green-banded sandal. As they worked silently at this small task, it struck her, as it often did, just how far these psoriasis-scarred, arthritis-racked feet had come.

On October 1, 1918, one day before Mahatma Gandhi's 49th birthday, in the small South Indian village of Vadamalapuram, Tamil Nadu, a child was born. His parents named him Govindappa Venkataswamy after his father, Govindappa Naicker, a well-respected contractor who owned land and cattle and was given to quoting the scriptures. His mother, Lakshmi, had dark-green tattoos on her arm and wore thick gold rings in her ears. She could add fractions in her head with ease, even though she had not been schooled beyond third grade. Only five of her eight children survived to adulthood; the others died in infancy.

First-born Govindappa was followed by a brother, Nallakrishnan— now a successful engineer turned businessman who is on Aravind's governing board. Then came a daughter, warm-hearted Janaky. A born nurturer, she helped raise her siblings' children while a dream called Aravind was being built. The youngest brother, G. Srinivasan (GS), came next: the one whose iron fist controls Aravind's costs, and of whom Dr. V says time and again, "Without Srinivasan, we could not have done this." Then came Natchiar, the youngest child, born a full 22 years after Dr. V. She was a little girl when their father passed away, leaving the young medical student, Govindappa, as head of the family. Natchiar grew up in her brother's care. He paid her school fees, sent her to medical college, and arranged her marriage. She would later be his chief support through the most painful years of his life. Their connection transcends words.

Fragmented memories from his childhood have stayed with Dr V: the thatched roof of the family home, the pair of bullocks he escorted to the grazing fields at dawn, the scorch of hot sand under bare feet (he does not remember wearing shoes until college), and lessons written first in sand from the riverbed and later on bark, with hand-fashioned twig-pens dipped in ink. But while the fabric and ethos of village life are dear to his heart, in telling his story Dr. V does not dwell on the details. In his words, these images from the past are mere "entertainment," irrelevant to the work of blindness prevention and, by that token, to him insignificant. But one incident does stand out from this period in his life, a sobering story with pivotal effects.

One morning, five-year-old Govindappa was awakened by the piercing cries of a young neighbor screaming in pain. Later that day, he was told that the woman had died in childbirth. "She was hardly 20 years old," he says, reliving that moment almost eight full decades later. "Such a young woman, and then you don't see her anymore." Soon after that incident, Dr. V would lose three cousins to eclampsia, an acute pregnancy-related condition. There were no doctors in his village and no help for complications during pregnancy or labor. These losses troubled him deeply. They seeded in him the resolve to become a doctor, an obstetrician trained to prevent the tragedy of such untimely deaths.

He was a sickly child who developed lifelong psoriasis early on (a painful skin condition that causes the skin to itch and peel, leaving raw layers below, red and aching). His frequent illnesses meant that keeping up with schoolwork was challenging. But what Govindappa lacked in physical strength he made up for in hard work. He was the first child from this sleepy, sun-baked village to pursue a higher education and the first to enter the white-coated dignity of the medical profession.

It was an extraordinary era in which to come of age. In the 1930s, India was in the throes of its struggle for independence. The voice of a man who proposed fighting the British with truth and nonviolence had swept across the nation. Dr. V recalls being ignited by Gandhi's vision and example. The call to simple living and self-reliance and the focus on inner transformation resonated deeply with him. "We started spinning yarn with hand *charkhas* [spinning wheels]. We boycotted foreign goods. There was picketing of liquor shops. I started wearing *khadi* [homespun cloth]," Dr. V says.

In 1944, Dr. V graduated second in his medical class and enlisted in the army as a medical officer. The pay was good, and as the eldest son, he felt a responsibility to support his family. But he had not forgotten his dream of becoming an obstetrician—a dream that was destined to shatter in his prime, accompanied by an exponential increase in his own experience with pain.

❦

RHEUMATOID ARTHRITIS IS a chronic autoimmune disorder. Its exact causes are unknown, but it is generally understood to be a disease that prods the body's immune system to attack its own joints, causing inflammation, pain, and stiffness. In extreme instances, it disfigures the shape and alignment of joints; fingers and toes move from their usual positions, drifting away from the thumb and big toe, to twist and freeze in aberrant formations. In 1948, soon after India's independence and just prior to his discharge from the army, Dr. V developed the first frightening symptoms of this disease. It was to irrevocably alter the course of his life.

The timing could not have been worse. He had just turned 30, was engaged to be married, and was to begin training as an obstetrician. Instead, he was hospitalized and bedridden for close to two years. All his joints were so badly swollen that he could not sit, stand, or walk. Even the slightest movement resulted in excruciating pain.

Natchiar was 12 years old when her brother fell ill. She left the village to take care of him. "In those days, a lot of places had signs, 'Lepers Not Allowed,'" she says quietly. "People mistook his psoriasis and arthritis for leprosy. Sometimes we weren't allowed into restaurants or trains. I used to cry myself to sleep on those days. How could people treat my older brother like that?" But Dr. V glosses over the intense physical suffering and emotional devastation of those years in telling the story of his life. When asked what it was like to witness his own crippling and to realize that it barred him forever from his chosen career in obstetrics, Dr. V smiles and says succinctly, "It was difficult, but then you move on."

Dr. V moved on. His recovery was very slow, but eventually he returned to medical school. On the recommendation of senior colleagues, he joined the eye department instead of the maternity department, for further specialization. Operating on the eye required more nimble skill than physical strength in the fingers. With determination and will, Dr. V persevered through his illness and trained his gnarled fingers to hold a scalpel and cut the eye for cataract operations. "That's how I ended up in eye care," he says. "Sheer accident."

After returning to work, he quietly called off his engagement. Whatever the reasons, Dr. V never married. "Severe pain has been my companion and it has never left me," he once said, in a rare, raw admission.[1] Perhaps this carved deep into him the capacity to feel the suffering of others. He would soon be known for his heightened power of empathy, and in the years that ensued, he worked like a man possessed—haunted by the magnitude of blindness, the unnecessary loss, and his newfound ability to do something about it.

IN THE EARLY 1960S, the government of Tamil Nadu became increasingly interested in eye care services for the villages, and the concept of mobile eye camps was born. Dr. V, who had helped influence this interest—and whose heart had always gravitated toward serving the rural poor—took on the responsibility of heading this new initiative.

Cataract treatment at that time required a weeklong recuperation, during which patients needed to be fed, tended to, and nursed. Dr. V, then working at a government hospital, had a budget of roughly $15 per camp (in today's currency). At each camp, he and his team performed 200 to 300 surgeries. To screen, operate on, and feed these patients; provide them with postoperative care, medicine, and spectacles; *and* cover staff costs within that slender allotment was next to impossible. But impossible had always been a rather dangerous word to dangle in front of Dr. V.

He took his medical team into the villages on this shoestring budget, and when costs went higher than they could afford, he dipped into his meager savings. Initially, villagers were suspicious, and the medical world, too, had its reservations. Dr. V was ridiculed for trying to popularize what colleagues derogatively referred to as "roadside surgery." But he steadfastly continued his work in areas of greatest need. *Identify yourself with all people in all villages. Not trying to exploit, but to grow with them,* Dr. V urged himself in his journals.

He and his team would begin operating at five in the morning and work without rest until seven or eight in the evening. Only then would they eat. And all of them would sit together—the doctors, the nurses, the cleaning staff, and the villagers—a highly unusual practice in India, where unspoken codes still segregate "low caste" menial workers from "upper caste" professionals. It was a rugged, bare bones operation. "We converted schools into operating theaters and sterilized the classrooms," says Dr. V with a chuckle, "no microscopes, sutures, or antibiotics. But the more operations we did, the more the demand." The eye camps taught Dr. V a lesson he would never forget: when you begin doing the work you are meant to do, unexpected resources will find you. Slowly, a powerful ripple of goodwill spread across these rural clusters. One by one, villagers came forward to help the young doctor. Community leaders offered to sponsor the costs of medicines and spectacles. Women told him not to worry about feeding the patients, declaring, "What are we here for? We'll cook for all of you." The rice mill owners offered rice, the oil factory gave them cooking oil, and others donated vegetables. "It was a people's movement," says Dr. V.

That movement laid the foundation for a lifelong relationship with the community. "I was not greedy to take someone else's money," says Dr. V. "I was honest, sincere in my work, and committed to helping the people who were poor. These things gave me a great advantage." In explaining his achievements, Dr. V highlights his humblest qualities. Perhaps it was these unassuming traits that captured the attention of a blind man named Sir John Wilson. He would be Dr. V's mentor, and their friendship would shape the future of blindness prevention in the developing world.

❧

JOHN WILSON WAS BORN in England in 1919 and blinded at the age of 12, when a teacher accidentally gave him the wrong chemicals to mix during a lab exercise. Wilson went on to obtain a double degree in law and sociology from Oxford University. Soon after graduating, he was hired by the Royal National Institute for the Blind—at the time governed by a board of sighted trustees. There, Wilson quickly earned a reputation for being a fearless advocate.

After World War II, Wilson, then in his mid-20s, was sent to tour Commonwealth nations to make a survey of people blinded in conflict. Everywhere he went, he encountered the suffering of the sightless and discovered a surprising truth: malnutrition and disease were responsible for far more casualties of sight than the war.

The field of blindness prevention was still in its infancy. In the mid-1900s, almost no national programs were in place to address blindness, much less a global initiative. In 1948, Wilson proposed forming the Royal Commonwealth Society for the Blind (now Sightsavers International), and served as its director for over three decades. He was knighted in this period and, along with his wife, Lady Jean Wilson, created organizations for the blind in 30 Commonwealth countries, pioneering scores of related programs in the field. Wilson was one of the most effective forces in the battle against curable blindness, and many people were inspired to join him. Among them was an Indian ophthalmologist with gnarled fingers, from South India.

They met in 1965 in New York, at a conference on rehabilitation for the blind. Between waiting for buses, taking elevators, sitting in meetings, and riding in taxis, the two men struck up a ready friendship. "One of Sir John's knacks was that he could meet anybody with ease, whether it was the president of a country or a beggar in the street," says Dr. V. It was not a gift that Dr. V felt he himself possessed. Writing in his journal, he revealed the surprising and deep-rooted sense of inadequacy that plagued him well into his career: *Lots of times I suffer from inferiority complex. I feel I am not an upper caste like the Brahmins. Then in the west that I am not the white class.*

Wilson's friendship with the young surgeon was instrumental in building Dr. V's confidence and strengthening his capacities. "Being brought up in a colonial country, you are all the time looked down upon," Dr. V reflects. "Sir John understood the problems. When I was a student and when I was a doctor, the British were ruling us. It didn't occur to us to feel that we could do something as well or better than them. We had to work hard in our own way and build that feeling of, 'Oh! We *are* as good as people in London.' Sir John used to pull me up constantly—he used to say, let's go see this WHO meeting, or let us see the prime minister."

Those blithely described invitations were part of a global movement. Wilson did not just go "see" a WHO meeting; he helped persuade the World Health Organization, along with all the funding agencies working in the field, to join forces and establish the International Agency for the Prevention of Blindness. He did not just have tea with the prime minister of India; he persuaded Indira Gandhi to launch India's National Program for Control of Blindness, the first nationwide program for blindness prevention in the world.[2]

"You see, as an eye doctor, I was not thinking of a national program or a global program," Dr. V says seriously. "I just wanted to be a good doctor and operate on the people who came to me—whoever I could reach. But when Sir John saw I was working with the community, he thought, 'Now here is a fellow who can be gradually molded to work at the national level.'" With disarming frankness, Dr. V credits Wilson's keen intuition and steadfast support for gently knocking the blinders off of his eyes. As Dr. V sees it, this relationship catalyzed his transformation from a government surgeon struggling to meet the needs of his immediate community into the man who believed he could help solve a global problem.

The Wilsons often visited India to be better connected with the work there. On one such visit, Jean Wilson remembers walking among the patients at an eye camp. "Venka [her name for Dr. V] was examining a patient, and as I walked past, I saw him turn away, and there were tears pouring down his cheeks. I said to him, 'Why Venka, whatever is the matter?' and he said, 'This child, if he had come to me 24 hours earlier, I could have saved his eyes.' It was a little boy with vitamin A deficiency, and it was too late for him."[3]

In cases of extreme vitamin A deficiency, the corneal layer of the eye starts to soften and dissolve, literally melting overnight—a blinding condition called keratomalacia. Dr. V recalls the tragedy of seeing hundreds upon hundreds of young children with melting corneas— children blinded for want of a simple dietary component. His journals reveal the searing questions he asked of each loss:

> *Who is responsible for this child's blindness. She is hardly three months old. Perhaps the first baby for her poor parents. Both eyes are blind. Right eye perforation of cornea with iris prolapse, left eye cornea hazy and dry. They must have spent lot of money to come to [the hospital]. What work are they doing. Where did they go first. Why did they decide to come. What were they feeding the child. Did they realize the danger or risk. How we can help such people hereafter.*

With Wilson's support, Dr. V started India's first residential nutrition rehabilitation center in Madurai. Children with vitamin A deficiency received extended treatment while their mothers trained in basic nutrition and taught how to prepare balanced, cost-effective meals using a kitchen garden. The project swiftly gained traction, and in a series of villages, similar centers were set up that helped improve child health and the early detection of vitamin A deficiency. After one visit, Aravind volunteer Susy Stewart, wrote, "A handful of greens can save the eye. Don't forget the grandfather holding a two-year-old the size of a newborn, already irreversibly blind, eyes murky white, never to see. Never forget the dedication of this staff, the nobility of their work. The Battle. Dr. V will set up camps throughout Asia. He is a man with purpose."[4]

The rates of vitamin A deficiency–related blindness steadily fell, and today, such cases are much rarer in South India. Word spread about the success of the program, and Dr. V found himself with a string of international speaking engagements. As his reputation grew, so did the number of projects that landed at his doorstep. Soon he was running more than half a dozen government programs.

In the midst of all this, Dr. V managed to support two brothers through engineering college, put his youngest sister through medical school, and arrange for the marriages of all his siblings. He talked unceasingly to all of them about the work he saw ahead. For as Dr. V's experience grew, so did his vision for blindness prevention.

# GET LESS, DO MORE

In 2005, a man from Turkey arrived in Madurai and announced plans to set up 20 facilities like Aravind in Egypt—now could someone please tell him how much it would cost, so that he could start buying the equipment and materials needed? If only setting up a system with Aravind's reach and impact were that simple. "Every day I meet some people who want to change the world in two days—or two weeks," Dr. V once wrote in an e-mail.

Most explanations of the Aravind model start at the middle of the story. They treat the founding of the Aravind Eye Clinic as the beginning and plunge from there into a fast-paced account in which a series of eye hospitals burgeon into existence, thanks to the financial viability of a revolutionary approach. But the truth is that Aravind was built on Dr. V's track record of more than two decades of pioneering work at the village, state, and national levels. By the time he was 58, India's mandatory retirement age from government service, Dr. V had served as an ophthalmologist, an educator, and a national public health figure. He had already personally performed over 100,000 surgeries, pioneered a hugely successful outreach model, trained hundreds of young doctors as vice principal and dean of the Madurai Medical College, and been awarded a Padma Shri (one of India's highest honors).

But this man was not built for retirement. There was too much unfinished business in the field, and as a 1976 diary entry reveals, too many burning questions within: *Is it possible to provide cataract operations at a cost that the majority of people can afford. What would be the cost. What sort of paramedical workers will be useful. What facilities can be provided. Suppose we operate 30 patients per week, how many beds do we need.*

First, he would need a place to examine and operate on patients. He would also need nurses and doctors, builders and managers. Naturally he turned to his family. In addition to Dr. V's own siblings, Dr. Natchiar's husband, Dr. Nam; Dr. Nam's sister, Dr. Vijayalakshmi Srinivasan (better known as Viji); and her husband, Dr. M. Srinivasan (known as MS) would form the founding team of Aravind. To manage the hospital, they formed the Govel Trust, a nonprofit body named after Dr. V's parents. "Everyone cooperated—that was our big strength," says Natchiar. "The dream was Dr. V's, but the dream became a reality only because of the family."

Aravind was started at a time when ophthalmology was an unattractive field. There was little money to be made in it, there was great need but low demand for cataract surgery, and specializations had not developed. Given this climate, one of the enduring mysteries of leadership at Aravind is how a retired bachelor with a punishing work ethic and no capital or business plan managed to sign up his entire clan to the task of eliminating needless blindness. "He was like a father to me, and there was more respect for him than a real understanding of his intentions," says Natchiar. She and her husband had both completed fellowships at Harvard University when they decided to join Dr. V. Cultural deference to the family patriarch was no doubt a part of what informed their decisions, but there was more to it than that. "He told us we should serve the poor rather than work in a corporate setting," she says. Natchiar's sister-in-law, Viji, speaks frankly: "To tell the truth, we didn't have time to think on our own, we only had time to do what we were told. And we believed what he told us was the right thing."[1]

"We must be the change we wish to see in the world," said Mahatma Gandhi famously. Dr. V's influence traces the outward spiral of a life lived in that vein. The suffering he had endured and transcended, his passionate commitment to serving the blind, and the ideals he lived up to imbued him with a special magnetism. The founding team did not understand where Dr. V was headed, but they trusted him. In an implicit way, they knew he connected them to something greater than themselves.

To BUILD THE first hospital, Dr. V mortgaged his house, and his siblings pooled their life savings. Each of them put in 500 rupees (roughly $11 in today's currency). When that was not enough, as his brother G. Srinivasan recalls, "I had to pawn jewels from the family in order to pay the construction workers every Saturday. We were not businesspeople. We did not plan ahead; we did not know anything about costing or budgeting. So in the beginning, we had a lot of problems."[2] Dr. V's team worked from dawn until well past dusk, a five-to-nine schedule, seven days a week. Operating at the hospital during the week and in the village eye camps on the weekend, they did everything that needed to be done, including cleaning patient wards and restrooms. In the early years, each of them moonlighted at government or private hospitals, supplementing Aravind's meager earnings with this income. They forfeited many of the conveniences of success and lived simply. It was not an easy choice to make.

Dr. Nam describes the challenge in the initial decade of watching his peers climb up the ladder of material success while the team at Aravind continued to count every rupee. "At that time, I didn't even have a bicycle, let alone a scooter," he says pointedly. "We would be at the bus stand and watch our former classmates drive by in their cars." For an ambitious doctor supporting not just his own young family but also parents and siblings back in his village, it was a difficult period. "Our marriage was not smooth," says his wife, Natchiar, frankly. "My husband was bright and knew he could earn more elsewhere. He adapted, but we had two young children, and the tight finances always made it difficult. At that time, we were not mature enough to fully understand the cause. So we would fight about why we were doing this for my brother. I would cry, but never tell Dr. V." What could she possibly tell the man who refused a salary from the organization he founded? The austere bachelor Dr. V made do with a tiny government pension. It did not occur to him that his siblings might have greater needs.

Ever since the early 1990s, Aravind's doctors have been compensated at roughly the market rate. But during the first decade, money was desperately tight, and the founding team drew dismal wages. "I used to secretly complain to Fred Munson [longtime volunteer and an old friend of the family's] about how tough it was," recalls Natchiar, breaking into laughter. "With his help, we finally got a raise in the late 1980s!" They would all struggle to rear their families in the midst of the unrelenting toil of those years. Viji stationed a crib outside the operating room and nursed her ten-day-old son between surgeries. Natchiar took her qualifying exams in a wheelchair, two days after a Cesarean-section operation.

Each of the founding team members would gradually be chiseled by a work ethic that had nothing to do with financial incentives. "Dr. V always told us we shouldn't have high charges," recalls Viji. "'Think of every patient who comes in as your aunt or your grandmother from the village,' he would say. 'Then automatically compassion will come. Once that feeling comes, then you'll naturally do a good job.' . . .

"When we started, I asked Dr. V, 'Why do we need *five* ophthalmologists in such a small place?'" says Viji, who now heads pediatric ophthalmology at Aravind. "And he said, 'Wait, wait, we'll see.' When I came back from my fellowship in the United States, I asked him again, and again he said, 'Wait, Viji, we'll see.' It was so frustrating . . . and then the growth started. Dr. V always seemed to know what was coming, *way* before we did," she says, smiling.

"One of our strengths was that all of us were from the village, so we knew how to talk to the villagers and they used to identify with us," says Nam. "The workload kept increasing because our reputation was growing." The team went to extraordinary lengths to make their patients comfortable. It was not uncommon for them to start surgeries in the villages at 1 a.m., "because the weather was so much cooler for the patients then," says Natchiar. When Viji thinks back to the alchemy and labor of that era, her face lights up. "It was fantastic!" she exclaims. "Now we don't expect the same amount of work from our staff, but people should know how this place came up." Then she offers up this gem of insight: "Dr. V always told us to keep charges low and see more patients to make it work. Get less, do more. That was our slogan." It was an approach that forced them beyond their comfort zone and demanded that they each trade in small, individual dreams for a bigger, shared one.

There is a gradual, catalytic force unleashed when people put aside personal gain in service to a higher vision, day after day, month after month, year after year. That is why money cannot explain Aravind's success. What the hospital has accomplished today is not by virtue of its bank balance but by, in some sense, its virtue—period. Like many of the founders, Viji's husband, Dr. M. Srinivasan (now a world-renowned corneal specialist), does not use the word *sacrifice*. A man with a sharp mind and little patience for small talk, he traces Aravind's work ethic to the founders' agricultural roots. "Coming from farming families, traditionally, we all worked hard," he says matter-of-factly. "That was not a problem. We had to work all 365 days. We weren't used to vacations. The Aravind culture transferred from the family to the hospital. It wasn't developed through special courses, education, or retreats. It's in the blood."

Decades later, people still pick up on that ethos. "Hardcoreness is one of the things I loved most about Aravind," says Arathi Ravichandran, a public health major from Harvard University who volunteered at Aravind in 2008. "There was an undeniable 'We need to do what we need to do' attitude. No cheesy, frou-frou notions of 'doing well by doing good.' It was kind of just—*doing*."

# THE POWER OF
# CREATIVE CONSTRAINTS

When Professor Kash Rangan first visited Aravind, he found a sophisticated working model that no one there had fully discussed or documented. Thulsi laughingly admits that the detailed strategic framework underlying Aravind's work was articulated in hindsight—to explain Aravind's success, not achieve it. But the absence of a traditional business plan does not make the organization a fortuitous accident. Its trajectory was directed by conscious, if unconventional, decisions and one man's extraordinary compassion.

"Dr. V was able to get into the lives of the patients," says Natchiar. "Before they suffered, he suffered. 'Blindness kills a person every day,' he used to say. 'It takes away their sight, respect, and decision-making authority. Our job is not just to bring them vision,' he would tell us. 'How do we get them back their *dignity*?'"

Dr. V's attempts to answer that question would decisively shape Aravind.

"ALL MEANINGFUL DESIGN begins with empathy," says Tim Brown, "and to me, Aravind is a model of what can be achieved through design."[1] Coming from him, this is no small praise. Brown is CEO of IDEO, one of the most influential design firms in the world.

In 2005, he visited Aravind on a tour coordinated by Acumen Fund, an organization that uses philanthropic capital for social investments (Acumen had supported Aravind in a telemedicine initiative). "What I saw in India, and particularly at Aravind, played a big part in how I've moved forward with IDEO," says Brown. How so? "Innovation, in some fundamental way, is linked to constraints," he says, "and Aravind is an organization that operates within a *very* unique set of self-imposed constraints. That automatically eliminates ordinary solutions."

Brown's argument is compelling: Empathy and self-imposed constraints can force you beyond obvious options. What you then get, he points out, is "the chance of a breakthrough solution instead of an incremental innovation."

The developing world faces constraints of money, skilled labor, and other resources. But Brown is talking about something other than these obvious limitations. "Dr. V brought in his own set of constraints when he insisted on a particular mode of delivering care. He said it had to be high-quality, compassionate care, and that it also had to be affordable and sustainable," Brown says. He is referring to the unwritten rules that Dr. V decided Aravind would follow:

1. We cannot turn anyone away
2. We cannot compromise on quality
3. We must be self-reliant

In summary, these rules meant that whatever Aravind chose to do, it would have to do it with uncompromising compassion, excellence— and its own resources.

Today, numerous initiatives in India provide free eye care to those in need, and at least a dozen of them offer quality that is world-class. Where Aravind differs dramatically from these other efforts is the magnitude of its work coupled with its astonishing financial self-reliance. No other eye hospital in the world comes close to handling Aravind's routine outpatient and surgical volumes. And no other organization in the field provides its services to the poor at this scale, within such a robustly *self-sufficient* model.

☙

OVER THE YEARS, Aravind has proved sustainable in multiple ways. It is an organization that has quadrupled its growth every decade, successfully navigated multiple leadership transitions, and consistently upgraded the quality and range of services provided. It demonstrates all the boons of sustainability: financial health, massive scale, continued relevance, and longevity.

Naturally it is Aravind's financial sustainability that attracts the most attention. In 2009–2010, Aravind made an operating surplus of approximately $13 million on revenues of $29 million.[2] A *Forbes* magazine article in 2010 reviewing Aravind's profitability called it "a performance worthy of any commercial venture."[3]

Oddly enough, financial self-reliance started out low on Dr. V's list of priorities. Certain unpleasant experiences bumped it up very quickly. Dr. V's first application for a bank loan to start Aravind was rejected, and his sole attempt at fund-raising yielded more embarrassment than riches. He had visited a neighboring industrial town to solicit donations, and "he came back with about 1,500 rupees [roughly $33]," says his brother GS. "He said, 'Because people don't know us, they thought that this was some sort of begging.'" The misconceptions came as a painful shock. It had not crossed Dr. V's mind that people might view his fund-raising efforts as an attempt to secure easy cash for his retirement.

In retrospect, the sting of that experience proved invaluable. It spurred Dr. V to explicitly redefine the role of money in his organization. "We're not going to ask people for donations anymore," he announced to his brothers and sisters. "We just have to do the work. The money will follow." It became one of his most-repeated phrases:

Do the work. The money will follow. This serve-and-deserve rule of Dr. V's forced the organization into an improvised independence and fostered some of its most novel systems.

IN THE FIELD of international development, money can be a touchy subject. To carry out their core work, many nonprofit organizations rely on external funding from individual donations or grants from foundations. An unspoken assumption that business and charity do not mix often gives rise to a tension between purse strings and heartstrings.

In this context, Aravind manages to hold two seemingly contradictory principles with ease: self-sustainability and universal access to its services. Dr. V seeded these "constraints" in the organization without a preset plan. But the founding team, over time, evolved effective systems for working within them. "In our experience, self-sustainability is a dynamic process, not a static destination," says Thulsi. "It emerges from a complex interaction of organizational, technical, and human factors." He maintains that Aravind's own financial health and independence are by-products of careful attention to pricing structures, free and paying patient volumes, effective resource utilization, standardization, and an extremely cost-conscious leadership. In other words, at Aravind, self-reliance is more of an ethos than an end goal.

"ZERO CAN BE a legitimate price point," declares Thulsi. This is his succinct response to the to-charge-or-not-to-charge dilemma. Aravind's pricing strategy goes beyond the traditional notions of free care. It positions free service not as a charitable handout but as one of many options in a self-selecting fee system. Its price range—from zero to market rates—is built around a culture that respects every patient's right to selection.

"Choice is fundamentally important," says Dr. Aravind Srinivasan, the hospital's adminstrator. "We all exercise it when we go to a supermarket and choose what we want from an array of options. Our choices are based on subjective combinations of aspiration and affordability. We believe in empowering our patients with that kind of choice."

The organization also believes that a pricing model offering free service as one option within a broader range can serve more patients in need than a system that does only charity. Aravind's consulting work with an eye hospital named Sadguru Netra Chikitsalaya, in the town of Chitrakoot in rural Madhya Pradesh, is a case in point.

Until 2002, the Chitrakoot hospital relied heavily on donor funding and focused exclusively on the very poor. The hospital's trustees believed that charging patients would corrupt the institute's charitable focus. Most of its patients paid nothing, and the hospital ran at a loss. But when Dr. B. K. Jain, the hospital's director, visited Aravind, he experienced the power of a different approach.

With Aravind's assistance, Jain persuaded the Chitrakoot trustees to adopt a tiered pricing system and to broaden its patient base to include wealthier patients. They sought Aravind's expertise to put together a detailed plan of action. Along with implementing the new fee structure, they developed the skills to do cataract surgery with intraocular lens implants (replacing a less advanced procedure) and also began running free eye camps in the community. The ripple effect was dramatic. Five years later, for the first time in its existence the Chitrakoot hospital was breaking even. And it was actually making a surplus.[4]

Most significant was the fact that the number of free and highly subsidized patients served annually had increased by as much as 45 percent, and the hospital's cataract surgery volumes had more than doubled.[5] The profits from paid services made it possible to provide cataract surgery with IOLs for its free patients as well—something it had not been able to do before. In addition, the hospital was able to develop specialty services and retain five times the number of ophthalmologists, drastically reducing its earlier dependence on volunteer medical expertise.

In these ways, the user-fee system at Chitrakoot, far from compromising the mission, proved a tremendous tool for reliably reaching more people in need. It also enabled significant upgrades to services and overall program strength. To Aravind's leadership, financial autonomy is important not in and of itself, but precisely because it allows for this greater command over the many dimensions of quality.

PEOPLE OFTEN WONDER if mistrust creeps in when organizations serving the poor charge market rates for some patients. "That kind of confusion doesn't happen at Aravind," says Thulsi, "because our prices are transparent and compare favorably with local markets."

Aravind's pricing strategy aims to make it easy for patients to seek treatment; there are no hidden costs. "We don't add on charges for individual tests—like refraction, ocular pressure, urine sugar," Thulsi explains. "To us, it is unethical to offer those services with separate price tags. These are basic tests that need to be done. They are all included in the $1 consultation fee that is valid for up to three visits." This outpatient fee (which applies only to paying patients) has not been increased in over ten years.

"From the very beginning, our systems have been designed so that there is no incentive for us to exploit a patient financially," Thulsi says. "For instance, we don't accept commission for patients that we refer outside for MRI or CAT scans." The management regularly reviews clinical protocols to eliminate any tests or medications that do not contribute to improving outcomes or patient comfort. Meetings are held to analyze the number of re-operations, lengths of stay at the hospital, and the reasons behind postponed surgeries. Prescriptions for medicines and tests are scrutinized to ensure that they are advised only when necessary and of real benefit to the patient. The overall goal is to reduce any needless cost and inconvenience to those seeking care. It is an approach that continuously builds fiscal and operational efficiency into the system, as well as patient trust.

There is an interesting flip side to the issue of public perception. Most of Aravind's paying patients, while aware of Aravind's vast work in the community, have no idea that by choosing to pay for services, they are indirectly contributing to someone else's care. Aravind deliberately steers clear of advertising this pay-it-forward angle to its high-end customers. Touting charitable services can work against your reputation in a world where quality and charity are not necessarily linked, and Aravind leadership believes that when it comes to personal health, value for money and quality of care are priorities that tend to outweigh generosity.

❧

"WHEN I FIRST arrived here, I got a strong sense that Aravind had a higher purpose than what was apparent from the outside," says Thulsi. "It was strongly committed to providing eye care to the community, and there were no boundaries to that commitment. It was very clear that whatever it did had to be done with a high level of integrity and transparency. Most places tend to have an internal focus, whether it's money, their own success, or fame. Aravind, as far as I could see, didn't focus on any of that. It was operating on a plane much higher than most organizations."

Thulsi is married to Chitra Ravilla, one of Dr. V's nieces. As a young husband and father, he walked away from a lucrative management position with a multinational company to join Aravind's team in 1981 as its first administrator. He attended the inaugural ceremony of the newly expanded Aravind hospital in Madurai literally a few hours before his own wedding.

Thulsi spent his first years with the hospital doing everything from ordering furniture for the reception area and changing lightbulbs in the operating theater to mapping out patient workflow. "I really grew with the organization," he says, smiling. Over the years, his in-depth understanding of Aravind's mission, his clarity in assessing its needs, and his gift for translating those needs into systemic solutions have turned him into an indispensable global leader in the field of blindness prevention.

"I would very much like to come to Aravind Eye Hospital to spend some time learning and to seek your advice" is a sentiment that Thulsi encounters in his inbox with increasing frequency. It is March 2010, and the man writing in today is Dr. Bharatendu Swain, a plastic surgeon with decades of experience at one of India's well-known corporate hospitals. His passion, however, is Aakar Asha, a grassroots, nonprofit initiative he founded. It performs free restorative surgery for people who are motor impaired and unable to afford the medical attention they need. Swain has studied Aravind's model from a distance and wants to learn more about it in order to better shape his own initiative.

The easy accessibility of Aravind's leadership would surprise most in the private sector. The door to Dr. V's office, for instance, is always open. Anyone can walk in without an appointment. Thulsi's response to Swain is swift, warm, and encouraging. He intuits a genuine dedication and resonance of approach, and soon after Swain's e-mail, a full two-day itinerary is set up, including meals and a stay at the Aravind guesthouse. In Madurai, Swain will tour the hospital, watch live surgeries, meet Aravind's senior management, and be escorted to an eye camp. This hospitality is typical of Aravind—even, as in this case, with a stranger whose work is tangential to its own mission.

SWAIN HAS A neatly trimmed salt-and-pepper mustache and a courteous air. Seated in Thulsi's office, he quickly turns the discussion to questions of scale. His team is now doing 500 complex reconstructive surgeries a year, at no cost to their patients.[6] Swain wants to expand to do ten times that number and asks Thulsi for his thoughts. Thulsi is candid in his answer: "Where large need exists, you can build a much more sophisticated organization with a roadmap aimed at scale. Boutique interventions, even if they bring some kind of personal satisfaction, won't make the needed impact. What's the estimated need where you are?" Swain has done his homework. "Roughly 415,000 people in my home state suffer from disability issues that we can treat," he says. "There's your case for scale," says Thulsi.

The people whom Swain's organization treats are typically healthy, apart from their motor impairment. All they require is a one-time surgical intervention. The needed intervention has low morbidity and next to zero mortality rates. The transformation in a patient's life is dramatic (in all these respects, the treatment parallels cataract surgery). But Swain must consider the issue of sustainability as his initiative grows. He is curious about Aravind's enviable patient equation that balances its services between the very poor and those able to pay.

"So how *did* you arrive at the 60:40 ratio between your poor and well-to-do patients?" Swain asks. Thulsi smiles. "It just happened," he says, adding, "that ratio isn't fixed—the break-up is actually slightly different now." In Aravind's initial years, he explains, free services were provided on an ad hoc basis at the discretion of its doctors. If the attending surgeon knew or suspected that a patient could not afford surgery, then he or she waived the charge. Often the hospital had sufficient income to cover the expense, but when it did not, Aravind's founders dug into their own pockets to make up the difference. By 1980, the leaders created a formal policy giving patients the freedom to choose whether or not to pay for services. The 60:40 ratio of nonpaying and ultrasubsidized patients to those paying market rates emerged organically from there. In recent times, with the growth of the economy, that ratio has shifted to 53:47.

"Currently at Aravind, for every 100 patients treated, the typical breakdown is that 47 will choose to pay close to market rate, 26 will come to us on their own and opt for care at very minimal cost [roughly $15], 27 will choose to come in through our outreach efforts and be treated for free," Thulsi tells Swain. "The annual growth rate in terms of patient volume is about 10 percent," he says, "but the revenue growth rate is much more, because we are finding in recent years there is a real migration from free to paying. Our eye camps influence health care–seeking behavior in the community. Now the percentage of patients opting for free treatment is coming down, and the percentage electing to pay steeply subsidized rates is increasing."

While the paying-to-free ratio is not set in stone, it is closely monitored. Trust must be built and maintained across the entire patient spectrum. If either end loses faith in Aravind's services, the entire ecosystem of the organization is thrown off balance. Losing free patients increases unit costs, affects Aravind's reputation in the community, and reduces training capacity. Losing paying patients augurs a different set of ills. The organization knows this from walking the delicate balance between the two.

Thulsi briefly sketches for Swain a situation in the late 1990s when the proportion of paying patients at Aravind plunged to 18 percent. Projections showed that in as little as two years that figure would plummet to 10 percent. Senior leadership held a series of emergency hospital-wide meetings. It wasn't just the percentages that triggered the red flag. "The real concern was that we were off-sync. We weren't reflecting the market," Thulsi says. There was an upward mobility in the environment that was not showing up in Aravind's patient trends. Once the crisis was spotted, patient surveys were conducted and the results scrutinized for insights. Aravind's leaders learned that the problem was not because something had changed— it was because *not enough had*. As India's economy had grown and standards of living had gone up, patients were willing to pay more for a more comfortable and modernized setting. But in the 25 years since its inception, Aravind's inpatient facility had not undergone any major renovations.

It was time to update more than the hospital's accommodations and amenities. Aravind's leadership also realized that it needed to place more emphasis on additional services beyond cataract. The market for cataract surgery had matured and was becoming highly competitive. Pushed by this reality and by its own mission, the leadership decided to identify other areas of dormant need in eye care. Community surveys for the potentially blinding conditions of glaucoma and diabetic retinopathy revealed a high number of undiagnosed patients. Not as common as cataract, these conditions would require a certain scale to make delivery viable and to develop the necessary treatment expertise. With its ability to provide high-quality, high-volume care, Aravind was well placed to provide such treatment. A more deliberate focus on subspecialties was thus born.

"We also looked at the surgical acceptance rate, patient counseling methods, waiting room ambience, and cafeteria food," says Thulsi. "Then we worked on improving all these different things simultaneously. It took us about two to three years to course-correct and bring the ratio back to healthy equilibrium."

The experience strengthened the case for paying patients in the Aravind system. While providing high-quality eye care to those who can afford to pay little or nothing is an integral part of serving its mission, Aravind's paying patients are key drivers for advancing quality, service breadth, and medical expertise. "We look at financial viability as an indicator of our relevance," says Thulsi. "If people are willing to pay [for something], then there is a need for it. Serving people who can pay helps keep you on your toes."

He has a word of caution for Swain: "The distribution of the disability in your field will be different." He draws attention to the fact that cataract affects both the rich and the poor, and that the well-to-do tend to be reasonably active in accessing care. Paying patients make up a reliable portion of Aravind's patient load, which is crucial for a cross-subsidization model. "In your case, there may be more trauma-related disabilities in the labor class that can't afford to pay for treatment," Thulsi tells Swain. "If incidence is primarily among the poor, then you may need to follow a model that exclusively does charity work. You will want to look into the trend of these disabilities and do some thinking on this front," he says.

"Do you have a donor strategy?" Swain queries. Thulsi breaks into one of his infectious laughs. "We're not a good group to ask that question to because fund-raising really isn't one of our strengths," he says. "Dr. V chose to grow slowly and with internal resources."

He shares that Aravind's core patient care services as well as all of its new hospitals are entirely funded by revenue from its paying patients. "The founders did not want the eyesight of the community held ransom by external resources," he explains. "In the past, we have even turned down people's offers to support our free surgeries." He then makes an important clarification: "But for other areas, like eye care research, we welcome outside funding, and for many of our pilot initiatives we often actively seek grants."

Over the years, Aravind has received funding and technical support from an array of foundations, grant agencies, companies, and individual donors. These contributions are expressly earmarked for areas outside of core patient services and represent only a small percentage of Aravind's total income. In 2009, for instance, grants and donations accounted for 6 percent (roughly $1.8 million) of Aravind's income, compared with the 72 percent that was earned through patient revenue.[7]

There are some exceptions to Aravind's funding policy. The organization does, for instance, allow well-wishers to contribute to its Food for Sight program, which helps cover meals for Aravind's free patients, and to its Youth Vision program, which provides free eyeglasses to schoolchildren at its screening camps. But as Thulsi points out, neither of these programs is dependent on external funding. "If the donations dried up, we would absolutely still continue to provide these services. They are not controlled by money from the outside."

Ultimately, in Thulsi's view, where money comes from is not nearly as important as how it is put to use. One organization might be extravagant with earned resources while another is frugal with donations. Based on Aravind's experience, Thulsi has come to believe that self-reliance is more about a mindset than it is about money. It is a particular way of viewing your resources and putting them to the best use possible.

Swain's initiative might require external funding, but his approach, as Thulsi sees it, bears strong parallels to Aravind's. "You have clinical competence with a broader vision," he tells the visitor. "Money will not be a problem. Maybe in the initial stages there's a bit of a struggle, but not for the bigger vision."

❧

THERE IS A certain charming paradox embedded in the Aravind founders' perspective on money. They are all extremely cost-conscious individuals, but "ask any of them, apart from GS [who manages Aravind's finances], what our annual turnover is," challenges Thulsi. "They will venture a guess but will probably be off by a factor of three or four." He is right. "I don't really know how much we made last year," confesses Dr. Natchiar, "but all of us know how many patients we reached, and that's what our focus really is." Her nephew, Dr. Aravind, smiles. "The founders' approach was a real blessing to the organization. Because it meant, in their heads, they weren't connecting their cause to money."

That early de-linking is perhaps what allows financial resources within the Aravind model to be treated with equanimity. Money here is neither an obsession nor an obscenity, but a tool (one among many others) that aids in the restoration of sight.

❧

AN EARLY PATIENT of Dr. V's, an English Christian monk who dedicated his life to work in rural India, remembers coming in for a checkup at a time when Aravind was still struggling to make ends meet. When he asked for the bill, Dr. V laughed and said, "Brother, for your fee you must send me 100 patients from the villages to be treated for free."[8] An unaffected generosity and lack of greed were hardwired into the organization even when resources were scarce. It spoke to a curious kind of faith. Dr. Jack Whitcher, from the Proctor Foundation in California, remembers discussing a research project when he first met Dr. V and "expressing my anxiety that we wouldn't be able to do it because we didn't have the money."[9] Dr. V told him what he would tell dozens of puzzled colleagues, partners, students, researchers, and volunteers: "You must do the work. The money will follow."

From a strategy perspective, it was about starting the work and letting its perceived value organize the financial resources. From a metaphysical perspective, it is explained a little differently. As the Mother (one of Dr. V's key spiritual inspirations) put it, "The true method of being in the stream of this money-power is the feeling that it is not something you possess, but that it is a force you can handle and direct." She goes on to say that if a person is in touch with this force, then, with respect to money, he "can make it act, make it circulate, and if ever he finds it necessary, receives from it as much power as he needs without there being externally any sign or any reason why the money should come to him."[10] To maintain that invisible laws direct the ebb and flow of money in a system seems a stretch. But it was certainly a part of Dr. V's experience. "It comes," he says simply. "The ideas, the money, the people. Today we have enough credibility to raise a lot of money, but we don't plan to. By and large, our spiritual approach has sustained us."[11]

That—and a man named G. Srinivasan.

IT IS 1:15 P.M., and Dr. V's youngest brother is on his way to lunch. As G. Srinivasan (who also goes by GS) crosses the empty inpatient area, he notices a ceiling fan running. He frowns, walks over to switch it off, and then shakes a fist at the front-desk receptionists. "If I see a fan on in here again when no patients are around—" he raps out menacingly, before breaking into a wonderfully sweet grin. The years and grandchildren have softened him—to some extent. But his displeasure in the face of carelessness, sloth, or extravagance can still cause staff members of all ages to quake in their boots.

The sign outside his office reads simply: "Secretary." (Aravind does not put much stock in impressive titles.) GS is secretary of Aravind's governing trust, but functionally he has also served, since inception, as its director of buildings and finance. He is the organization's biggest implementer of cost-containment measures.

GS has strong features and a face that looks as if it had been carved from dark stone. His lips press together in an almost habitual expression of disapproval, and he speaks in terse, rapid sentences, as though impatient with both the people and the words he employs. But when a family friend cannot afford to send a child to school or an acquaintance in hard times is in search of a job, when the village needs a new marriage hall or the budget for a project is finally tight enough to stand up to his scrutiny, GS can be counted on for support.

In India, land purchase and construction is a tortuous process, ridden with corruption. With a combination of moral integrity and hardheaded perseverance, GS manages all aspects of Aravind's infrastructure and building projects (across its multiple hospitals) single-handedly. He was trained as a civil engineer, and his knowledge is encyclopedic in matters of appropriate building materials, the impact of architecture on workflow, designing for flexibility and growth, and much more. He is an expert at getting durable hospitals up in record time at the lowest possible cost. But that is not all. "At a macro level, he brought in a tremendous amount of financial prudence," says

Thulsi. "That cost culture of everyone thinking three times before asking for money." That mindset is part of Aravind's self-reliant approach. "Sometimes, particularly in donor-driven organizations, there can be pressure on you to spend," continues Thulsi. "You need to eat through a certain amount [of funding] within a set time. This can create a different mindset around resource utilization. But GS's style is to really drill into the details of every purchase request—an ethos that has trickled down to all levels."

Thulsi points out that money within the Aravind system tends to stretch much further than at other hospitals. Many factors contribute to making this possible. For one thing, Aravind's doctors are paid a fixed salary. There are no incentives based on the number of patients they see. This means that once all fixed costs are covered (including salaries), all surplus goes to the organization.

The size of that surplus depends on the margin Aravind is able to maintain, based on the market price. "In Madurai, the market price for midrange cataract surgery is approximately $220," says Thulsi. But Aravind's incurred costs are driven very low: a paid cataract surgery costs the organization (by its own estimates) on average about $75.

Thulsi goes on to explain how Aravind uses its favorable proportion of paying patients and its efficiency-bought gains to strengthen its cross-subsidies. "When a patient chooses to pay in the market-rate range, then we can use the margins to serve more needy patients. But if our incurred cost was, say, $200, we wouldn't have as much freedom to do that," he says.

The market price is set based on an average provider's cost and throughput. This is where Aravind's phenomenal productivity gives it a decided edge. "Say the average practitioner uses his surgical microscope 20 times a month," says Thulsi. "At Aravind, our utilization is actually 20 or 30 times higher. So our average cost per case is drastically lower than his. The considerable downtime that most practitioners have means their average cost per case is much higher than ours."

Aravind abhors downtime.

❧

WHILE THE INITIAL investment cost in terms of equipment and infrastructure is similar to that of other hospitals, the utilization rate at Aravind (that is, the ratio between actual use and maximum potential use of existing infrastructure) is drastically higher—around 80 percent, which far surpasses the global estimate of 25 percent for resource utilization within eye care services.[12]

One of Natchiar's favorite examples of downcycling and waste mitigation at Aravind is how bed linen no longer in use gets converted into tablecloths and then, later still, into washcloths—three uses for one resource. "When we started, we never had any extra resources," she says. "We used to cut up packing material for sponges and even made our own cotton swabs. Now we don't have the same challenges or constraints, but the values are still the same and come from these sorts of experiences."

According to the World Health Organization, at any point in time, roughly 50 percent of medical equipment in developing countries is unusable or in disrepair.[13] Sourcing spare parts for imported medical machines and instruments can be a lengthy and expensive process, as can repairs. Aravind learned this the hard way in its early days, before tailoring its own solution. The organization hired V. Srinivasan, a retired physics professor with a passion for making things work, to begin an in-house maintenance division. That division is now a 35-person team that works across Aravind's network of hospitals.

If a company cannot sell them a spare part, Aravind's maintenance division will find a local machinist who can make it for them. The division's trained team also, for example, cleans and sterilizes retinal forceps, rendering a $1,000 use-and-discard instrument good over several cases without compromising safety. They tackle surgical debris on $36,000 phaco machines, change lightbulbs in slit lamps, identify local substitutes for spare parts and costly consumables (such as imported eye-cleaning solutions), and have even custom-built equipment for special clinical needs. Their constant behind-the-scenes efforts help Aravind to process high patient loads with ease. Aravind openly shares this expertise through six-week training courses on instruments maintenance for eye care, which are typically waitlisted a year in advance. Five weeks of the program are onsite at Aravind. In the sixth week, students travel to an outside hospital and repair its instruments (and those brought in from surrounding facilities) at no charge.

THE 65TH GRADUATION ceremony of the instruments maintenance class is under way at Aravind–Madurai. It is early 2010, and to date the department has trained 414 technicians from 36 countries, including Papua New Guinea, Eritrea, Nigeria, and Cambodia. Very few technicians in developing countries receive training specific to optical instruments and machinery. Ziyanda Zigayi is a slender young South African with high cheekbones and a luminous smile. As she steps forward to receive her certificate, she says, "I used to have to pretend I knew what to do when people in my eye department asked for help. Now, after this training, I actually *do* know." When Aravind's team goes to Johannesburg later in the year to educate technicians, Zigayi will be one of their trainers.

OUTSIDE ARAVIND–MADURAI, an orange bus rumbles down the street, lopsided with four young men hanging on for dear life in the open doorway. Behind it comes a man on a bicycle, with egg crates stacked higher than his head, wobbling precariously. There is a widespread talent in India for carrying more than what is considered sensible, and doing so with unruffled ease. You see it at Aravind too. Throngs of patients that would overwhelm many care providers are considered par for the course here. Aravind's hospital in Madurai alone sees roughly 2,000 patients every day. Collectively, its entire network of hospitals examines 7,500 patients daily.

While the large volume of patients at Aravind forms the engine of the model, the system needs a *regular* flow of patients in order to be optimally efficient. "Managing demand fluctuation is critical to maintaining quality and controlling costs," says Thulsi. Patient volumes are regularly scrutinized. Using data from past years, seasonal trends, and real-time monitoring, the management works hard to smooth out demand patterns and protect against dramatic peaks and troughs that stress the system. For the convenience of their patients, Aravind's hospitals have a walk-in, no-appointment-needed policy that makes it harder to control volumes. This vulnerability is further compounded by Aravind's practice of conducting eye camps.

In the mid-1980s, the surgical load on Mondays would shoot up drastically because of the busloads of people brought in from weekend camps. By Wednesday, patient numbers would drop back to a more normal level. Dealing with this spike-and-dip cycle was frustrating for staff and created inefficiencies. Aravind's approach to the situation was interesting. Instead of doing the most obvious thing and redistributing camps across the week to comfortably flatten the spike, it looked for ways to significantly *increase* patient volumes throughout the whole week—so that old "surge" numbers would be the new norm.

To pull this off, Aravind's leaders first analyzed the bottleneck in patient admissions. Looking at the data, they realized that a considerable number of patients were dropping out of the system after being told by a doctor that they needed surgery. Further investigation revealed a missing step in the process. Patients needed an opportunity to have their doubts and fears about undergoing surgery addressed at length by a staff member. A cadre of counselors was promptly conceived and a new division for patient counseling implemented.

Aravind's hospital network now has 164 patient counselors. Its systems ensure that a counselor meets with each patient advised to have surgery; she explains the entire process, along with all the various options available, and fields any questions the patient might have. Within two years of introducing counselors, direct admissions per week increased fourfold. In the same period, Aravind's eye camp volume also increased by 20 percent. But by then, the systems in place were robust enough to handle the increase without a hitch.

This approach to bottlenecks and capacity barriers at Aravind leaves no room for complacency. Dr. Usha Kim, one of the organization's senior doctors, recalls walking into Dr. V's office with two other colleagues in 1999 after first hearing of his plans to build a fifth hospital in Pondicherry. "We said to him, 'Look, this is a bad idea. We don't even have enough doctors in Madurai right now. We have four hospitals already; we're not interested in starting another one,'" says Usha.[14] Dr. V listened to them quietly and nodded his head. "If you feel that way, we won't do it," he said. "But then after that, he called us each in to meet him individually," says Usha, laughing at the memory. "He called me the next day and said, 'You know, when you think you've grown enough, that's when you start to decline. It means you're walking downhill instead of climbing.'" Aravind–Pondicherry was inaugurated in 2003, and Dr. V's perspective on growth would slowly filter through the organization's leadership. "I've matured into the idea that when you're in a comfort zone, you start to deteriorate," Usha says. "You need to have some kind of pressure or you don't evolve. Dr. V was right—it isn't about staying where you are and feeling cozy."

# YOU DON'T FIND PEOPLE, YOU BUILD THEM

D r. Bharatendu Swain, the visiting plastic surgeon, has been at Aravind for half a day and is still reeling from the wealth of information he has received, but his stream of questions continues unabated. He is now with the administrator of Aravind–Madurai—Dr. Aravind. Revisiting the issue of scale, Swain describes chasing the Indian government for two years in hopes of obtaining free land to expand his charity work—efforts that were in vain. "What is an appropriate size for me to aim for now?" he asks.

"We started with 11 beds," Dr. Aravind says with a smile. "I'd say, do a pilot, and if that works, then build off of it. For us, scale has always come later. Building in phases is more practical. Your time and energy needs to be invested in inspiring people, patients, and staff. Start with a microcosm of what you're dreaming of. Seeing it in motion will give you the energy you and your team need. Commitment on the ground goes a long way, even if it's a modest effort."

Aravind leadership's approach to expansion was without haste—or complacency. "As we made more money, we built more floors," Dr. V explains. The Madurai hospital, now a five-story building, was built floor by floor, over a period of five years. The founding team at Aravind favored a slow and steady pace over rapid expansion, which mitigated not just financial risk but also quality variation and the dilution of values. Construction of additional hospitals in the Southern Indian localities of Theni, Tirunelveli, Coimbatore, and Pondicherry was funded by patient revenues and staggered across more than 20 years. "I'll take this phasing input seriously," says Swain. "It's been a real issue, the question of size, but this sounds like the right approach."

He mentions then that a renowned business school and a financial company have stepped forward to assist him with strategy development. Dr. Aravind offers a good-natured caveat. "External resources are great, but they can complicate things. Push the kid in the swimming pool, and he'll swim. He doesn't need ten people telling him all the ways he can drown—that way, he'll never get in the water." Dr. Aravind then goes one step further with a recommendation. "I'd suggest something like this: commit a certain percent of your time, one day of the week or whatever you can manage, and then just *start*."

The conversation surges forward into more questions around hiring, reporting structures, and how to attract and retain talent. They cover a lot of ground. Before he takes his leave, Swain says tentatively, "I'll keep communicating with you, if you don't mind?" "Please. We'll be in touch," replies Dr. Aravind, before echoing Thulsi's sentiments from earlier in the day: "You have the clinical skills, and you have a vision for the bigger picture. You are off to a great start."

And then, almost as an afterthought, he adds, "You know, Dr. V built this place at the right time. He wasn't competing for anything at that stage in his career. He was building competence in others. You have to be completely out of the rat race to build an institution like this."

❧

"IN 1978, THE HEAD of a big company came to us and said he would like to donate a large sum of money to Aravind in memory of his wife," says Natchiar. "All we had to do is name the new hospital wing after her. We were very tempted because money was short then. But we said no. It was a harmless request, but we figured if we started doing things just to get someone else's money, then we wouldn't have the same kind of energy. The purpose behind our work would start to get lost."

Natchiar sees patients in a cubicle adjoining her office. It is not the kind of workspace you would imagine for the joint director of the world's largest eye hospital. She served Aravind in this capacity for 15 years, all from this 8-by-12-foot room. In 1965, she was among the first women in India who qualified as ophthalmologists. Chief of Aravind's neuro-ophthalmology division, she has worn multiple hats through the decades, including that of commander in chief of Aravind's vast outreach activities and its paramedical program. She has always been, and continues to be, the unofficial keeper of its culture. As Fred Munson jokes, "Natchiar believes in the Aravind culture more deeply than anyone in the whole organization. And she would like to, I think, sometimes go around with a club and beat the culture into it because that is her favorite way of operation." (Munson's friendship and respect for Natchiar run deep. He adds with a twinkle that she has now found "more effective" modes of working.)

Like Dr. V and all his siblings, Natchiar is deeply good—but not always nice. As one of Aravind's senior nurses put it, "People get scared when they see her because she looks at all the details. You suddenly notice the little things that are wrong as soon as she comes in the room. She shouts a lot, but she also teaches us a lot about how to work, and how to do the best for our patients." Natchiar is a woman with a phenomenal organizational consciousness and a vividly personal style. She is equal parts tyrannical, generous, and concerned.

Her morning is spent examining patients and doing hospital rounds. In the span of a single hour this afternoon, she has reviewed a list of nursing staff members and their transfer locations, counseled a nurse departing on maternity leave, met with the head of housekeeping, responded to a speaking engagement request, and looked over the schedules of doctor-volunteers visiting from other countries. Natchiar delves into particulars with the thoroughness of a clinical investigator, focusing always on the practical. Take the housekeeping meeting, for instance. "How are other organizations doing recycling?" she wants to know. She wastes little time on debate and is quick to action: "All recyclables can be sold. We must stop thin plastics," she declares.

Natchiar grabs a pad and sketches the kind of trolley she wants to use for transporting food waste from the hospital. It will be composted for farmland. The discussion moves on. A hospital, Natchiar maintains, has to "look nice like a hotel" but has to pay a lot more attention to disinfection. This morning, she noticed the way Aravind's floors were being mopped and was unhappy with the process. Her dissatisfaction immediately translated into recommendations for color-coded buckets, standardization of equipment, and additional training of janitorial staff. To all these areas, Madam (as she is known to her staff) brings more than a streak of deep maternal interference and caring. On this particular day, she has already had food delivered to a young doctor with a newborn baby, arranged for the hospitalization of a nurse's ill mother, and gifted a voluminous apron (specially purchased on a trip to England) to the hospital's gardener.

Between patients and meetings, Natchiar composes an e-mail to Aravind's senior leadership regarding the passing away of a volunteer whom she had taken under her wing. Mangammal was a widow who volunteered with Aravind for 28 years and considered it her home. She worked at the patient inquiry counter and lived on the premises in the nurses' dorms, a surrogate grandmother to the young women there. Natchiar had once invited Mangammal to eat lunch with her in her office, a gesture that meant a great deal to the elderly woman. The shared lunch sessions soon became a daily custom. When Mangammal died, she surprised the organization by leaving it over a million rupees in her will. No one, least of all Natchiar, had been aware of her assets. "I have handed over the money to GS, and we think it can be used for the Food for Sight program, for feeding our free patients," writes

Natchiar. "We are very grateful to Mangammal for serving us physically when she was with us, and helping the poor after her death."

Natchiar is wearing one of her vibrant handwoven saris. It is olive green with a narrow red border shot with *zari* (gold thread). She has the same strong features as her siblings, a radiant smile, and a healthy suspicion of sophistication that she often phrases in unforgettable ways. "These people from the West, they talk a lot about 'value addition.' I don't know what that means," she says. "When a nurse holds an elderly patient's hand and leads her where she needs to go— to me that is value addition. But that's not what these people seem to be talking about."

❧

FROM HIS EARLY DAYS in the field Dr. V recalls women in the villages draped in tattered saris who had no change of clothes. Because of this fact, with a mixture of fear and shame, they refused to travel to hospitals in town for much-needed treatment. In a society that is hierarchical in almost every aspect, it is not easy for a poor, unschooled farm laborer to approach a hospital without feeling intimidated. *There is an unnatural atmosphere,* wrote Dr. V in 1978 after a visit to a reputable medical institute in Delhi. *It has not got Indian traditional hospitality and culture. How to bring that hospitality and culture in our hospitals and camps. The ordinary man must feel at home.* At Aravind, the nurses—themselves from villages—are beacons of comfort, guiding patients through the maze of medical care. Their specialized skills, honed by repetition, not only enhance quality and allow for high patient throughput but also nurture a sense of individualized care.

In India, you never address an older or elderly person solely by his or her first name. People are commonly addressed by a relational term. "*Paati* (Grandmother), come this way," "*Thatha* (Grandfather), look over here." You hear these phrases again and again in the corridors of Aravind and in the eye camps, as young nurses guide the elderly through the process. The nurses themselves are referred to as "sisters." There is quaintness to this easy assumption of relationship between the staff and patients. It lends a note of grace to interactions that in many hospitals can be brusque. At Aravind, patients are never more than a few steps away from a competent professional in sari uniform who speaks their language and treats them with compassion. There is far more to the role of these women than mere assembly-line efficiency or a financial bottom line. They are the scaffolding that holds the Aravind model in place and the most pervasive conveyors of its culture. Each one of them is carefully selected for this role.

A SEASONED INTERVIEW panel sits at a wooden table in a basement classroom of Aravind–Madurai. Alongside Dr. Natchiar are Nursing Tutor Alees Mary, Head Nurse of Surgery Aleykutty Varghese, and Nursing Superintendent Radha Bai. The three nurses are imposing in crisp white saris. Radha Bai is in her early 50s, with salt-and-pepper hair pulled into a bun. She oversees the work of more than 500 young women, and her air of calm authority makes it hard to believe that she first came to Aravind as a timid teenager. "I was 19 when I joined here in 1979. I grew up in a village and didn't know about town life or hospitals," she says. "But here, I was treated like family."[1]

The founding team's respect for and connection to villagers has had a profound impact on its approach to recruitment. In the early days, they encouraged young women from poor families in their own and neighboring villages to apply for jobs at Aravind. As the hospital grew, so did this invisible network. Since its inception, Aravind has recruited over 5,000 women for various paraprofessional roles, including ophthalmic nursing.[2]

All along the corridor and in multiple classrooms, chairs have been arranged for the candidates. Gazing across the sea of young, expectant faces, one fact leaps out: none of these women have come alone. An unusual practice at Aravind is its insistence that prospective candidates attend the interview accompanied by parents or grandparents. Even more unusual is the content of these interviews. "We ask questions not relating to medicine, [but] relating to the farm," says Natchiar. "We ask them about rainfall, about manure, and the value of their crops. We look at the family background, the common sense in the girl, her attitude." She chuckles, describing the naiveté of parents who often interrupt the interviews to make innocent corrections to their children's exaggerations. The honesty of this sort of interaction appeals to Aravind.

In this system, natural empathy and a demonstrated willingness to work hard (be it milking cows, taking care of siblings, or helping in the fields) can count more than high grades. Even though some of the panel's questions may seem startlingly irrelevant to the job description, the combination of experience, intuition, and the very strong practical grounding of the interviewers ensures that they very rarely miss the mark. When watching them in action, it becomes increasingly clear that the panel is focused on not one but two questions.

The first and more obvious one: What does she have to offer us?

The second and equally important one: *What do we have to offer her?*

There is a deep recognition within Aravind's senior management of the impact of hiring on the female candidate and her family. If not for their jobs at Aravind, many of the women employed here would have been grazing cattle, working in match factories, or forced by their families to marry within the year. Being hired by Aravind transforms not just their lives but those of their siblings and extended family as well.

Eighty percent of Aravind's employees are women, and the majority of them are paraprofessionals.[3] Aravind prefers women because, as Natchiar says with her usual directness, "they are better with patients and less prone to distraction." When hiring them, Aravind's focus is on value-fit over skill-fit. It looks not for accomplishment, but for people suited to its pattern of working. "Our task is to make an ordinary person extraordinary," says Natchiar briskly. "We make them activists at 18."

The organization assumes guardianship in a manner that could seem intrusive in other parts of the world but is in keeping with the local culture and has mutually beneficial results. "They've taught me about savings," says Parveen Banu, an attractive 22-year-old refractionist at Aravind–Pondicherry who speaks with candor about her five years here.[4] "We were compulsorily made to open a savings account. At the end of the first year, I helped buy back our home. In the second year, we bought some jewelry for me. In the third year, we arranged my sister's marriage," she says with a glow. In a country where debt to the local moneylender often traps generations, these are significant milestones that Aravind has helped thousands of women cross. Many of its senior nurses are the chief breadwinner at home.

Over a two-year period of training, a metamorphosis takes place. The intensive residential program combines lessons in the classroom with on-the-job training and specialization. At the end, these young women will no longer be fluttering, insecure new recruits but self-assured members of the extended Aravind family. Many of them possess enormous strength of character. Some are single mothers whose husbands have deserted them or are unemployed alcoholics. Working at Aravind provides these women with a measure of dignity, stability, and control over their lives. It also reveals their considerable potential for leadership.

Senior nurses are the chief decision makers for 70 percent of all the activity that takes place in Aravind's operating rooms and patient wards. This includes daily staff allocation, equipment, and sterilization planning, as well as caseload distribution among the doctors. Aravind relies heavily on its nurses' sharp-eyed judgment and familiarity with protocol. They play an integral role in the training of postgraduate ophthalmology students. Senior nursing staff members assign patients to individual residents based on case complexity and the student's skill level. Student doctors often find themselves following the nurses' cues in the examination and operating rooms, and are answerable to them for patient follow-up. These women are fierce guardians of patient well-being, as well as encouraging mentors.

"We watch the younger doctors in each step of the operation," says R. Sundari. She joined Aravind in 1992 when she was 17 and fell in love with the complexities and stringent demands of working in surgery. She is now one of the most respected operating theater nurses in the system. "If they are struggling with a particular technique, we point them to training videos and have them practice particular steps in the wet lab to increase speed and perfection of suture techniques," she says.

A. R. Jeeva, assistant nursing superintendent, has been with Aravind since 1986. She encapsulates what she has learned from the system in two words of Tamil: "*Surrusurrupu, sikkanam,*" which roughly translates as "Briskness and thrift." "I learned these things here, and I don't know why but I can't imagine working anywhere else." Jeeva is clear about how the transfer of values happens. "When someone so much older, like Madam [Dr. Natchiar], works so hard and does so much, then we know we can do it too," she says. "We want to make the trainees who come after us do the same kind of work with the same spirit—they have to enjoy the work like we did. If there's even a little bit of bitterness or resentment about handling the load, you can't stay here as long as I have."[5]

Most nurses cycle out of the system relatively early, but for a different reason. When a new cohort of trainees enter the Aravind system, they are usually fresh out of high school and have four or five years before, as is the custom in India, their families arrange their marriages and they relocate to where their husbands live. Rather than posing an unequivocal threat, there are aspects of this relatively high turnover at Aravind (roughly 10 percent in 2010) that work to its advantage. The turnover ensures a natural agility within the system and keeps the average age of the workforce young. For those who do stay on, the organization strives to create career tracks. Depending on their ability, these women become tutors, supervisors, or managers in various departments across Aravind's network of hospitals. Some even become trainers who help transfer best practices from Aravind's nursing program to hospitals across the globe, in places like Bolivia, Congo, and Bangladesh.

Aravind's experienced nurses are highly regarded and sought after in the field. A dearth of well-trained medical assistants across the country heightens this demand. Every so often, Aravind loses a few of its nurses to private practitioners promising higher salaries. The leadership knows that the efficiency and sustainability of the organization depend heavily on these women. Behind every one of Aravind's phenomenally productive surgeons stands a team of highly competent nurses. "All I do is diagnose, then in surgery open the eye, operate, close the eye, and follow up the next day," says Dr. Usha Kim, who now oversees the entire nursing program at Aravind. "These women take care of all the other steps, before, during, and after. They are the real heroes in our system."

THE ENORMOUS SCOPE of the mission that Dr. V set necessitated invention. It pushed the founding team well beyond self-centered, complacent solutions and fostered what global activist Lynne Twist, author of *The Soul of Money*, calls "sufficiency," "an intentional choosing of the way we think about our circumstances, an act of generating, distinguishing, making known to ourselves the power and presence of our existing resources and our inner resources."[6] It is this mindset of sufficiency that spurred Aravind to identify resources and create relationships in unexpected places—from community leaders and high school–educated village women to grateful patients and retired physics professors.

Being rooted in sufficiency also prompted the leadership to use these resources in original ways and account for them with a high degree of integrity, whether in making their own swabs, repairing their own instruments, monitoring surgical volume fluctuations, or calculating the case-finding cost per patient at each of Aravind's camps. And ultimately it unleashed a generative force that helped Aravind build a highly skilled, resonant workforce.

"Anyone can have a vision," says Natchiar, "but to keep that vision in action, you need people." Dr. V had his brothers and sisters to put his dream into motion, but it would take far more people-power to sustain it. India has only a little over 13,000 ophthalmologists for a population of 1.2 billion.[7] (The United States, by contrast has over 18,000 for a population roughly a quarter the size of India's.[8]) Dr. S. R. Krishnadas, one of Aravind's leading glaucoma surgeons, remembers complaining to Dr. V in the early years about a lack of personnel. Dr. V had chuckled and replied, "Doctor, you don't just find people, *you have to build them.*"[9]

RATHER THAN DEPEND on externally trained staff, Aravind took an innovative and self-reliant approach to recruitment and training—not just of nurses, but of doctors too. More than 90 percent of Aravind's ophthalmologists are products of its own training. The management has a strong preference for employing doctors groomed within its walls because they have already absorbed not just the technical aspects of its system but also the cultural ethos of the organization. "They have less to unlearn," explains Natchiar, smiling. "And it doesn't happen in a day. The buildings, the money, even the technology, can happen quickly. But the values—they have to be *cooked.*" The founders see this kind of tempering as crucial to the organization's sustainability.

Dr. V spends a great deal of his time mentoring Aravind's doctors. He has a way of grooming people into significant leadership positions despite themselves. The ability to envision the full capability of a person and spur him or her to living it is one of his strengths. "Just as if you are training somebody for the Olympics, you train everybody every day," he says, speaking with sweet, almost comical, simplicity of the hands-on way he mentors staff at Aravind. "You coach him, guide him, and play with him. So you can develop him quickly as a top player."

"The great thing about Dr. V is that, as a teacher, he transfers everything," says Dr. MS, a renowned corneal surgeon and one of Aravind's founding team members. "He guides you in diagnosis and surgery; he encourages you to attend conferences, present papers, and visit other hospitals, other models; he speaks highly of you in the field. In order to stay on top, many other leaders won't do this. We try and do the same thing Dr. V did with us, with our students. This is why we get such good doctors from all over the world."

MS's wife, Dr. Viji, dissolves into laughter remembering how Dr. V's small caring gestures went hand in hand with putting them all through the grind. In the early years, every morning on Dr. V's orders, a flask of hot coffee would arrive at their doorstep at 5 o'clock sharp. "We had no fridge to store milk in, at the time," says Viji. "The flask would come for two reasons: one, to make sure we had a cup of coffee in the morning. And two, to wake us up and make sure we were on time for surgery!" By 5:30 a.m., husband and wife would be in the operating theater alongside Dr. V.

The relentless coaxing toward excellence is multifaceted, and Dr. V is clear that the demands of the job go beyond medicine. "Doctors here must develop physical stamina, mental capacity, and *a vision*," he says firmly. But a vision that soars doesn't come naturally to everyone. Dr. R. Ramakrishnan, or RK, as he is known, is a prime example of someone who was mentored far beyond his own aspirations.

A well-liked surgeon with a soft-spoken manner, RK specialized in glaucoma, the third-largest cause of blindness in the world. With assistance from Dr. Alan Robin, a professor of ophthalmology from Johns Hopkins University, he founded Aravind's glaucoma department. In 1996, when Aravind leadership transferred the director of Aravind–Tirunelveli to the new hospital in Coimbatore, Dr. V identified RK as the man to fill the vacant slot. RK's retiring nature, coupled with many a surgeon's typical aversion to management, made him shrink from the considerable promotion. "I told him I would be a bad fit because I'm not good at scolding people," he says.[10] But his spluttered protests were in vain.

This is a classic example of how Dr. V's word is heeded as law, often overriding personal preferences—but what is interesting is how Dr. V himself processed their discussion. *I had a talk with Dr. Ramakrishnan yesterday*, he wrote in his journal. *He is keen to stay here and develop himself as a Glaucoma expert. He feels he is not good in management. There was a certain amount of bitterness and misunderstanding in our discussion. How to develop people. How to bring spiritual development—integral development, to a large number of our people.*

As a leader, Dr. V is not impervious to the perspectives of other people. He listens, but more often than not, he comes to the conclusion that they are arguing for their own limitations. Because he is deeply interested in not just the professional but also the spiritual, emotional, and intellectual evolution of his staff, his lookout point is perched on high ground. The fact that everyone understands this plays into the curious culture of acquiescence to Dr. V's orders at Aravind.

So, in 1996, RK, who had just built a beautiful new house in Madurai, moved with his wife and two young sons to Tirunelveli. The job waiting for him was not easy. But RK, true to Dr. V's intuition, rose to the occasion. The reluctant administrator surmounted his own lack of confidence and went on to build extensive community ties for outreach, increase focus on the hospital's specialty services, and ramp up its medical training.

Mentorship is often a baton—those who receive it tend to pass it on. RK shaped others in the same determined and intuitive way in which he himself had been shaped. "When I first joined, I was very insecure about my surgery," reminisces Dr. R. Meenakshi, a former student of RK's. "I used to watch his surgeries, and one day I said, 'I don't think I will ever get the confidence to do surgeries like you.'" "You don't know how many years I took to get here," RK told her firmly. "You're just at the beginning of your learning curve. Believe you are good and you will be good. You can do it." He steadily mentored her and many others through the years. Meenakshi, the once-unsure surgeon, now heads the pediatrics division at Aravind–Tirunelveli, and RK, the leader still loath to harshly reprimand anybody, is her role model.

Leadership is not always quite so benign within the organization.

# THE QUESTION OF THE GREEDY DOCTOR

"You'll be drilled, fried, boiled here." Dr. Prajna Venkatesh's clear voice rings through Aravind's conference room where the institute's 2009 class of postgraduate students in ophthalmology are gathered. "But we're interested in you. We care about you and about making you shapers of research, education, systems, and processes."

In Aravind's first decade as a government-recognized postgraduate institute (which began in 1982), the organization's overwhelming focus was on eye care service delivery and outreach camps. Teaching was done in an ad hoc manner, squeezed in while attending to the urgency of service delivery. Since the turn of the millennium, however, Aravind has increasingly refined its teaching facilities, course structure, and methodologies to attract the country's best students. Today, it is one of India's most esteemed training institutes for ophthalmology, prized for its high-caliber instructors, its advanced specialty departments, the hands-on surgical experience, and the case exposure provided by its large volume of patients. On an annual basis, Aravind currently takes in 35 ophthalmology residents and 55 fellows (in specialty areas), and provides more than 350 ophthalmologists with short-term courses. By 2011, as many as 15 percent of all the ophthalmologists in India, 10 percent of those in Nigeria and Nepal, and 100 percent of those in Bhutan had undergone some form of training at Aravind.[1]

In India, many people outside the field of ophthalmology are unaware of the breadth of Aravind's contributions, and its near-celebrity status in the international business school community and public health domain. Dr. Prajna is out to set the record straight—at least for this group of new students. He zeroes in on Aravind's recent front-page accomplishments: the Gates Award for Global Health in 2008 and its 2009 listing in *Fast Company* magazine as one of the world's 50 most innovative companies.[2] "Aravind has won global awards that no other organization in India has even been nominated for," he raps out sharply, referring to the Conrad N. Hilton Humanitarian Prize that Aravind received in 2010.

The students regard Prajna with a mixture of uncertainty and awe. He is chief of medical education for the Aravind system, head of the cornea department at Aravind–Madurai, and a Fellow of the Royal College of Surgeons (he is also the eldest son of founding members Natchiar and Nam). His slick and snazzy style is a departure from the self-effacement of the earlier generation. "Other institutions like to boast that they are a center for the exams of the International Council of Ophthalmology [ICO]," says Prajna, and then with a touch of self-congratulation, "I help set the questions for the ICO exams. Such is Aravind's presence in the sphere of international ophthalmology." Humility is not his strongest suit, Prajna admits with a grin. But his lordly manner is backed by considerable professional competence.

"When doctors from the United States see what surgeons from Aravind do, they are blown away," says Dr. Christine Melton, a Manhattan-based ophthalmologist. "I had Prajna give a presentation at the New York Eye and Ear Infirmary on corneal ulcers one year. After his talk, the faculty advisor told his residents, 'The amazing stuff you just saw—don't try it here. We don't have that kind of expertise.'"[3]

Christine came to Aravind in the early 1980s and witnessed the beginnings of the model taking shape. She performed cataract operations illuminated by flashlight and caught a spark from Dr. V's vision. Upon her return to the United States, she helped formalize and oversee a process that sent two to three residents from New York to Aravind for training each year. Over a period of 35 years, more than 100 surgeons would visit Aravind in this way. "They each stayed three weeks to a month, during which time they would typically do 30 to 40 operations. The requirement for their *entire* residency is between 70 and 80 cases," says Christine, "so in terms of their confidence and adeptness, this really got them over the hump. Not to mention the opportunity of seeing so many textbook specialty interest cases!"

Each year, Aravind hosts a number of foreign residents from some of the best medical schools in the world and offers them training opportunities at no charge. In return, its own doctors and students gain informal exposure to Western systems, techniques, and policies. "Aravind's success goes beyond training others. It has a really open mind to learning whatever is out there from other people," says Christine, who dedicates a considerable part of her time to Aravind's cause. She has arranged for many of its surgeons to undergo training and observation visits at some of the finest eye care facilities in the United States. If the training is in New York, she hosts them in her own home. Her deep commitment to and continuing relationship with Aravind is characteristic of many of the early visitors to Aravind who found themselves unexpectedly moved by Dr. V and his team.

Part of Christine's own motivation in staying involved stems from wanting to pass on that experience. "For the residents from the U.S., the Aravind adventure is a life-changing thing," she remarks thoughtfully. "It's extremely humbling because it comes at a time in their careers when they are used to a routine, insular world and the illusion of having everything under control. Then you see this much greater challenge being addressed with such excellence. It's very empowering, in terms of redefining what you think you can contribute."

DR. PULIN SHAH was raised in Louisiana. His was an idyllic Southern upbringing that included catching rattlesnakes in the sugarcane fields surrounding his school and sailing the family boat in the Gulf of Mexico. Later he applied to medical school, and as a final-year ophthalmology resident at San Francisco's California Pacific Medical Center, he was inspired to train at Aravind after meeting Dr. V.

Describing the experience of treating patients there, his voice grows increasingly animated: "A lot of the patients who come to Aravind are truly blind from cataracts. They have advanced cataracts in both eyes; so you look at them and you'll see just two big white pupils—cataracts like *idlis*," says Shah.[4] (*Idlis* are steamed rice cakes, a popular South Indian dish). "You just know these people haven't seen anything for a very long time.

"First day after operating, I'm looking very carefully through the slit lamp at my patient's right eye. Everything looks great; then I take a quick look at his other eye. He still had an eye patch on, since I'd done the operation just six to eight hours ago. So I took the patch off and he started to look around, and I didn't think much of it. And then I realized—this is the first time this man is seeing in, probably, years!"

Poetry and practicality blend in that moment, when a surgeon lifts a patch to stare into an eye newly sighted by his hand. Shah muses over his own experience, "The patients in India, they don't react a lot. I mean, it's a cultural thing. I think in the States, people would be like, 'Oh my God—look, I can see!' Here they're very quiet, they're very solemn. I think they're ecstatic inside, but it's not all over their faces. But if you look beneath the surface, you can see this happiness that they have. They start to light up. I got the satisfaction of seeing *that*. And it's a daily occurrence at Aravind."

DR. PRAJNA VENKATESH is still pacing in front of his captive audience of postgraduates. "So what's in it for you if you join Aravind?" he asks, and without pausing for an answer he continues, "You can do much more while you are here than just passing an exam." He makes this announcement in the manner of a calm oracle before launching into a string of impressive achievements by previous students at Aravind: publications in prestigious journals; presentations at high-profile conferences; and deployment to foreign countries to assist with replication efforts. The postgraduates of yesterday now run some of Aravind's hospitals, and as Prajna points out, it did not take decades for them to reach those executive positions.

He is pitching Aravind to these young professionals with a clear understanding of their aspirations. Prajna and others in his generation at Aravind recognize that it takes more than an inspiring mission to draw in and retain young ophthalmologists. In general, retention of its doctors is one of the bigger challenges that Aravind faces.

Later that day, seated in his office, Prajna reflects on the situation. "The peril of India's growing economy is the abundance of opportunity your employees have elsewhere," he says. "Our salaries are competitive but can't beat private practice or corporate salaries." The fact that none of Aravind's hospitals are in India's metropolises is an added disadvantage for doctors seeking higher incomes and an urban lifestyle for themselves and their families.

Given these realities, the tongue-in-cheek question of incentives for "the greedy doctor" often comes up when people are first introduced to the Aravind model. There is a natural curiosity to know what keeps talented professionals who "want more" at an organization whose driving ethos is to "do more."

A surgical residency at Aravind lasts two or three years, depending on the choice of program. Typically, 60 percent of Aravind's postgraduates leave for jobs outside as soon as their residency is complete. Those who do stay on are often drawn in by specialization opportunities and other unique career choices the organization affords. Aravind's specialty departments each screen tens of thousands of patients, providing doctors with first-hand experience not just with routine cases but with a wide range of rare conditions as well. They offer a chance to build skill and expertise levels that would be hard to come by in smaller institutes. As private practitioners in metropolises, the doctors might earn more, but Aravind's international visibility, along with its teaching, research, and management opportunities, is not easily dismissed.

Dr. Dhananjay Shukla is a strapping retina specialist at Aravind–Madurai with a trim goatee, a rigorous gym routine, and a passion for ophthalmic research. In a largely mild-mannered organization, he stands out for his short fuse, outspokenness, and general disdain for cataract surgery. To him, the relative simplicity of these operations, their more or less assured outcomes, and the minimal variation between cases amount to a professional rut. "It all gets a bit pedestrian after a while," he says.[5] "The only thing cataract surgeons can talk about after a morning of operating is the number of operations they did." To Shukla, the high-stakes complexities in his chosen field of retinal surgery are infinitely more compelling. "I remember as a student watching Dr. Nam operating in the retinal surgery room. It's generally darker than other operating theaters, so the vitrectomy instruments with the lasers light things up, and, you know, it looked really nice and jazzy," says Shukla, beaming.

The surface glamour may have reeled him into the field, but the challenges and intellectual rigor kept him there as an avid researcher. Shukla is unsentimental about why it makes sense for him to stay with Aravind. "Volume is key for research. In the retina department here, we see 350 patients every single day," he says. "I've compared that with other top institutes in the country. They see only half or one-third of our numbers. Also, I've worked out an arrangement with the management that allows me to spend a large percentage of my time doing research. In private practice, this just wouldn't be possible. I used to think after I'd published 30 papers, I'd leave to make more money in private practice," admits Shukla with a chuckle. "Now I think maybe I'll have a hundred publications and still be here."

❧

"CLINICAL RESEARCH IS Aravind's greatest strength," says Dr. Carl Kupfer decisively. "It took Aravind less than a year to recruit the 3,400 patients who participated in an intraocular lens study we did. In the United States, it would take five years to get that number."[6]

For 30 years, Kupfer stood at the helm of what is today the largest and most comprehensive center for vision research in the world—the National Eye Institute (NEI) in Bethesda, Maryland. "India was a main focus in my research; in ten years I made 40 visits to the country. They always took such good care of me at Aravind," says Kupfer warmly.

He first visited Aravind in 1979 on a WHO assignment and was struck by what he found there. "I couldn't fathom the will that Dr. V had. He was very debilitated and yet continued to do surgery, and did it remarkably well. The second thing was that he didn't call upon organizations to help. He waited for them to ask to be involved."

This "don't ask" approach was novel to Kupfer. As was another trait: "Dr. V really picked and chose from what we offered," he says. The discernment with which Dr. V often refused money, even when Aravind was a small, struggling hospital, intrigued him. It led to a strong collaboration based on complementary strengths and mutual respect. "Meeting Dr. V had a profound influence on my life," says Kupfer simply.

"My feeling was that the NEI had an awful lot of knowledge that could be applied to the problems Aravind was facing, and that we could provide some credibility to their work. And we had a lot to learn from Aravind," he says. "Serving the underserved is a universal problem. If I hadn't agreed to work with Dr. V and Aravind, I don't think I would have slept very well."

❧

NOT ALL ARAVIND doctors feel the same fervor for the organization as Kupfer. "Some doctors are unhappy at Aravind because they don't really know what they want or where else they would go," says Shukla briskly. "They stick around, but basically they want to escape work." Shaking his head, he says, "You can't survive at Aravind with that attitude. Dr. Natchiar tells every recruit up front, 'Being at Aravind is about *hard, hard, hard, hard, hard work.*'" Not everyone has a predilection for that kind of environment.

There is no doubt that along with their towering dedication and compassion, Dr. V's generation brought a driving severity to the work culture at Aravind. The dictatorial vein in the founding generation's mode of leadership would intimidate many and offend some. Their imperious rages and exacting demands are legendary among old-time employees. Most of them interpret this harshness as stemming from the founding team's extraordinary commitment to the well-being of patients.

Shukla's own take on it is interesting. "You have to be fearless in order to appreciate these seniors," he says of the founders. "If you're scared in front of them, then you're resentful behind their backs." He appreciates their work ethic but also believes that their authoritarian style can stymie genuine inquiry. "Strictness shouldn't mean that juniors don't ask questions," he says. "If you look at the postgraduates here, they don't really push their instructors. They are too scared of being disrespectful. When I'm teaching a class, I have to tell them not to just sit there like cattle."

Shukla has an engaged but matter-of-fact perspective on working at Aravind, and a tough self-confidence that has allowed him and his wife, who is also a surgeon here, to find their own equilibrium within the system. There are scores of doctors across Aravind's five hospitals who have been able to find firm footing here as well, and who cannot imagine working elsewhere. Dr. Rathinam Sivakumar, the petite head of uveitis services at Aravind–Madurai is one of them. She points to the founding members as her role models. "I was really inspired by their dedication and by the high quality of the institute," she says. "I didn't want to work anywhere else after studying here, because I really don't think other hospitals place such a strong a focus on delivering high quality—and I'm a person who doesn't like to compromise."[7]

"Basically, to be at Aravind, you have to be able to link your own growth with the hospital's growth," says Shukla. "It's interesting, when I talk to old school friends at this stage, I realize that at a basic level, what they and pretty much all of us really want out of life is to make a difference. And we can do that either by creating something like Aravind or by supporting something like Aravind," he says, smiling. "Being here, it is easy to make a real difference."

ℭ

ARAVIND'S PATIENT POOL requires 60 percent of its surgeons to focus on cataract treatment. For this to work seamlessly, Aravind must maintain a higher ratio of residents and junior doctors to senior specialists. Surgeons like Shukla (with his good-natured scorn for cataract surgery and preference for spending more time doing research), if too broadly mimicked, could throw the model out of balance. But there is also the recognition that he and others of his ilk add crucial value to Aravind's ecosystem. They run the competitive specialty services that address other forms of treatable blindness, and their research publications and rare clinical and surgical expertise raise the organization's profile on the national and international scene. These surgeons steadily build the value of the Aravind brand in the field. Their contributions play a role in attracting both wealthier patients and professional talent. Ultimately, they help fuel the organization's long-term sustainability and relevance.

To serve its mission, Aravind clearly needs this body of professionals with diversified interests in teaching, research, community outreach, specialty care, surgery, and clinical work. But how do its leaders ensure that these multiple motivations all operate within a framework that stays true to Aravind's founding values?

"Dr. V is a very unusual person in that, as a doctor, he really sees systems as important," says Fred Munson, who worked closely with Thulsi to set up some of the early administrative systems at Aravind. "Trying to put people within a framework is something that doctors really resist, and here is Dr. V recommending it very strongly for himself and others," says Munson. From Aravind's very beginnings, Dr. V wanted to create systems that would drive and reinforce the core values of equitable care, high quality, compassion, and transparency. He knew that strong, mission-aligned processes and protocols could mitigate the threat introduced by individual deviations. In an organization that functioned at such a massive scale, this was all the more important.

The systems at Aravind are thus designed to operationalize certain core principles. So to ensure equity of care, for instance, the organization intensively monitors clinical outcomes across paid and free services, and all of its surgeons are rotated between free and paying patients. To help ensure universal access to its services, Aravind mandates doctors' participation in eye camps and follows an innovative, nonexploitative pricing model. Its emphasis on a values-fit over skills-fit when recruiting paraprofessionals, as well as its practice of hiring doctors groomed internally, help it to build and maintain a work culture in line with its mission. And a priority for patient-centric care and transparency leads Aravind to regularly evaluate treatment methods to ensure that only procedures that are gainful to the patient are carried out. In these and many other ways, Aravind leadership uses the authoritative power of systems, protocols, and policies to carry and convey its key values. It is an approach that tends to serve as a natural filter.

"From the view of Dr. V's world, if you do more for more people— that is good for you, as a person. It's a blessing you have got, and it doesn't have to translate into more money in your pocket. Not everyone likes this philosophy; those people move on," says Dr. Aravind. "Good people in a bad system typically go bad. Bad people in a good system become good. That sounds simplistic, but it's true. For the majority of us, the system becomes your *dharma.*"

Dr. V's approach was to create virtuous systems that corrected for individual variations. By doing so, he steered a return to the heart of what medicine is all about.

❧

THE SELF-IMPOSED CONSTRAINTS of quality, compassion, and self-reliance that Dr. V chose gave Aravind's founders the liberty to pursue their outlandish mission with integrity. Yes, they had to work exceedingly hard in the early years, but within the framework they set for themselves (we cannot turn anyone away; we cannot compromise on quality; we must be self-reliant), the pressure of their mission would not push them in directions that compromised their principles. Today these constraints and the systems they gave rise to provide Aravind's doctors, nurses, managers, and other employees the freedom to stand by the original values of healing that draw people into this field to begin with.

Health care delivery in much of the world is fundamentally driven by the notion of limitation—an underlying assumption that there is simply not enough to go around for everybody's needs. That its model defied this notion (even in the years when its own resources were scarce) is perhaps Aravind's most potent and paradoxical quality. It is clear that much of the model stems from the precedents set by the founding team—a group led by a man for whom selflessness was a daily aspiration and whose deepest asking was always for others. In a 1988 journal entry, Dr. V wrote:

*To have no attachment to the result of action.*
*To have no ego. Mentally I plead for some actions.*

*1. Better health for all people.*
*2. Basic needs for all people.*

And in another two-part entry that followed:

*What are you. You represent only a little bit of consciousness and a little bit of matter. It is that you call myself.*

And then comes a brief sentence of flaming sincerity and surrender to the greater forces for good that he called the Divine:

*Make of me what you want.*

TO TRULY UNDERSTAND the conditions that gave rise to Aravind, it is not enough to examine the founding team's history of sacrifice, their self-imposed constraints, and the approaches that emerged. You must trace the fruits of Dr. V's vision back to the fertile soil that gave rise to that intrepid proclamation. *Make of me what you want.*

He did not mean it lightly, and the evidence is buried in plain sight across the organization. The patient reception area of each one of Aravind's hospitals displays the same daring assertion—a large, mounted print of a quote by the Mother, written in her graceful, spidery hand:

"Finally it is Faith that cures."

## PART III

# A Vast Surrender

## On Innovation and Inner

## Transformation

*In a contrary balance to earth's truth of things*
*The gross weighs less, the subtle counts for more;*
*On inner values hangs the outer plan.*

—Sri Aurobindo, *Savitri*

# HUMANKIND IS A
# WORK IN PROGRESS

D r. V is in his office. He is wearing thick, black-framed spectacles, and his head is bent attentively over a massive book. Approaching 24,000 lines, *Savitri* is reportedly the longest epic poem ever written in English. Composed in unrhymed iambic pentameter, its lines hold a rumbling grandeur.

All he had done was to prepare a field;
His small beginnings asked for a mighty end[1]

On the wall behind him are two black-and-white photographs. When Dr. V is at his desk, the portraits seem to look out over his shoulders. To the left is Sri Aurobindo, the man who penned the lines being read; he has a flowing white beard and a noble bearing. To the right is a woman, her gaze direct, her smile deep and warm. Mirra Alfassa is the name she was given at birth, but she is better known as the Mother.

The story of *Savitri* can be traced back to an old legend tucked into the labyrinth of India's celebrated epic, the *Mahabharata*. In the original telling, Savitri is a beautiful princess who, by the tidal force of her love and purity of spirit, vanquishes Yama, the Lord of Death, to win back her husband's life. In Sri Aurobindo's symbolic treatment of this tale, Savitri's quest represents the adventure of life and consciousness on earth, an evolutionary journey in which mortals transition through successively higher planes of consciousness, setting the stage for a total transformation of life as we know it. *Savitri* was composed over more than 20 years, and Sri Aurobindo (a prolific writer who earned nominations for the Nobel Prize in Literature from Pearl S. Buck and Aldous Huxley) is said to have written each stage of this vivid, spiritual epic from the level of consciousness it describes.

> This Light comes not by struggle or by thought;
> In the mind's silence the Transcendent acts
> And the hushed heart hears the unuttered Word.

These three lines hint at the subtle framework Dr. V leans on in his decision making. In an active mode of stillness and surrender (labeled meditation or prayer in the world's spiritual and religious traditions), Dr. V frequently experiences a sense of inner clarity and guidance.

> A vast surrender was his only strength.

Dr. V uncaps his pen and carefully inscribes that last line in his journal. Then he shuts the book and reaches for his cane. "It's a wonderful blessing to start the day with a reading from *Savitri*," he says simply.

In some ways, it is "The Big Book of Everything." *Savitri*, as the Mother put it, covers "the history of evolution, of man, of the gods, of creation, of Nature." It is by no means an easy read. Sri Aurobindo's writing is decidedly esoteric, his style mazelike and über-literary. And yet, framed between the gazes of two spiritual teachers, this is how Dr. V has greeted his day—every day—for the last 40 years. Each time he reaches the end of the book, he turns to the beginning and starts all over again. He does this with a wisdom that knows some forms of understanding cannot be hurried. "It is very difficult to understand *Savitri*," says Dr. V with a smile, "just like it is very difficult to realize the soul. But you keep trying, and sometimes you get an inkling of it."

*Soul, stillness,* and *surrender*—these are difficult words to fit into organizational strategy, and they do not make it into most public analyses of the Aravind model. The spiritual underpinnings of the organization, if written up at all, are treated as decorative detail: Sri Aurobindo is given a perfunctory nod as the organization's namesake, end of story. But when asked what he attributes Aravind's success to, Dr. V has an unequivocal response. "Grace," he says. "It all happened by grace."

It is an answer that might be dismissed if Dr. V were an ineffectual personality or if his faith translated into some kind of dreamy rapture. But to meet Dr. V is to know the sharpness of his mind, to see the practical bent of his purpose, and to recognize that there is nothing vaporous about Aravind's work.

Every organization operates with a set of reference points that reflect its ultimate motivation. Aravind too, through Dr. V, has a touchstone. If left unexamined, explanations of Aravind's work and what it offers the world will always be incomplete. Dr. V believes Aravind's work is a manifestation of Sri Aurobindo and the Mother's influence. Whether or not this is true is irrelevant. The objectives, systems, and culture of Aravind certainly do not demand belief in spirituality. But the fact remains that they were created and distinctly shaped by one man's sense of an inner reality. This is why you cannot give short shrift to Dr. V's spirituality when tracing the path of Aravind's evolution. It threads through everything: his priorities and perspectives, his vision for Aravind, his leadership practices, and the unique impact he has on the people who work with him. It is what linked this man's individual quest to the evolution of the largest eye care facility in the world.

❧

Born in Calcutta in 1872, Aurobindo Ghose (Sri Aurobindo) was shipped to England as a child by an Anglophile father, determined to have his son bred among the English. In his teens, Ghose won a scholarship to Cambridge University in classics, where his gift for languages led to prodigious mastery of over half a dozen Romance languages. But when newspaper clippings from colonial India brought him a whiff of the country's tumultuous political scene, his focus shifted. Ghose joined the Lotus and Dagger, a dashingly named underground society whose members pledged to work for India's independence. At age 21, he turned his footsteps back to his homeland for good.

Ghose took an administrative position with the ruler of Baroda (a princely state in West India). In his spare time, he pursued an in-depth study of India's languages, history, classical art, scriptures, and politics. A self-proclaimed atheist, he came to a curious bend in the road when a *sannyasi* (holy man) saved his brother from a fatal illness. An unshakable intuition arose within him then—that a vast, untapped power dwelled in humankind that could be put to use for India's freedom.

Following the ancient traditions and techniques of the East, Ghose began a process of inward focus and meditation that accelerated into a series of revelations and profound experiences. During this period, he also began to dedicate his public life to India's independence movement, shooting with meteoric speed to the top ranks, although only in his early 30s. As editor of a fiery and influential national publication, he urged the country toward radical noncooperation with the British government. Ghose's hard-line stance on self-rule and his rising popularity did not go unnoticed. He was arrested and jailed multiple times on charges of conspiracy and sedition.

It was while serving a period of solitary confinement that he received a powerful inner intimation that the freedom of India was certain. He felt commanded to shift the focus of his work to liberation of a different nature. In 1910, in answer to this inner voice, he escaped to Pondicherry, a French enclave in southern India where the British could not arrest him. The move signaled the abrupt end of his political career and the beginning of the concentrated spiritual pursuit that would occupy Sri Aurobindo, as he came to be known, for the remainder of his days. "Man is a transitional being," he would declare, "he is not final." A conviction that evolution is incomplete, that humankind as we know it is a work in progress and that it is destined to realize a collective and radical transformation of consciousness, is central to the approach Sri Aurobindo developed and termed "Integral Yoga." According to him, this ascent to the top of the evolutionary staircase is inevitable, because it is both "the intention of the inner spirit and the logic of nature's process." In other words, it is a journey that is being worked out by our own deepest purpose, in conjunction with the natural unfolding of the universe.

Sri Aurobindo's philosophy differs from most traditional Eastern belief systems in two ways. First, awakening, or enlightenment, is not the end goal. Sri Aurobindo was pioneering the idea that humans have the capacity to shape their lives in harmony with the deeper forces at play, and that by doing so, they actively help all of creation make an evolutionary leap to its summit potential. Second, he did not advocate retreat from worldly activity and renunciation of material concerns in pursuit of realization. He defended life on earth as the real field of growth and progress. His Integral Yoga proposed a sweeping canvas that included all spheres of the human experience: mental, physical, emotional, and spiritual.

"The evolution of consciousness and knowledge cannot be accounted for unless there is already a concealed consciousness in things, with its native and inherent powers emerging little by little," wrote Sri Aurobindo. In his framework, nothing comes from nothing, and *everything* contains a seed of a higher, cosmic intelligence. He termed that hidden seed the Divine.

"Aurobindo is a stupendously great guy," Michael Murphy, co-founder of the Esalen Institute, is quoted as saying in a spirited 2002

*EnlightenNext* magazine article titled "Why Sri Aurobindo Is Cool." "He opened up so much. Hardly anyone has this vision that puts the two together—God and the evolving universe. Hardly anyone!"[2] This capacious framework led to a more decentralized global movement.

Many consider Sri Aurobindo's work foundational to the field of integral studies, popularized in the mid- to late 20th century, encompassing, among other fields, psychology, religion, cultural anthropology, environmental sustainability, and organizational behavior. To Murphy and many other modern-day thinkers, Sri Aurobindo was an influential pioneer charting an exciting course to the birth of a new planetary consciousness.

In 1920, a woman named Mirra Alfassa joined Sri Aurobindo in Pondicherry. She was a Parisian of Egyptian-Turkish descent and an artist who had undergone a series of deep spiritual and psychic experiences since early childhood. Alfassa would become Sri Aurobindo's spiritual collaborator, and he named her "the Mother." In 1926, when he retired into semi-seclusion (a period that lasted until his death in 1950), Sri Aurobindo entrusted her with the practical manifestation of Integral Yoga—including oversight of the Sri Aurobindo Ashram, the care of its residents, and directorship of its diverse initiatives.

Legendary among disciples for her force of compassion and intuitive faculties, the Mother was a skilled administrator and an avant-garde educator with astonishing capacities for organization building. She and her writings are less well known than Sri Aurobindo's in the West. But it was her progressive views on the future of society that mapped out Auroville, a unique international township founded near Pondicherry in 1968, centered on sustainable living and the social, spiritual, and cultural needs of humankind.

The Mother's flowerlike symbol is composed of two concentric circles divided into 16 "petals." Each petal represents a unique spiritual quality—such as wisdom, harmony, generosity, and aspiration. It is this symbol that is carved into the gates of Aravind's hospitals and that Dr. V, his siblings, and many members of his extended family wear on their rings.

○

ONE OF THE most intriguing things about Dr. V's connection to his spiritual teachers is that he met Sri Aurobindo just once, and the Mother only a handful of times—with a minimal exchange of words and never for more than a few minutes at a stretch.

For the last 24 years of his life, Sri Aurobindo appeared in public only on limited occasions. Dr. V arrived in the quaint seaside settlement of Pondicherry on one such darshan (sacred viewing) day in 1950. On these days, the Mother and Sri Aurobindo offered their silent blessings to the thousands of people who filed past them. Dr. V recalls the experience briefly in his journal:

> *Sri Aurobindo's skin was a golden color. He was wearing a dhoti with a big red border like that worn by priests in the Vaishnava Temple. He had his eyes closed. Mother opened her eyes to see me. I did not have any reaction or [feel] a Force.*

No flash of recognition or visions of divinity, and yet there was something to the experience and in the teachings that led him back to the ashram again and again. Dr. V became well acquainted with many of the ashram's oldest disciples. Burdened by the early challenges of his work in eye care, he took comfort in their counsel and turned to them for guidance in the practice of Integral Yoga.

Sri Aurobindo and the Mother did not codify a set of techniques in their teachings. Maintaining that the path to transformation is specific to each person, they instead emphasized an ecumenical approach comprising skillful aspiration, rejection, and surrender as means to progress. In this trifold framework, aspiration is defined as a sincere dedication toward realizing truth and perfection in all aspects of living. Rejection is the diligent refutation of hindrances—any movements of thought or action that cloud the consciousness and impede an alignment with truth. And surrender is the deep, unconditional opening to the influence and will of our highest nature.

The secular idea of working to be an instrument of emerging perfection within the field of daily living is the gateway through which people from different backgrounds and religions come to Sri Aurobindo and the Mother's teachings. It was an approach that appealed deeply to Dr. V. For him, the framework of Integral Yoga was a natural continuation of lessons seeded in him by his father, a stern disciplinarian, and later, by the wisdom of Swami Vivekananda and Mahatma Gandhi, who both maintained that work is elevated to worship when carried out with an attitude of inner attunement.

ENTER THE FRONT DOOR of Annai Illam ("Mother's Home" in Tamil), the house where Dr. V lives with his brother GS and GS's family, and you will see two large black-and-white portrait photographs mounted high up on the wall. They are of Dr. V's parents, the simple farmer and his wife, who birthed the architects of a revolution in eye care. The photograph of Lakshmi shows an elderly woman looking directly at the camera with composure. Her face is wrinkled and very kind. She lived to see the beginnings of Aravind and was the only person with whom Dr. V could be caught sharing news of his own achievements. Beside her is a photograph of Govindappa Naicker. He sits in his chair with the ramrod-straight back and the unsmiling gaze typical of an era when having your picture taken was such a rare occasion that it merited a starched solemnity.

This man had little tolerance for shoddiness. Whether it was sowing the fields or feeding the cattle, his aim was to inform the task with perfection. In building a house, he would not hesitate to pull down an entire wall if it was slightly out of line. He carried over this attitude to parenting as well, often asking his firstborn why he wasn't at the head of his class. When the young Govindappa replied that it was too hard to attempt, his father would retort tersely, "Hard work is what you're meant to do." The boy took these words to heart.

The more one examines Dr. V's life, the clearer it becomes that what set him above others was not broad strokes of genius or recurrent flashes of brilliance. His accomplishments were made up of a steady succession of disciplined moments accumulated over a lifetime—moments inhabited by empathy, a passion for excellence, and the stamina for hard, humble work. *I have been doing yoga since 1936, from the age of 18 years, consciously, or unconsciously,* he once wrote in a journal entry.

He uses the word *yoga* to define any movement toward perfection. In medical school, Dr. V had a professor who upheld Sri Aurobindo's maxim "All life is yoga." "Whether it was sharpening a scalpel, studying, or dissection, this professor had maintained that one should always aspire to 'do yoga.' These things helped me," says Dr. V reflectively. "These things became a part of me. Discipline became a part of me, hard work became a part of me, and the aspiration for perfection, too, became a part of my nature."[3]

Friends of Dr. V remember the poignant sight of him sitting on the floor of his dorm room patiently drawing and redrawing anatomy diagrams with his afflicted fingers until they were exactly right. With rheumatoid arthritis, it is common to have sudden flare-ups of inflammation and acute pain after the disease appears to have gone into relative remission. Simple tasks of everyday living become difficult: tying shoelaces, opening jars, and buttoning a shirt, to say nothing of performing cataract surgery. It would take the young Dr. V time and much effort to pick up the surgical skills and speed needed in the field. He worked patiently at the operating table day after day, using the same instruments as other surgeons but holding them at a different angle in his disease-wracked fingers.

"People often notice that he is a surgeon with gnarled fingers," says long-term Aravind volunteer Dr. William Stewart, "and yet he is a surgeon of perfection; and where his fingers may not be aligned, where his fingers may not be perfect, his soul is perfect, and a soul is a much more powerful tool for the surgeon than his hands."[4]

In this contemporary age, the word *perfection* can conjure up notions of an unfeeling flawlessness that compromises our sense of what it means to be human. But in Sri Aurobindo's framework, it denotes something different. "That perfection, whether you call it 'God' or 'divine' or 'wisdom' or 'love' or 'universal spirit'—the label doesn't matter—it is the consciousness that surpasses any form which we can give it," says Vijay Poddar. Poddar grew up in the Sri Aurobindo Ashram and is a teacher at its International Centre of Education. "The entire focus in Sri Aurobindo's yoga is on this inner consciousness and a belief that, unless one changes oneself, no outer fiddling with the environment is going to work sufficiently."[5] He continues, "This principle applies to everything; sports, education, the arts, business, architecture, economics, politics, medicine—nothing is exempt from this vision. And this is why the Aravind Eye Hospital is significant." Poddar's voice deepens here with emphasis. "Because it is *not* just an eye hospital in Madurai. It is an extension of this spiritual movement in the field of eye care."

In a 1990s journal entry, Dr. V makes his perspective clear. *My interest in my profession is how to make this work a field for inner growth and perfection.* And in another entry he writes firmly, *Aravind Hospital aims at bringing higher consciousness to transform mind and body and soul of people. It is not a mechanical structure repairing eyes. It has a deeper purpose.*

# DR. V'S PRACTICE OF PERFECT VISION

Thresholds are important in India because the place where edges meet is seen as both vulnerable and powerful. The evil eye is warded off with masks tied above doorways. At dawn, and again at dusk, propitious forces are invited into the home by lighting brass lamps. The flame is a symbol of higher consciousness, and implicit in this ancient custom is a reminder to live a life governed by light. This relationship woven between truth, light, consciousness, and vision is common to many of the world's cultures.

On a morning in 2005, wearing a crisp cotton sari, Chitra Ravilla heads up the front steps of Aravind–Madurai and makes her way past the bustle of the front desk to the hospital's meditation room, where a lamp has already been lit. Chitra is Thulsi's wife and Dr. V's niece, and heads Aravind's communications department. A few minutes later, she emerges from the meditation room with a small white line of freshly applied *vibhuti* (sacred ash) on her brow. It is 9 a.m., and this short stop is part of her workday routine.

Many in Dr. V's family value Aravind's connection to the Mother and Sri Aurobindo and harbor a sense of devotional gratitude to these teachers; several of them spend a few minutes in the serene space of the meditation room at the start or end of their day. Relics of Sri Aurobindo are installed here and in the meditation rooms of all of Aravind's other hospitals. There are woven mats on the ground and pale floor-length curtains. The housekeeping staff arranges fresh flowers in intricate patterns on its prayer table, where sticks of incense stand, releasing their fragrance.

Dr. V is one of the earliest visitors to this room. He is a man of morning ritual. Each day, rising at 5 a.m. in the spacious but simple bedroom he occupies on the ground floor of his brother GS's house, he drinks coffee, reads the newspaper, bathes, and dresses. Aravind is less than a three-minute drive down the street, and Dr. V (a cautious driver) honks his horn almost the entire way. In his office, he lights two sticks of incense and carries them to the meditation room. Once back at his desk, he begins a reading session that typically lasts 45 minutes, opening with *Savitri* and following with other writings of Sri Aurobindo or the Mother. Siblings drop by with assorted grandchildren, a welcome and not-unusual intrusion. Then he returns home for a quick breakfast and is back at the hospital by 8:15. One of the first things he does is check the patient registration and admission numbers.

There is a rhythm to his simple routine that he carries out in the spirit of consecration. This structure and discipline is part of how Dr. V honors his ultimate priorities every day.

HIS COMPUTER SCREEN displays a rock-hewn statue of the Jain saint Mahavir seated in meditation. Dr. V often marvels at the perfection of the carving. "Hundreds of years ago, those fellows were able to create masterpieces like this!" he is wont to exclaim. "Those fellows" is an endearing Dr. V-ism. It can, depending on what he is discussing, refer to Western doctors, CEOs of companies, sportsmen, politicians, or modern youth. In this context, it refers to India's ancient sculptors, who had it in their power to create such indelible works of art. The possibility of tapping into such intellectual, spiritual, and artistic capacities for present-day use excites him. He has a gift for yoking apparent polarities and putting them to service for sight.

A hallmark of Sri Aurobindo's Integral Yoga is its synthesis of diverse traditions, cultures, religions, methods, and mindsets. Dr. V attempted to bring this approach to the practical work of blindness prevention. It helped him find relevance to Aravind's mission everywhere—in the ancient and modern, East and West, science and spirituality, grassroots charity and corporate empires.

"In Frankfurt, we were at the airport together, and he called me to watch a plane land," recalls Dr. Ramachandra Pararajasegaram, a consultant with the World Health Organization.[1] "You could see one trolley coming to take baggage, another for loading the trash. 'That's how we should run our operating theater,' Dr. V said. He is able to pick up cues like that. He even asks housekeepers at hotels about their training curriculum and the proper method of bed making. He has that kind of inquiring mind, and he applies the lessons he learns to Aravind."

"I absolutely remember my first encounter with him, because it is very unusual to find a man like Dr. Venkataswamy," says Dr. Larry Brilliant.[2] "I was teaching international health at the University of Michigan. Dr. V came to my office, and when he talked about eliminating blindness, you got the feeling that this man was either a saint or a complete nut. He kept talking about McDonald's and hamburgers, and none of it made any sense to us." Brilliant's voice ripples with laughter before turning serious. "But as you began to understand what he had already done in life, he moved you beyond imagining."

For the hundreds who would step forward to work alongside the Aravind team, one of the compelling aspects of the partnership was bearing witness to a visionary whose driving force was a spirituality firmly anchored in practical action. "*The Bhagavad Gita* says you're entitled to the work; you're not entitled to the results. You're not entitled to the fruits, the successes, rewards, the name, the fame, the money, the power. And Dr. V embodies that approach. He takes nothing and wants nothing for himself," says Brilliant. "He is a spiritual warrior as much as an ophthalmologist. But he doesn't then just stop and say, 'I am a spiritual warrior, so we don't need to have the best infrastructure, we will just wave our hands around.' He brings in the best techniques, the best equipment, and builds cutting-edge infrastructure because he is so *practical*. It's an unbeatable combination."

Brilliant himself is no typical amalgam. A poster child of the 1960s, he was a champion of Native American rights and personal physician to Jerry Garcia of the Grateful Dead. From a mountainside ashram in India, he was sent by his guru on a mission to wipe smallpox off the face of the planet. Two and a half eventful years later, the young epidemiologist led his team to the successful eradication of smallpox in India (its last outpost in the world). Brilliant then returned to the United States to a series of dazzling second careers that included cofounding the world's first virtual community, the Well; heading Google's philanthropic arm; and serving as president of the Skoll Global Threats Fund (his current position).

His journey includes another defining event. In 1978, close on the heels of their time in India, Brilliant and his wife, Girija, called for a small gathering in the United States. "We wanted to get the people together who had eradicated smallpox, and give ourselves the chance to do something else like that again," says Brilliant. Among the eclectic assembly of spiritual seekers, musicians, public health experts, and peace activists that evening was a retired eye surgeon from India named Govindappa Venkataswamy. He and a few others cast strong votes in favor of tackling curable blindness. From this meeting, Seva Foundation was born, and its first partner would be the man its founders soon dubbed Dr. V.

It was a collaboration born of serendipity and mutual resonance that shaped both organizations. Seva was a kaleidoscope of quirky, talented counterculture individuals with star-studded Rolodexes. Fresh from conquering a killer disease, they were energized about this new project and looking for a place to start. At that time, Aravind occupied negligible space on the international stage. It had very few partners in the United States, a no-name clinic in South India, and crazy notions about what was possible. The alliance with Seva was a perfect match.

This was not the usual donor-agency-funds-developing-world-charity relationship. Dr. V was not interested in raising money. He wanted help building long-term internal capacity in terms of crucial skill sets and know-how. He wanted equipment that could not be procured in India and regular upgrades in technology. He wanted trainers, systems thinkers, and curriculum builders. "In the early years, Seva functioned as a fill-in-the-blank," says Brilliant. "Whatever Dr. V or Thulsi needed, we would get. A YAG laser or a specialist in administration or a marketing manager, a computer or a network designer or strategic planning support—we would find those missing pieces and send them to India."

The partnership crisscrossed the globe, with the founders attending each other's board meetings, staying in each other's homes, and a steady stream of volunteers from Seva making their way to the old temple city of Madurai. Seva raised Aravind's profile in the West, and over time, all of the big players in the field of blindness prevention began to partner with what was no longer an insignificant enterprise. Notable among them were Sightsavers International, CBM, and the WHO. These international organizations offered various forms of support to Aravind early on. And in an uplifting reversal of roles, Aravind, as it continued to grow, contributed to their programs in turn.

"Seva was fortunate to meet Dr. V when his ideas were first getting formed," says Brilliant, who is quick to acknowledge the existence of Aravind's multiple other partners. "It would not be fair to say we discovered Aravind—everybody lays claim to Aravind and values the relationship, because it represents this amazing confluence of ingredients," he says. "It's a way of working together. Rich and poor, doctors and patients, East and West, everyone contributing— and it really works."

DR. V FIRMLY BELIEVES that action motivated by love exerts a force and organizing power of its own. He makes the cultivation of unconditional compassion for all beings a daily goal—a Dalai Lama-esque endeavor not always easy to pull off. In an early journal entry, he detailed the petty dynamics that can hijack a doctor's best intentions, before diving into a stream-of-consciousness meditation on the nature of the mind:

> *You feel drawn to a patient because he's from your village, known to you, and then you try to do your best for him. But at times, a patient is aggressive and demands some privileges. He says "I know what my trouble is. I do not want to go through all the formalities. Could you see me first?" This upsets you, and with that feeling of annoyance, you treat him. You are not able to disassociate him from his mental or emotional aggressiveness.*
>
> *Somebody asked Ramana Maharshi [a renowned Indian saint] what he felt when he saw any person. He said, "When I see somebody, I see his soul and I worship it. It may be clouded by ignorance, meanness, selfishness, greed, jealousy, hatred, but I can see the love in him." If you could develop that attitude and not react to a person's defects, and try to help his inner being, you will automatically do your best for him. To do this you must bring into your own being silence, calmness, and quietude. This needs constant practice. It needs enormous practice to realize the experience of silence in you. You may have it occasionally, and then you hanker for it. It seems to elude you. Your being is accustomed to agitation and it wants it. I can feel it every day, moving in me. I want to live in silence but something else in me wants excitement and runs for it. It feels perhaps the more I get agitated, then the more hard I work. So I shout, give commands to people around me. Perhaps all this helps me enjoy my agitated vibration. You aspire for calmness and peace and you want to love all, but to express it is not easy.*

*Gradually get out of superficial consciousness and go deeper to meet the soul. Live in the soul and be guided by it.*

❧

DR. V ASPIRES to perfect vision. He wants to be able to see with incisive clarity into the heart of people, problems, circumstances, and most of all himself. He is keenly aware of how unguarded patterns of the mind can form into habits and cloud his line of sight, and he understands the constant effort required to transcend those patterns. In Integral Yoga, an inner poise and self-awareness is the foundation on which you build. As a young surgeon, Dr. V began to use his day-to-day work to sharpen these qualities. To him, this was not an intellectual exercise but one that required operating from the *soul*—a word that typically comes loaded with religious connotations.

Though the soul is commonly interpreted as the spark of divinity within each being, in Sri Aurobindo's framework, it can also be defined in nontheistic terms as the inner center that holds each individual's highest evolutionary calling. It is the seat of what he called "true being," and it is from here, he maintained, that a power and wisdom arises that sees perfectly in every instance what *is*, what must be done, and by what means to realize its ultimate purpose. These cues, he says, are typically muffled in layers of ego, conditioning, and negative tendencies. But through persistent aspiration and effort, one can encounter the presence of true being and increasingly dwell in it.

Dr. V found it an elusive but fulfilling residence. *Today I had a nice experience of living in the soul,* he recorded candidly. *Experienced the richness of it and its persuasiveness over all.* Not only did he begin to strive for this depth of being in himself, but he also aspired to connect with that part in others as well. *Seek the soul of the person, not his money or power,* Dr. V urged himself in his early journal entries.

His sister shares a charming story of berating a janitor at Aravind, in Dr. V's presence, for some minor infraction. Dr. V said nothing at the time, but later he asked her, "Did you shout at his body or at his soul, Natchiar?" Not knowing how to answer, she remained silent. "Shout at his body," Dr. V told her. "His soul belongs to God. If you shout at his soul, you are shouting at God."

Holding a vision for each person's highest potential, whether employee, patient, or partner, shaped Aravind's model in important ways. It created a density of interconnections that were built not on transaction but on trust. This is what first enabled the organization to see surgical assistants in village women, outreach advocates in indigent patients, and partners in its competition.

IN INTEGRAL YOGA, the state of consciousness from which any action is generated is believed to determine its transformative power. This means that even good ideas geared to charitable outcomes, if they originate from a low level of consciousness, are not maximally effective. Which is what makes the quality and depth of one's aspiration so significant in this framework.

According to Sri Aurobindo, aspiration, the first element in his trifold approach, is vital for approaching the soul. This aspiration is a deep thirst, a commitment to one's own evolution or self-perfection, and a determination to move in the direction of one's highest purpose. Dr. V writes of the frequent internal tug-of-war he experiences between pure aspiration and restless ambition. In his journals, he often calls himself out on the distracting impatience of his desire to serve:

*Lots of times I get lost in small things like a better order for seeing patients in camps or hospital, better training of doctors, building a better kitchen for patients, etc. There was a sweepers strike. Got mentally worried. To watch yourself by stepping back is interesting. Normally mind gets frequently bogged with needless problems, confusions. You get Ambitious of having more and more Health jobs, Hospitals etc. To keep the mind absolutely still, to understand the reaction, impulse and attitude and to work from the Soul is the Aim.*

❧

ACHIEVING PERFECT VISION requires a diligent stepping back from conditioned reactions, biases, and the unwholesome internal movements of anger, jealousy, impatience, and the like. To see things as they truly are and to have that transparent consciousness organize your actions requires persistent self-examination. In a journal entry, Dr. V observes:

*You want to live deep within, but you get upset by so many superficial things, or you get elated because of some superficial achievement. How will you guide Aravind, Seva or other service organizations. First thing to do is for you to live in your soul. Do not allow mental prejudices to cloud your thinking. To surrender yourself to the higher qualities in you is your constant effort. Do not limit yourself to small things.*

This process of skillful rejection is the second element in Sri Aurobindo's approach, and one that flows into its third, and perhaps most challenging, aspect: surrender. The word here does not mean passive submission but rather an active and dynamic giving of one's entire being in service of goodness, love, perfection, divinity, or whatever represents the place of "true being" within. Dr. V zeroes in on how strong identification with our minds leads to loss of perspective.

*It is difficult to understand surrender. Constantly your mind has got its own fixed ideas or opinions. You get strongly attached to what you think is right and come into conflict with people who differ from you. You are not able to step back and watch your ideas. Lots of times, these ideas are based on the impressions of the mind, and not the higher spiritual consciousness.*

Dr. V persistently observed the nature of his mind and came to a startling conclusion. *I realize that reason is a very poor tool for finding out Truth*, he writes simply. And this is where Dr. V's spirituality gets particularly interesting.

The mechanics of how Aravind works are covered in some detail by business case studies, but they fall short on the more abstract questions of what created, and continues to animate, the model. Through a continued process of aspiration, rejection, and surrender, Dr. V was able to tap into an intelligence that went beyond the thinking mind. Seeking a realm of awareness stripped of ego, fears, and preconceptions often provided him with answers, ideas, and convictions that ran counter to the rational and dominant paradigm.

Dr. V has made several crucial decisions for Aravind that were rooted in the inexpressible logic of his deeper awareness. Take, for example, his insistence on inclusive services and self-reliance, his turning down of various attractive partnership opportunities, and his squelching of seemingly favorable expansion plans, not to mention his selection and grooming of doubtful candidates for key leadership positions. His approach often works inversely, with decisions coming long before any rational justification. Initially this took some getting used to. But Dr. V's team possesses a rare degree of tolerance and trust that has paid off time and again. The organization has grown accustomed to seeing reality catch up with his preposterous ideas.

In pragmatic terms, Dr. V's ability might be called foresight. He has an uncanny knack for intuiting decisions that yield tremendous benefit—sometimes 5, 10, or even 20 years down the line. His journal entries through the decades bear evidence of this. In the late 1970s, when he was still paying off the mortgage for the first hospital and struggling to pay staff salaries, he writes of intentions to set up 100 hospitals across the country, of the possibility of training village women to assist surgeons, of the urgent need for good administrators, and of a target of doing a million surgeries a year. He mentions plans for centers in places where land will be purchased and Aravind hospitals built decades later, and records glimpses into the nature and potential of young staff members who are now part of the senior leadership team. The language he uses is telling: *Last night there was a revelation . . . I had a dream or vision of . . . Today an idea came to me . . . I had a feeling or experience that . . .* These phrases are all indicative of tuning in to something other than the analytical mind, which even Dr. V himself cannot fully explain. *All my actions are not based on reason. I have been guided mysteriously all my life,* he once wrote in a laconic journal entry. Though deeply internal, this space of receptivity was a foundation for his powerful and far-reaching sense of compassion.

Drawn equally to Sri Aurobindo and the Mother as teachers, Dr. V has a more personal sense of connection to the latter (a not-uncommon asymmetry among their disciples, given Sri Aurobindo's long seclusion). She became a channel for the devotion that is part of Dr. V's spirituality, and that is often his refuge and strength. The last time he saw the Mother, she was 94 years old. A longtime disciple had arranged for a private audience, and Dr. V recalled the searing, silent encounter in a journal entry nearly 20 years later: *I can never forget the last blessing in 1972. Mother had such a penetrating look. She intensely gazed in my eyes for a long time. It felt like three or four minutes I had no thoughts. It was a big experience. What she did in me I do not understand.*

Dr. V received a benediction of love that would continue to reverberate and ripple through his spirit, thought, and action long after this last encounter. He has experienced, at multiple times in his life, subtle physical sensations that he correlates to this source, such as the ones detailed in this entry from 1991:

*Last night I had a clear indication of Mother's Force entering me. I felt a wide space inside my inner being. I felt deep inside me there was a presence with a small light, just a spark. I felt*

*it must become a fire burning strongly. Felt a good will, feeling
of benevolence. I could stand up strongly without being moved
by anything.*

IN 1992, DR. V was invited to give a lecture at Harvard University's
School of Divinity, titled, "Living a Spiritual Life in a Contemporary
World." Standing at the podium, dressed in an ill-fitting brown suit
purchased from a thrift store, he put words to his experience of grace:
"You feel that sometimes you get illumined or inspired. They say the
higher your consciousness goes, that consciousness is able to plan out
everything, set a base for you to do your work. With the awareness
that your intentions come from a different consciousness level, you
are not egoistic and you are able to work with the great confidence
that comes only with that faith and realization. And so we attempt, at
Aravind, to bring in higher levels of consciousness and to work in a
different method, as an instrument in the hands of a higher force."

To Dr. V, the cultivation of empathy, the effort toward equanimity
and self-awareness, the stepping back from ego, and the attempts to
align with a clear-sighted, inherent wisdom are all part of his larger
aspiration to be a perfect instrument. While many spiritual traditions
advocate the practice of working selflessly as a channel of a higher
force, not everyone relates to this aspect of Dr. V's vision. In fact, not
even all the senior management at Aravind resonate or practice it to
the same degree.

But there are other people whose lives have been architected in a
similar vein. Among them is a remarkable contemporary of Dr. V's—a
man who has absolutely no doubt that this form of agency works and
that it plays into Dr. V's abilities as a leader and institution builder.

RAM DASS, born Richard Alpert, is the former Harvard psychologist whose controversial research on psychedelic drugs and human consciousness got him booted out of academia and eventually sent him wandering up a mountain path in northern India to the feet of his guru (the same teacher who ordered Larry Brilliant to the front ranks of the battle against smallpox). Neem Karoli Baba was a unique teacher with a trademark plaid blanket, endearing smile, and profound mystical depth. This guru, described by many as a staggering force of love, encapsulated his teachings thusly: "Love all. Serve all. Feed all." It was he who shredded Alpert's academic concepts of consciousness by prodding him toward deeper realizations of the spirit, and gave him his present name. Ram Dass went on to become a teacher in his own right, inspiring millions across the world with the touchstone book of the '60s generation, *Be Here Now.* He is also a cofounder of Seva Foundation.

With his white hair and penetrating blue eyes, Ram Dass is an arresting sagelike figure. In 1996, he suffered a massive stroke that he now refers to as an act of "fierce grace." He indicates how that dramatic brush with mortality and suffering is common ground between himself and Dr. V. "He was a budding doctor when his arthritis took hold . . . and then he became an eye surgeon. He just saw it as grace, and I think perhaps that his example helped me with my stroke," says Ram Dass, chuckling softly, "because he worked with what he got— and now I work with what I've got."[3]

His first meeting with the doctor who had an 11-bed clinic and multistoried vision left a strong impression on Ram Dass. "We at Seva were trying to be *karma yogis* [people who have perfected the art of selfless service]," he says. "Then a real one came along: Dr. V."

Like many others, Ram Dass was struck by Dr. V's ability to lasso people with his vision: "Your life would be going in one direction, and then you'd meet him and go in another direction," he says, laughing. "His will was the bottom line." Ram Dass turns serious while speaking of Dr. V's intuitive interactions. "When I was with him, my role, my potential through his eyes, was clear," he says slowly. "Nobody else except my guru treated me that way. My personality pushed away my spiritual role. Dr. V reinforced the role by treating me as a soul."

Ram Dass does not beat around the bush on the subject of being an instrument. "I have a feeling that Sri Aurobindo runs Dr. V. Just like my guru runs me," he says calmly, stating the metaphysical as a matter of fact. "Dr. V's enterprise could not have had this success by normal ways. He performed, in the world of blindness, *a miracle*. Institutions, rules, and procedures, he treated them like Silly Putty—he could mold them. He has a vision from a next level. I saw how his faith worked. Even when everybody knew what the situation called for, he would hear offscreen that we should do it a different way. He was dancing to a different drummer."

Dr. V repeatedly set the direction of Aravind to that tune. His inner attunement informed many of the organization's most radical innovations, and one of the most controversial and ambitious decisions in its history. A decision made against the better judgment of the overwhelming majority, and one that nobody in Aravind's early days had anticipated for the tiny eye clinic.

# ELEVEN

# MANUFACTURING A REVOLUTION

In Madurai today, there is usually a long line of people outside the free section of the Aravind Eye Hospital. It is not uncommon to find an elderly patient among them, wearing a crooked pair of spectacles fastened around the head with a piece of string. The lenses of these glasses are as thick as your index finger. They magnify the eyes, giving the wearer an air of absurd gravity.

These are cataract patients from the fast-dwindling era of aphakic surgery, a procedure that emerged in the mid-18th century and remained the standard for over 200 years. It involved making a large slit along the rim of the cornea and removing the clouded cataract lens. This lensless condition was referred to as *aphakia*. To replace the lost focusing mechanism, patients were given "soda bottle glasses," heavy spectacles with a high refractive power. When Aravind was founded in 1976, the standard for cataract treatment in India was a particular type of aphakic surgery. It was relatively quick, straightforward, and inexpensive. Because the patients operated on were almost blind, the results of the surgery were dramatic and had an immediate, positive impact on their quality of life. But the surgery also had serious drawbacks.

Early-stage cataract is too soft to be easily extracted by aphakic surgery. Often, patients were advised to postpone surgery until the cataract was hardened and "mature." Because operating on one eye resulted in mismatched image reception, surgery was further delayed until both eyes were affected. This unfortunately meant that the patients' vision often deteriorated to complete blindness before they were treated. Following aphakic surgery, patients had to stay in the hospital or eye camp for a full week under close medical supervision. Complete recovery took another six to eight weeks. And then, for people accustomed to working in rural settings, the spectacles were problematic: heavy, breakable, scratch prone, easy to lose, and hard to replace. But without them, the patients were functionally blind.

When Dr. V first started doing cataract operations, there were no good alternatives to this technique. By the 1980s, however, this was no longer true. Across the Western world, a dramatic advance was transforming the field of cataract surgery . . . but it was still far from the shores of India.

◈

In the aftermath of World War II, while treating several patients who had been injured in combat, an English eye surgeon named Harold Ridley made an inadvertent discovery: Pilots whose eyes were wounded by plastic shrapnel from the cockpit canopy of fighter planes seldom developed eye infections. Time and again, the surgeon saw that an acrylic shard could lie inert in the eye for long stretches of time with no adverse reactions. Ridley had stumbled upon a possible implant material—nonreactive, transparent, and light.

On a November morning in 1949, Ridley implanted the world's very first intraocular lens (IOL) in the eye of a woman who had just had her cataract-clouded lens removed.[1] He knew he was treading on dangerous ground. Ridley's invention was the forerunner of a new field of biomedical engineering. His IOL arrived decades before the first pacemaker or artificial kidney found its way into a human body. This surgery was a radical departure from the way medicine had been practiced for centuries. Before then, surgeons had focused on skillful *extraction*—of tumors, foreign bodies, and toxic substances.[2] Now here was a procedure that had the audacity to do the opposite: replace a flawed product of nature with a working, manmade substitute.

In the academic and medical worlds, the opposition to this discovery was as fierce as the implications were tremendous. The IOL's evolution and eventual acceptance in the West took three decades and involved a slow series of advances in design, manufacturing process, and surgical technique—advances that successively ironed out the kinks in the original invention and made the benefits of the new technology increasingly clear.

The intraocular lens is undeniably one of the greatest innovations in ophthalmology and a gift to humanity. Today, more than 10 million IOLs are implanted every year and have directly helped more than 50 million patients worldwide.[3, 4] And yet, its early history in the West, beleaguered by professional opposition, would be strangely mirrored on the other side of the globe, with Aravind right in the eye of the storm.

Dr. Richard Litwin sits in a wicker chair on the shaded steps of Harmony, the Aravind guesthouse in Madurai. With his black beret and white beard, he looks more like a fashionable, summertime Santa Claus than a practicing ophthalmologist from California. Like most longtime friends of Aravind, Litwin can vividly recall the first time he met Dr. V. It was in Pondicherry, the year was 1981, and the occasion was a surgical eye camp. Litwin's soft voice threads this story and tugs it gently into the present.

"Dr. V had control of this very large movie theater. It had been converted into a hospital, and there were what seemed to be hundreds, perhaps thousands, of people neatly in line, moving through. It was mind-boggling to me. I come from a country where procedures are done one at a time," he says. "People were marched up to these operating tables, a quick transformative procedure was done, and by the end of the week they could all see. It just seemed—magical. A transformation of the way medicine could be done."[5] Shortly after that camp, Litwin himself would be the harbinger of another crucial transformation at Aravind.

"We saw an elderly man in Madurai with white pupils; totally mature cataract. Now you could remove his cataract and give him aphakic glasses, but that wouldn't help this man," recounts Litwin. "He was a carpenter, and Dr. V told us that no one would hire him after surgery. The results of aphakic surgery would be insufficient to reintegrate him into his line of work. I demonstrated the new IOL surgery on this guy for Dr. V, with Dr. Natchiar assisting," Litwin recalls. "Now a good surgeon can just look at something, and he knows instinctively, 'This is a go.' Dr. V saw it and he knew: 'This man will be able to go back to work!' he said. It only took one demonstration for him to know that *this was it.*"

It was a defining moment. Aravind was not performing IOL surgeries at the time, and hardly any hospitals in developing countries were. But now Dr. V had witnessed firsthand how a new technology could enable Aravind to better serve those in need. Unlike aphakic surgery, IOL surgery could be performed on early, still-soft cataracts without needing to wait until both eyes were affected to the point of complete blindness.[6] IOLs were implanted using a precision-enhanced technique made simpler by sophisticated microscopes. It involved making a smaller incision in the eye than that required for aphakic surgery, and the healing time was much faster.[7] Most important, the implanted lenses could be tailored to the precise power required for each individual eye, yielding superior postoperative results and allowing patients to do day-to-day tasks without the need for glasses.[8] Litwin's wife, Judith, also an Aravind volunteer, interjects, "Dr. V didn't know how it was going to happen. He always said the money would come and the technology would come. He didn't know how, but he knew that IOL surgery had to be made available to the villagers."

In the 1980s, India was not considered a viable market for IOLs, and there were no credible local manufacturers. At that time, a single implant in the United States was priced at $200.[9] Rapidly changing technology made it viable for American manufacturers to get rid of their excess stock by selling it at discount rates, or donating it to eye care programs in developing countries and claiming tax benefits. Seva Foundation played a key role by building the necessary relationships and coordinating these transfers, as well as arranging for visiting ophthalmologists to volunteer time training Aravind's surgeons in the technique of IOL surgery. The IOL lenses arrived at Aravind packed between Lonely Planet travel guides and mosquito repellent in the suitcases of medical residents and volunteers from America. This ad hoc method worked for a while, but when Medicare forced down the price of IOLs in the United States, manufacturers lost their profit margins, and the supply of donated lenses began to dry up. Meanwhile, many patients were willing to pay for this new form of implant surgery, and so demand at Aravind was steadily increasing.

"You can't run a public health program on leftovers," says Dr. Suzanne Gilbert from Seva. "It was one thing for us to support an eye hospital that was doing 10,000 surgeries a year," she says, "but when that number went up to 80,000 at Aravind, it was quite a different equation. Asking companies to donate that much was uncomfortable."[10]

Senior management at Aravind was also uneasy with the donated-lenses arrangement. It made them externally dependent and seriously compromised their mission of providing affordable, high-quality eye care to all, rich or poor. The prohibitive cost of the lenses meant that Aravind could not offer them at scale for free. As a result, the superior surgery benefited only its paying patients. Patients being treated for free continued to receive aphakic surgery, the conventional treatment for cataract in all developing countries at the time. Thulsi says, "We strongly felt that the IOL was even more relevant to a poor man than a rich man, because his living environment is less predictable. We felt the poor would benefit immensely by the new technique, and we had to figure out how to make it affordable for them."

Aravind's leadership reached out to international IOL manufacturers, but the widespread feeling was that India was just not a viable export market. In any case, these companies were unwilling to make the IOLs available at a price that Aravind calculated to be affordable for all. In 1989, the conversation on the growing need for IOLs took a seminal turn. A rather giddy, high-risk solution was starting to make sense: if no one was willing to manufacture lenses that India could afford, then Aravind would just have to do it on its own. "I'd never heard of anything like it," says Litwin with a chuckle. "A bunch of doctors were going to take on manufacturing."

Aravind had always enjoyed the support of local and international bodies. However, with this new venture, several ties were tested. Thulsi recalls, "It was a big struggle because the government was against it and felt that Aravind was derailing the national eye care program by working at a tangent. Several international funding agencies were also against it—some who had partnered with us [in the past] backed out at the last minute."

Announcing the idea of manufacturing the lenses in India sharply divided those working in the field of international blindness prevention. Litwin recalls, "A pinnacle figure in ophthalmology wrote this very long article with 18 to 20 points, some of which were contradictory, about why IOL technology was inappropriate for developing countries. This inspired a spate of articles in [ophthalmic] journals." Those most fiercely against it were powerful, policy-level bureaucrats. The high cost of the lenses, the advanced production technology, the specialized surgical training required to implant them, and the investment in the necessary equipment seemed obvious barriers. The World Health Organization, the World Bank, and other international agencies maintained that using IOLs in developing countries was not merely unsustainable but irresponsible. They could not advocate the use of such technology in regions of the world where there was no regulatory body in place to monitor quality of production or surgical outcomes. Harsher criticism accused IOL advocates of encouraging an "addiction" that these countries could ill afford.

Those in favor of IOLs in developing countries like India were clinical practitioners like Richard Litwin, who had "already been there and done that." From personal experience, they knew that IOL surgery could work in India. "Appropriate technology doesn't mean doing the same thing for 200 years," he says staunchly. "To Dr. V, the principle of delivering the best possible quality to the patient was key." The question now was how to bring down the prices and scale production of IOLs in order to reach the people in need.

Aravind leadership listened politely to the informed opinions of the majority but did not participate much in the public debate they had helped trigger. As Dr. V says, "It was difficult for us to argue with them. So we just quietly went ahead and did it." His spirit of compassion and dedication to excellence, aligned with the ultimate authority of an internal compass, was all the green light needed. This decision to move forward in the face of overwhelming opposition may have seemed perverse to many, but it also underscores how the self-sustainability constraint helps breed innovation. "Having monetary success gave Aravind the freedom to chart its own direction," says Thulsi.[11] Litwin reflects on the lesson in prototyping that Aravind's initiative held for him. "It really taught me that if you're going to do some kind of innovative work, the way to go about it is to do it," he says. "And do it on the smallest possible scale that you can manage, so that you can say, 'This is how it works.' Otherwise, every theoretician will debate endlessly about the hypothetical results of that action."

SIMPLICITY HAS ALWAYS characterized Dr. Bala Krishnan's life, but if you ask him, he will admit with a chuckle that he once had dreams of owning a Porsche and vacationing in Acapulco. When he was a young man, taking on directorship of an intraocular lens factory in Madurai had never featured on his to-do list for this lifetime. Born in a village, Bala graduated from the Indian Institute of Technology, one of India's premier engineering colleges. Soon after, his marriage to a young woman named Varalakshmi was arranged. Her family lived in Madurai, where her maternal uncle had recently opened a small but well-respected eye clinic called Aravind.

Bala went on to get a Ph.D. in mechanical engineering at the University of Wisconsin–Madison. After graduating, he moved his family, which now included two young daughters, to Ann Arbor, Michigan, where he worked as a research scientist. They braved the cold winters of the Midwest, bought a house and a new car, and took a trip to Disneyland. Their lives echoed, in many ways, those of the thousands of other Indian couples who emigrated to the United States. Except that most other couples did not have an uncle visiting them every so often, talking about the urgent need to eliminate curable blindness in the world.

In 1990, after more than a decade of building a life in the United States, Bala and his wife sold their home, packed their belongings, and moved the family back to Madurai. They rented a house about a mile away from Aravind, and Bala began to study the intraocular-lens-manufacturing process. Working with him was David Green, a young, energetic Seva Foundation recruit who, like Bala, had no experience in the field of IOL manufacturing. For many years, Green had been the point person in the West for procuring the donated lenses that Aravind needed. When Aravind made the decision to start manufacturing the lenses, he was the first on board to help and would be an instrumental part of the process.

Together, Bala and Green did the extensive legwork that was required before production started. Aravind had lined up the space and was confident that the resources would be in place to buy equipment and hire the necessary engineers and technicians. What it lacked was access to a key component: the lens-making technology. Procuring it was tricky. IOL surgery was still new enough to be considered a state-of-art procedure, so the lens-manufacturing process was heavily patented and closely guarded by major medical-device producers.[12] Seva Foundation, through Green, played the crucial role of broker at this stage, initiating discussions with manufacturing companies to find someone willing to enter into a professional partnership with Aravind. It was not an easy sell; partnering with an eye hospital in the developing world that had zero experience in manufacturing made the project easy to oppose. Manufacturing IOLs required precision machinery, sterilized environments, and high levels of quality control. And making the venture operationally and financially sustainable required hardcore business acumen. Says Seva's Suzanne Gilbert, "We were told we were crazy and that the plan wouldn't work. That it could never happen outside of the U.S., Europe, and Australia. That India's heat, dirt, erratic electricity, and low worker productivity would compromise our efforts."

It took two years of searching, but finally a small lens-manufacturing facility in Florida, IOL International, agreed to work with Aravind. It was a good fit and, despite the delay, perfectly timed. IOL International had reached its full production capacity and was on the lookout for a production partner. "Three hundred thousand dollars for the machine and know-how, and then they were willing to take about $50,000 worth in lenses. We went there for two weeks, and then they came here for two weeks to train our staff," recalls Bala.

But even as plans for a production facility raced forward, internal doubts began rising to the surface. By 1990, Aravind was a well-established organization with high standing both locally and internationally. Entering an unfamiliar arena against the advice of the global community could potentially jeopardize its hard-earned reputation. What if its doctors were not up to the challenge of high-volume IOL surgery? What if demand petered out? What if the opposition was right and India simply did not have what it took to be able to pull off high-quality manufacturing? What if rural patients didn't want a foreign body implanted in their eyes? The risks attached to the unknowns were dauntingly high. With this new direction, the hospital stood to lose money, face, and the faith of the communities it worked with.

In a delayed crisis of confidence, other ethical implications of the venture became apparent. Dr. V was familiar with the workings of the medical industry and deeply disliked the culture of cutthroat competition and kickbacks that was often part of the package. As a nonprofit dedicated to serving the poor, would the hospital be compromising its integrity by financing this venture? Dr. V figured it just might. At a meeting of the team that had done the extensive groundwork for the manufacturing plant, he made an off-the-cuff pronouncement that left the group reeling in disbelief. "No hospital money will be used to fund this," he said.

Suzanne Gilbert, who was present in the room, remembers the helplessness of the moment. "I loved the idea of Aravind funding this on its own and felt it was in its self-interest to do so. To show the world that it could be done. We'd already come so far—Bala had gone through all the training, moved his family back from the U.S.; so much planning on so many different levels. There we were, all gathered from different parts of the world in Madurai, just for this. And then, without warning, Dr. V puts his foot down. We listened incredulously. It was very uncomfortable in the room," she recalls.

It is not unusual in Aravind's history to see the brakes slammed on a project at an advanced stage of planning by the same person who set the wheels in motion. Dr. V was as beloved as he was notorious, for calling shots based solely on inner guidance, and at certain times he was not to be reasoned with. "Sometimes when there is an important decision to be made, he'll say, 'Let me ask Sri Aurobindo and the Mother [who by then had passed on],'" says Natchiar. "Then a couple of days later he comes back with a very clear answer. But there are also times when, if you ask him about taking a particular step or changing some plan, he will just look at you for a long while and not say anything; then he will respond with something completely unrelated, like, 'Shall we go eat now?' and that signals the end of pursuing your idea," she says, laughing. But good-natured submission was not always her response.

In this case, as strongly as he believed in the cause, Dr. V was convinced that Aravind would be making a false move by putting money into the IOL factory. "That was when Dr. Natchiar spoke up," says Gilbert. "It's the only time I have ever heard her speak so forcefully to her brother." In Natchiar's mind there was no debate. The hospital had to have IOLs. The respectful deference of a younger sister made room for the conviction of a compassionate surgeon who could no longer tolerate having Aravind perform a lower-quality procedure on its patients. "If I hadn't done everything you told me to all these years, I would have lots of money and jewelry by now," she told her brother, "and I would give all that money and sell all that jewelry now, to be able to get IOLs for this hospital."

The uncharacteristic outburst was followed by silence. No extended debate about funding followed. But in the wake of Natchiar's passionate declaration, Dr. V's categorical "No" eventually softened to allow for partial funding to come from Aravind. The rest would have to come from external sources. A scramble for collaborators ensued. Seva Foundation, Sightsavers International, Seva Canada, Combat Blindness Foundation, and a number of valiant individual well-wishers worked feverishly to fill the gaps.

Forty-three years after Ridley's first implant, on a morning in 1992, the dream that had seemed unwise and impossible to so many was finally realized. With a ten-person team of production staff and engineers, including Bala and Sriram Ravilla (Thulsi's youngest brother), the Aravind Eye Care System's modest factory division was inaugurated on the fourth floor of the Aravind–Madurai hospital. It was named Aurolab, after Sri Aurobindo. Incorporated as a nonprofit, it adopted the mission of delivering ophthalmic products of world-class quality, at affordable prices, to help eliminate needless blindness.

Aurolab initially aspired to produce 150 high-quality lenses a day, enough to meet Aravind's in-house needs for intraocular lenses. It was a cautious production target to reduce the risk of low market response. With Aurolab's lenses, Aravind now had the ability to offer modern cataract surgery to the poor for a minimal fee or for free. Its deeply subsidized IOL surgery was offered at Rs. 500 (about $11). At the time, the price for imported IOLs was around $80 to $150 per piece.[13]

Aravind's steeply discounted price was calculated based on surveys of what villagers estimated they could afford to pay for restored sight—it averaged out to a little over ten days' worth of wages, at the daily wage rate of $1.

No one anticipated the explosion in demand that was to come. By 2009, Aurolab was producing 7,000 IOLs per day—more than 2 million a year. In a research paper on Aurolab, a team of business school students from the University of California, Berkeley, wrote, "This socially-driven organization produces ophthalmic technologies more cost effectively than any other comparable manufacturer, delivering their products to over 120 countries and owning 10% of the global market for intraocular lenses."[14] By the dawn of 2011, 10 million people around the world would see through Aurolab IOLs.[15]

Aurolab, it turned out, would do much more than manufacture lenses. It would produce a revolution—one that was rooted in, and driven by, compassion.

# TWELVE

# MAXIMIZE SERVICE, NOT PROFIT

Like the rest of Aravind, Aurolab presents an uplifting conundrum. It is a factory whose products compete in a fierce, international market. Yet it is run as a nonprofit by founders with no prior production experience, driven by a bottom line that aspires to provide access to the poorest of customers.

The biggest innovation at Aurolab was not technology based. Aurolab purchased the same equipment and trained in the standard production techniques of its Western counterparts. The real innovation was around pricing strategy. As David Green points out, Aurolab chose to lower prices not merely because its production costs were lower but because its goal "is maximizing service rather than maximizing profit."[1]

The need for businesses like Aurolab is immense. Technology developed in the West does not cross borders easily or quickly. "You end up having two classes of care—first world and developing world," says Thulsi. What blocks the dissemination of technology is not just the expense but also a series of related issues, including underdeveloped markets, lack of trained personnel, inefficient delivery systems, rigid mindsets, and indifferent competition.

To start with, Aurolab needed skilled technicians for a series of precise machine-supported tasks that included cutting, calibrating, sterilizing, quality checking, and packaging of the delicate lenses. Seasoned at training high school graduates from South Indian villages to assist in the operating theater, Aravind calmly reapplied to manufacturing the assembly line approach it had borrowed from industry. It used its existing recruitment channel and focus on value-fit over skill-fit for hiring Aurolab's mainly female team technicians.[2] "We have not taken ambitious people, but simple people with a commitment. And then we grow them," says Sriram Ravilla, Aurolab's passionate and quietly proficient director of operations. These young women operate everything from computer-aided lathes to robotic cleaning systems.

Lower labor costs account for some savings at Aurolab; however, the bulk of its manufacturing costs are similar to those in the West. Most of its inputs, such as specialized machinery and 80 percent of its raw materials, are imported. And in raw materials, Aurolab's costs are actually higher than those of its Western competitors, due to high transportation costs and import duties.[3]

Adopting Aravind's tiered pricing structure, Aurolab offers separate brands and discounted prices for charitable organizations (Aravind included), while also catering to customers who predominantly serve paying clientele. Nonprofit organizations and governments buying in bulk account for as much as 65 percent of its revenue.[4]

In Bala's words, Aurolab is "an experiment to see how advanced technology and products can be brought to developing countries quicker, to not have to wait until the market matures but to proactively drive that demand."[5] In retrospect, Aurolab's timing was ideal. When the dust from the international debate over IOLs for developing countries settled, several blindness-prevention agencies found themselves ready to accelerate the advent of the advanced surgery in the developing world. And Aurolab was ready for them.

In 1994, the government of India borrowed $110 million from the World Bank to ramp up a nationwide cataract-blindness-prevention program. The multiyear loan helped hospitals cover some of the cost of providing free IOL surgery to the poor.[6,7] This program kick-started a considerable spike in IOL demand that coincided beautifully with Aurolab's steady production of high-quality lenses.

The handful of IOL manufacturers in India that were making reliable lenses at the time charged high prices for them. By introducing high-quality IOLs for the low end of the market, Aurolab helped increase the market size by millions of customers.

Its launch was also the catalyst that helped blow the lid off of Aravind's potential. Over the five years leading up to Aurolab's creation, Aravind's free and deeply subsidized cataract surgery volumes went up 69 percent. The next five years saw those numbers increase by a staggering 162 percent.[8] The proof-of-concept stage had clearly been crossed. IOL surgery offered a huge jump in value for impoverished patients. A growing number of them were choosing to undergo cataract surgery, compelled by the improved visual outcomes and the fact that the newly affordable procedure not only abolished the need for heavy glasses but also shaved three to four days off of post-operation time in the hospital.

In this way, Aurolab added tremendous momentum to Aravind's market-driving approach. It leveraged the strengths of Aravind's existing demand and delivery systems and played a pivotal role in driving up Aravind's quality, volume, operational efficiencies, and program sustainability. By 2003, 98 percent of Aravind's cataract patients were receiving lens implants, compared with the 35 percent who had received them in 1992.[9]

The affordable lenses also allowed for a landmark shift in surgical training. In the early 1990s, the high cost of the lenses severely limited the number of IOL surgeries being done, so there was little incentive to provide training in the implant technique. Aurolab's lenses helped change that reality. Now that hospitals and patients could afford the lenses, the demand for IOL training rapidly increased. Aravind wasted no time in creating an intensive skill-transfer program for IOL surgery. Launched in 1993 in partnership with the U.K.-based charity Sightsavers, the program flung open the door to surgeons from across the world. Trainees began streaming in from such countries as Afghanistan, Mongolia, Pakistan, and Indonesia, as well as Switzerland, Germany, Israel, the United States, and New Zealand. Now, each year, the heavily waitlisted two-month program graduates more than 100 surgeons.[10] To date, it has trained well over 1,900 ophthalmologists. By making both lenses and training accessible, the Aurolab–Aravind team brought about the mainstreaming of IOL surgery and the phasing out of inferior techniques across hundreds of hospitals far beyond its own geographic borders.

Along with its concern for accessibility and high-quality standards, Aurolab had a personal, low-key approach to marketing that was also vintage Aravind. In its first eight years, exporting to hundreds of non-profits and hospitals across dozens of countries, Aurolab had a one-man marketing team—the serene, white-haired R. Duraisamy (Thulsi and Sriram's father). In the following five years, that team increased to a grand total of two. Rather than invest in high-profile and expensive promotional activities, Aurolab chose to let word of mouth organize distribution. Its products found an organic distribution network via Aravind's hospitals, its partner agencies, and Aravind-trained doctors who joined other hospitals or went into private practice.

FOR THE FIRST 13 years of Aurolab's existence, IOL production was unregulated in India. "Nobody questioned what quality you gave—nobody inspected," says Sriram.[11] Rather than view the absence of a regulatory body as a chance to cut corners, Aurolab saw it as an opportunity to create a benchmark. Its early lenses were tested in American labs by Dr. David J. Apple, a close friend of Harold Ridley's and one of the most renowned IOL researchers in the field.[12] In 1995, in a noted ophthalmology journal, Apple passed the following verdict: "[Aurolab lenses] clearly meet and often exceed the standards of many lenses manufactured in the United States and European countries."[13]

Aspiring to set world-class standards, Aurolab was the first Indian company to receive an ISO certification for IOLs in India and to be awarded the CE mark (ISO is an international certification of quality, and CE approves a product's sale in Europe).[14] The implications of certification went far beyond the eligibility to export. "Other manufacturers were forced to follow us, which meant they had to raise their standards," says Sriram. "So we brought about healthy competition in India—competition that resulted in better prices *and* better quality."

Today, India is the biggest consumer of IOLs in the world, and there are more than a dozen other IOL manufacturers in the country, at least four of which have met the quality of the CE mark.[15] In this changed environment, Aurolab is the nation's third-largest player and no longer the lowest priced. Its least expensive IOL now costs $2 in the market, but other brands can be purchased for even less. Having blazed its own trail in service of affordable products for all patients, Aurolab does not always keep up with price wars and sees its role more in terms of value leadership.

Inviting competition and improving quality, while keeping prices affordable, has pushed Aurolab to stay nimble. Like Aravind, it deeply believes that serving both ends of the economic spectrum is central to its progress. It used the rapid advancements in IOL technology as a spur to diversify its product line, which now contains nearly 20 different base models with over 1,000 different variations. It produces lenses that are rigid, foldable, hard, soft, three-piece, one piece, hydrophilic, and even hydrophobic (the latter requires a rare, high-end production capability). The scaled-up manufacturing processes are developed in-house, but basic product development is sometimes outsourced.

Even as Aurolab responds to high-end demands, its growth centers on its founders' ethos of empathy-driven development. "When Aravind comes across new technology, it looks to bring down the price so that it can be used for the masses," explains Bala. He adds, "The key has always been to identify the most expensive part of an operation and try to lower its price." After IOLs, the next most costly consumables for cataract surgery are sutures.[16] In 1998, the price was $240 for a box in the United States—too expensive for developing countries. Following a process parallel to its IOL set-up, Aurolab, with close support from David Green and other Western collaborators, began production of sutures that same year with technology obtained from Germany. The price for a box of Aurolab sutures was soon set at $30.[17]

Two years earlier, in 1996, a visitor from Moorfields Eye Hospital in England, impressed with Aurolab's production quality, had recommended that it enter the field of ophthalmic pharmaceuticals and offered to collaborate, thus setting the stage for Aurolab to become India's first nonprofit drug company. Aurolab's choice of intervention in this arena is telling—not only does the company tackle the most expensive ophthalmic drugs to bring their prices down, but also, as Sriram points out, "We make drugs that other companies don't want to make." Certain drugs with high impact but short shelf life and narrow demand are typically ignored, or eventually abandoned by big companies because of their low margins (for example, an antifungal drug used to treat corneal ulcers caused by tropical infections). Such "orphan drugs," though commercially unattractive, meet a clear need and suit Aurolab's ethos perfectly. Most of its formulations are no longer under patent protection, making production easier.

Today, Aurolab produces over 50 different ophthalmic drugs, ointments, drops, and tinctures, making it a convenient one-stop shop for clients.[18] It uses this wide range to create innovative packages that help address the inefficiencies of India's supply-chain infrastructure. For instance, Aurolab produces a popular cataract surgery kit that conveniently bundles together all the consumables (including lenses, sutures, and pharmaceuticals) needed for up to five surgeries. The organization has diversified even further and now also manufactures an assortment of ophthalmic equipment, ranging from sophisticated lasers to surgical instruments and diagnostic aids—including an LCD vision chart with remote controls for measuring not just visual acuity but also color vision and contrast sensitivity, eliciting considerable interest among European institutions.

There is no doubt that Aurolab's partnership with Aravind helps it in the marketplace. The latter's reputation for quality carries over to Aurolab products. Also, Aravind's doctors provide an immediate feedback loop that is valuable for rapid prototyping, and they occasionally even initiate new design ideas. Although Aurolab's initial raison d'être was to serve Aravind's needs, it has long since surpassed that role, and the relationship has matured in interesting ways.

Braided together by virtue of origin, a shared philosophy, and overlapping governance (the Aurolab board is a subset of Aravind's senior leadership), the two operate as independent entities, with no cross-subsidization between them. And as far as pricing goes, Aravind pays the same rates as Aurolab's other nonprofit customers. It is also free to purchase products from rival companies (and regularly does this for certain high-demand imported brands). In fact, in 2010 Aravind accounted for only 13 percent of Aurolab's $12 million revenue.[19] That same year, Aurolab's governing board turned down a purchase offer from one of the world's largest medical-device companies.

☙

THE WROUGHT IRON GATES with the familiar flowerlike symbol swing open. The sleek four-story facility, all 110,000 square feet of it, rises against a sunset sky. Aurolab is built on a beautiful property roughly four miles from its first home at Aravind. Visitors to its manufacturing areas don sterile coats and slip covers on head and feet before entering. Walking through its passageways, they can examine some processes up close, while other hyper-sterilized zones can be viewed only through windows. More than 460 employees work here. Everywhere there is the steady hum of machinery. Each room is occupied by rows of young women in pale blue lab coats, their hair tucked under matching caps. A wide range of detail-oriented activity is going on: some are peering through microscopes, and others are programming complex machinery, cutting, cleaning, checking, and packing thousands of the sight-restoring implants that look like clear plastic buttons. They work with diligent grace. Within the chambers of Aurolab is the same sense of fully absorbed tranquility that pervades the operating rooms of Aravind.

Aurolab is the prodigious child that grew up to exceed all expectations, including its own. A nonprofit hospital system creating a non-profit medical-products factory is a rare innovation. It is clear to the leaders of both organizations that the richness and value of this connection transcends the transactional. Together, they have done what so many considered impossible. In Aurolab's high-ceilinged lobby, an arresting black-and-white portrait of Dr. V is mounted on a granite plaque. His words are etched into its surface:

Intelligence and capability are not enough.

There must be the joy of doing something beautiful.

Dr. V's head is tilted to one side and he is smiling broadly, as if pleased to see how this maverick venture, armed with a generous mission, has made good.

# THIRTEEN

# THE FLIP SIDE OF A VISIONARY

One day in the late 1970s, when Aravind's small clinic examined a record-breaking 100 patients, Dr. V treated the staff to ice cream. As the treats were passed around, he urged everyone to aim for the day when they would see 1,000 patients. Even his most experienced staff members thought he was joking. Today, the Aravind Eye Care System sees more than 70 times that original milestone every day. "Throughout the time that I have known Dr. V, his vision for what was possible was *way beyond* what was anything reasonable," says Fred Munson, his voice rich with amusement and awe.

Aravind's growth was hardly one-dimensional. At different turns, it unfolded new and unexpected capacities. "I have read a little of Sri Aurobindo and of his idea that we are evolving," says Aravind research partner Dr. Jack Whitcher thoughtfully. "I think that's what's happening with Aravind. I see an evolutionary process going on. That's why people will always be able to learn as much as they give here."

"There is no more benumbing error than to mistake a stage for the goal or to linger too long in a resting place," wrote Sri Aurobindo.[1] Dr. V's passion for continual improvement protected Aravind from the dangers of stagnation. He encouraged people to test assumptions and question their success. This approach is what led Aravind leadership to put its screening eye camps—one of its most notable areas of achievement—under intense scrutiny. Camps have long been viewed as the crowning glory of the Aravind model. But in 1999, a joint study between Aravind and the London School of Hygiene & Tropical Medicine punctured that belief.

The study sought to determine what percentage of people in Aravind's service area in need of eye care were actually accessing it. The answer that surfaced was shocking: less than 7 percent.[2] While the absolute number of patients treated through Aravind's camps was high, their overall penetration rate, as shown by this study, was appallingly low. "Until then, we had only looked at how many people we were serving, not the number who needed care. We were deceived by the high numbers we were seeing [at our hospitals] into dealing with just the numerator," says Thulsi.

Though Aravind runs roughly 40 camps every week, when spread across the 600-odd towns and villages that serve as hosts, camps were reaching each community on a bi-yearly, quarterly, or monthly basis at most. To improve its reach, Aravind would have to come up with an intervention to reach potential patients year-round, one that could function alongside its hallmark eye camps and eventually perhaps even replace them.

☙

DR. V SITS at his desk in front of a new computer with a flat-screen monitor. "You have to pay two rupees to look at it," he says impishly to anyone who walks in the door. Technology excites him with its possibilities—this boyish octogenarian who still makes 50-year plans. The first time someone showed him how to use Google's satellite maps, he spent an entire afternoon excitedly looking up all the obscure cities and towns he had ever been to. Not an unusual fascination when you remember how much of his work has involved putting forsaken people and places on the map. His curiosity is eclectic but never frivolous; everything connects back to being a perfect instrument and helping people in need live better lives. On this morning in 2003, he is reading up on an Alaskan telemedicine project. "We need something like that to reach our villages," he says matter-of-factly (as if it were a one-click Amazon purchase away).

At the turn of the millennium, the magic wand of information technology began to wave in the direction of rural India. No one was more excited about the implications of this on eye care than Dr. V—except perhaps his brother-in-law Dr. Nam. Under their joint leadership, a string of IT projects geared toward outreach were set up in partnership with various technology companies and social venture funds. But the most spectacular success came from unexpected quarters.

In 2004, Sonesh Surana, a lanky Ph.D. student from the University of California, Berkeley, arrived at Aravind to explore a potential research project. He was part of a Berkeley initiative called Technology and Infrastructure for Emerging Regions (TIER), which focused on designing solutions for the challenging realities of the developing world. Surana wanted to explore the possibility of setting up a scalable, high-bandwidth, wireless computer network link between Aravind–Theni and a small Aravind vision center that had just been launched as a pilot in Nam's native village of Ambasamudram, ten miles away.

The idea behind the vision centers was to provide rural and small-town populations with permanent outposts for diagnosis and primary eye care. Aravind aimed to get people to proactively seek eye care as soon as they needed it, instead of putting it off until an eye camp was held in their area. Dr. V and Nam envisioned these centers using teleconsultations to eliminate unnecessary hospital visits. There was a good deal of internal debate on the approach—it was not clear whether the technology was feasible, and even if it was, whether patients would be comfortable with remote diagnosis.

Surana and TIER had no firsthand experience working in the social sector, let alone rural India. Whether this novice group would be able to reconfigure expensive Wi-Fi technology (traditionally designed for distances of about 100 meters) reliant on a stable power supply, and make it work for long-distance communication in regions of frequent power outages and poor infrastructure, was doubtful. The rampant poverty in these regions also made the financial sustainability of such a venture uncertain. But Dr. V was firmly convinced that this new technology could reshape the future of eye care—there was no debating with him on the subject. And so Aravind plunged resolutely ahead with the collaboration.

Over the next two years, Surana and his small band of associates clambered on top of village rooftops, water tanks, factory chimneys, chicken sheds, and schoolhouses in search of the perfect line of sight required for a working point-to-point wireless connection. They adapted software protocols, mixed cement, built towers, and mounted directional antennas and routers. All of this eventually resulted in network speeds of up to 6 megabits per second at distances up to 40 miles.[3] Their redesigned technology was affordable and robust, and recovered easily from electrical outages. A mere 17 months into the partnership, the adventurous pilot had proved so successful that Aravind announced plans to expand the vision-center model. Its goal was to set up 40 such centers (built with support from the Lavelle Fund for the Blind and other partners) to serve a rural population of 3 million year-round. Each center would be linked to one of Aravind's hospitals to receive long-distance, high-quality care.

Aravind's vision centers are set up as primary eye clinics. Nurses from Aravind who are trained in comprehensive examination, refraction testing, and spectacles dispensing run these centers. There are no doctors onsite. Real-time video consultations with an Aravind doctor are carried out through telemedicine links. Doctors at each Aravind hospital are responsible for up to five vision centers and have immediate online access to patients' case sheets. The vision centers are entirely paperless and maintain all records in a centralized database.

Today these centers have dramatically increased the rate at which eye care is accessed. For instance, Alaganallur is a little town in Tamil Nadu that used to host two Aravind eye camps a year. These camps screened fewer than 1,000 people in all. The town now has an Aravind vision center. Within the span of a year, the center examined 5,000 new patients; fitted more than 800 people with eyeglasses; and referred more than 250 cataract patients, and an additional 400 patients requiring specialty care, to Aravind–Madurai.[4]

By 2011, Aravind was running 36 fully functioning vision centers that had been in operation for over a year. The centers collectively process over 550 telemedicine consultations every day and generate income that covers roughly 90 percent of their operating costs. Patients are charged a fee of Rs. 20 (less than 50 cents), which covers three visits—less than the travel expenses they would incur for a single visit to the nearest eye hospital. The centers collectively receive roughly 160,000 patient visits in a year.

By reducing the necessity of traveling to major cities for eye care, the vision centers collectively save the community close to $1 million in travel fare each year.[5] Most significantly, these centers have, on average, increased market penetration to about 30 percent of those needing eye care, within the first year (for centers that have been functioning longer, this figure is as high as 75 percent).[6]

Surana talks about how closely Dr. V followed the progress of each vision center in the first couple of years. "On one of my visits, I went to see him right after I landed in Madurai. As soon as he saw me, he said, 'I want you to look at something.' Then he pulled up information from the vision centers, pointed to one of them, and said, 'Look, we have only a few people coming to this one—what do you think is happening?' I hadn't even said hello yet! But he was so excited about this project and so sure we could figure this out together."[7]

Surana was tickled by Dr. V's utter lack of small talk but also touched by his ready spirit of partnership. "It stems from people like Dr. V, Dr. Nam, and a few key others, and creates this second-order effect," he muses. "Because of the way they are and the way they connect with people, it generates a lot of goodwill that comes back their way. I saw this in Theni when we were trying to find land on which to erect our towers. I had a coconut farmer come up to me and say, 'Look, I know Dr. Nam and all the good work Aravind does here, so I'm going to dig a six-foot pit in my field just so you can put up your 40-foot tower.' I mean, who does that kind of thing?" he exclaims. "That's the power of goodwill capital at Aravind—and it's generated in a way that's not calculated."

☙

NOBODY WHO HAS worked closely with Dr. V doubts the influence of his spiritual mooring on Aravind's evolution and success. But they also know he has his share of fallibilities. His journals reveal the private corridors of a beautiful mind that was often seized by doubt, turned rigid by fear, or plunged into despair by conflict and obstacles. Behind Aravind's crown of lustrous achievement is a history riddled with gritty, ordinary battles. There was much to overcome in the early years.

As Aravind built additional hospitals in the rest of the state of Tamil Nadu, each faced numerous challenges: competition, leadership gaps, low service uptake, and the need for each hospital to develop an individual identity within a shared mission. There were political tussles with the government over accreditation of Aravind's postgraduate institute and ideological conflicts with partner organizations on the decision to produce IOLs. Dr. V wrote about these and much else in his journals. Staffing proved to be one of the organization's most persistent issues. *6 doctors are leaving*, reads one short, despondent entry from 1980. Another, which is almost comical in its scope, reads: *Recent challenges: 1. Doctors 2. Nurses 3. Operating assistants 4. Hospital administrators 5. Optical technicians.*

In his journals, Dr. V is candid about the struggle to control his negative tendencies and bursts of impatience with staff. *I feel something is wrong with me. I develop fixed ideas and strong prejudices,* he writes. *So much tension, anger and reaction sometimes.* He writes, too, of heated disputes between members of the family. The challenges inherent in having multiple generations of a clan working under the same roof were great, but Aravind was blessed with counterbalances that prevented irreparable rents in the fabric.

Dr. V's sister Janaky Ramaswamy was one of them. She and her quietly supportive husband lived next door to the house that served as the first Aravind clinic. The two properties were connected by way of a cowshed in the back. Janaky was given to slipping across to the clinic, bearing steel cups of freshly brewed coffee for the staff. Warm, generous, tireless, and sharp-tongued, Janaky Amma (who succumbed to cancer in 1998) was in the early years a powerful binding force and a maternal refuge for the young, overworked team of doctors. She helped raise their children along with four of her own.

There is no job description for the role she played, but the founding team remembers her as a vital anchor. Janaky never went a day without seeing her eldest brother. A visit to his office was a ritual part of her morning. When she learned of upsets between any of her siblings, she always hurried over to smooth ruffled feathers and try to mediate a truce. Her presence helped restore equilibrium.

All the founders of Aravind built their homes within a few minutes of each other, and there are few formalities between them. A fierce loyalty and an undemonstrative affection hold them together through professional differences and unavoidable spats. The everyday lives of this family are intertwined on multiple levels, and Dr. V, the white-haired bachelor of the clan, deeply cherishes this closeness. He is always the first to show up at the doorstep whenever someone in the family has fallen ill, and loves buying small treats for the grandchildren. *Nothing compares to a joint family*, he once wrote in his journals. *I would not have survived had I lived alone.* This sense of indebtedness perhaps is part of what disturbs him when altercations do arise.

The founders are all close-knit, but each can be headstrong in argument. In a telling entry from the mid-'90s that records the tragicomic drama of close human relationships, Dr. V writes:

> *T feels very bad because I wanted to make a change in his training program. R feels bad that T is feeling bad. N feels bad that her recommendation was not heeded. P feels bad that his desire was not satisfied. They are all individual opinions and ideas. Attachment is so strong that it causes lots of friction. I feel that my idea is correct so there is controversy. T feels that I don't encourage people to develop. R also feels the same. How as a leader can I help to solve the problem and lead them to a clear goal. I feel tired and weak. I want to escape and leave this scene and go somewhere else.*

His despair is palpable, but the charges against him are not unfounded. The flip side of Dr. V's ability to tap into a higher plane of consciousness and his sense of being guided is that he often finds it hard to abandon his own point of view and does not always trust others to make independent decisions. His tremendous gifts are speckled with the stereotypical faults of older generations. He can be narrow-minded and rigid in outlook, and his intentions to coach are sometimes overtaken by an unfortunate tendency to command. The man's contradictions are occasionally called out by a brother, sister, nephew, or niece. But outside of the family, Fred Munson is the person at Aravind most often dispatched to beard the lion in his den. Speaking truth to power (and getting away with it) has been a consistent part of his role here.

&#128488;

IN 1980, MUNSON was professor of hospital administration at the University of Michigan. On a visit to the school that year, Dr. V dropped by to talk to him. Intrigued by the quality of the surgeon's presence and his hunger to better understand hospital systems, Munson accepted an invitation to visit Aravind the following year. He and his wife, Mary, fit like long-lost pieces into the intricate jigsaw puzzle of India, the organization, and Dr. V's clan. For more than 30 years since that first visit, they have both spent a month of each year volunteering at Aravind.

The Munsons are of the same generation as Dr. V and his siblings, and share their natural affinity for hard work, practical thinking, and unpretentious living. Fred is a farm boy at heart who, in his 80s, still drives a tractor and chops wood for their furnace. Mary is a whirlwind of caring activity with a gift for making people feel special. They both swiftly won the trust and affection of the founding team. Fred's appreciation for democracy, gift for deep listening, and tact have also made him a valuable confidant for Aravind's younger generations.

"This family can be pretty abysmal when it comes to communicating with each other," says Munson, disclosing one of the open secrets at Aravind. "A part of it is the culture of deference. The elders got used to that and demanded it without realizing how it can also cut off communication." He smiles in detailing the interrelated complexities of the situation. "They complained how the next generation didn't tell them anything and wasn't showing initiative. That made young people like Prajna strike a blow in favor of open conversation, by being as blunt as possible!"

"Fred plays the role of an insider-outsider," Thulsi explains. "He's been here frequently enough that he knows what the real issues are but is also distanced from the actual dynamics. He has a perspective that's suited to asking all those awkward questions that can help resolve things effectively." It was Munson, for instance, who initiated the first breakthrough discussions with G. Srinivasan on salary hikes for the doctors. And Munson who prompted Dr. Natchiar to tone down the sharpness in her interactions with nurses and student surgeons, and who eventually broached the delicate subject of a succession plan with

Dr. V. He also has a track record of successfully intervening in tricky situations on behalf of younger staff members.

"I really was troubled on this visit by the number of people in responsible positions who felt that any significant decision would be made by you," wrote Munson to Dr. V in a lengthy letter in the mid-1990s (a letter that includes convivial details of grandchildren, and leaf raking). "Right now my feeling is that you are more interested in [people] making the right decision than you are in them making their own decision." Very few people in his life can speak to Dr. V with this degree of frankness.

"I am extremely thankful to you," Dr. V wrote back. "It is true that I have been constantly focusing on right decisions. Now I am making increased effort for human resource development, and decision making by our people in all levels will be a priority." To his (and Munson's) credit, Dr. V genuinely worked on modulating aspects of his leadership style. But there were certain elements to his approach that he dearly wished to pass on.

In his journals, Dr. V writes repeatedly of a keen aspiration: *We brothers and sisters and our families should not live in small worlds, bound up in small things. We must make wider progress.* He often lists the advancements at the external level that he and his siblings made, but follows that up with a poignant admission: *I do not know how far we have grown spiritually.* It is worth noting here that Dr. V never mentions a desire to have his family follow Sri Aurobindo or the Mother. They each resonate (or not) to different degrees with his teachers, a fact that does not perturb Dr. V. He does not force his special connection on others. But he does insist that *to get things done in a big and permanent way it must be done spiritually.*

In Dr. V's worldview, certain conditions of mind and heart are of utmost importance in any form of work, and must be actively cultivated. He believes that when selfless intentions drive an undertaking, and when people truly attempt to understand themselves and their work within the vast interconnectedness of the world, they can effect profound change. He does not look for shortcuts to this process, and understands it to be the slow and necessary work of a lifetime—a process that does not bear direct fruit but fertilizes the soil, so to speak. By practicing at the boundaries of your compassion, by following disciplines that progressively dissolve personal biases that cloud your judgment, and by consciously seeking to align with your deepest purpose, you create the conditions from which truly transformative action and innovation arise. These are Dr. V's beliefs, and they are rooted in his experience.

*All work in the outside world reflects the action of life inside,* writes Dr. V. *Work must become* sadhana *[a practice of self-evolution]. It is not about buildings, equipment, money or material things, but a matter of consciousness.* His abiding aspiration is to have family and other staff members at Aravind engage with their work in this spirit.

On February 14, 1994, Dr. V entered a few impassioned lines from *Savitri* in his journal. Perhaps they echoed something of the beautiful dissatisfaction that raged within him:

> *In me the spirit of immortal love stretches its arms out to embrace mankind.*
> *Imperfect is the joy not shared by all.*

PART IV

# Training Your Competition

## On Replication and Self-Awareness

*Yaadhum oore, yaavarum kelir.*
("All countries are my home, all people my kin.")

—From the *Purananooru*, an ancient collection of Tamil verse

# FOURTEEN

# IF WE CAN DO IT, SO CAN YOU

The story of blindness prevention in the 20th century was brought to life by an ensemble cast of passionate strangers, people who dedicated their lives to restoring sight in far-flung corners of the world, inspiring hundreds to join them. There was the German missionary Ernst Christoffel, who began treating sightless children in Turkey; and the New Zealander Fred Hollows, who journeyed across Africa, Asia, and the Australian outback treating curable blindness. In the United Kingdom, there was Sir John Wilson, who spurred entire nations to launch blindness-control programs and cofounded the International Agency for the Prevention of Blindness. There was the strong-willed French-Swiss doctor Nicole Grasset, who along with Larry Brilliant and others of smallpox-eradication fame took on the cause of sight restoration. There was the Texan ophthalmologist David Paton, who created the Flying Eye Hospital. And in India, there was a retired ophthalmologist with an unpronounceable name, bent on building eye hospitals modeled on McDonald's.

All of these paths and many others intersected over the decades to create a loosely defined coalition for sight, comprising country governments, grassroots charities, medical teams, activists, public health experts, management consultants, and volunteers. Together, they bent the boughs of possibility. As a result of their combined efforts, the elimination of curable blindness is low-hanging fruit in the 21st century. It is achingly within reach, which is what makes the following Vision 2020 statistic doubly incriminating: Every five seconds, someone in our world goes blind, and a child goes blind every minute.[1]

Ninety percent of the people affected live in developing countries, where blindness often cuts short earning potential, decreases life expectancy, and destroys an individual's sense of dignity and independence.[2] The chilling facts of the situation bring us face to face with what a young research student aptly termed "The Tragedy of Easy Problems."[3] Millions of people still suffer from diseases for which we have reliable treatments *and* demonstrated models that deliver those treatments in economically viable, medically excellent, and practically scalable ways. Cataract surgery hovers near the top of this list. In 2008, a World Bank assessment found it to be one of the most cost-effective and justifiable of all public health interventions. By their calculations, a patient's economic productivity in just the first year after a cataract operation yields 1,500 percent of the cost of the surgery.[4]

The continuing magnitude of the problem shaped Dr. V's approach. Early on, he recognized that Aravind's direct surgical contributions alone would never be sufficient to address the scale of the problem. This awareness fueled his belief that the real power of the Aravind model lay in its potential for replication across states, countries, and even continents.

*To get universal consciousness*, writes Dr. V. *In a small way how can we make a Global effort to conquer cataract blindness.* There is a glimmering oxymoron in Dr. V's approach. He treated Aravind's work as a microcosm of the solution: To make a *global* effort—in a *small* way. In this quiet, deliberate manner that spanned decades, he lifted Aravind's relevance from the provincial to the planetary. *Last night I dreamt of expanding the work of Aravind Hospitals to other places*, he wrote in an early 1980s journal entry. *Get others involved.*

DR. V IN HIS OFFICE: A visitor's first glimpse of Dr. V—framed by his spiritual teachers, the Mother and Sri Aurobindo. Photographer: Raj Kumar, 2006

**IN UNIFORM, 1940s:** Dr. V served four years as an army doctor before crippling rheumatoid arthritis set in. Photograph courtesy of the Aravind Eye Care System (AECS)

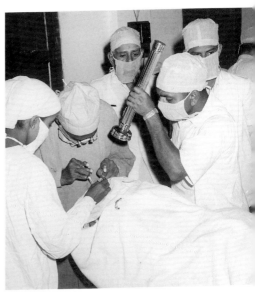

**DR. V OPERATING UNDER FLASHLIGHT, 1970s:** With extraordinary willpower and dedication, Dr. V went on to personally restore sight to over 100,000 people. Photograph courtesy of AECS

**DR. V AND SIR JOHN WILSON, 1980s:** Wilson (*right*), blinded at age 12, was Dr. V's friend and mentor, and a unifying force in the field of global sight restoration.

Photographer: Rameshwar Das

❧ ARAVIND EYE CLINIC, 1976: The original 11-bed clinic, founded by Dr. V and his siblings, which grew into the largest eye care system in the world.
Photographer: Murugan

❧ DR. V AND DR. NATCHIAR, 1977: Dr. Natchiar (*right*) is a force of compassion with a formidable organizational consciousness. Dr. V was her teacher in eye surgery. Photograph courtesy of AECS

❧ ARAVIND CONSTRUCTION SITE, 1980s: G. Srinivasan's genius for cost management played a large role in Aravind's growth, allowing it to make a surplus even while giving away the majority of its services for free.
Photographer: Thulsi Ravilla

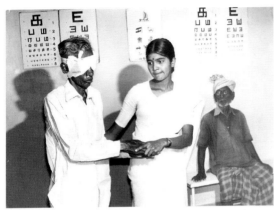

✻ ARAVIND NURSE WITH PATIENT, 1970S: Highly trained high school graduates recruited from local villages are the backbone of the model. "To me, a nurse leading a patient by hand—that's value addition," says Dr. Natchiar. Photographer: Murugan

✻ FOUNDING TEAM, 1980S: "Do more, take less" was the hardworking, selfless ethos of the early years. *Left to right:* seated, Dr. Natchiar, Dr. V, Dr. Viji; standing, G. Srinivasan, Dr. Nam, Dr. MS, Thulsi. Photographer: Murugan

✦ CROWD AT AN EYE CAMP:
Aravind sends medical teams to
the doorstep of rural India to
screen patients in need of eye care.
Photographer: David Heiden, 1994

✦ CHART READING: A line of villagers
wait their turn as Senior Nurse
Kavitha tests a young girl's vision.
Photographer: Moses Ceaser, 2003

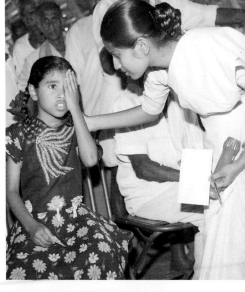

✦ REFRACTION TESTING: Senior
Nurse Podhumani tests a woman
for eyeglasses.
Photographer: Moses Ceaser, 2003

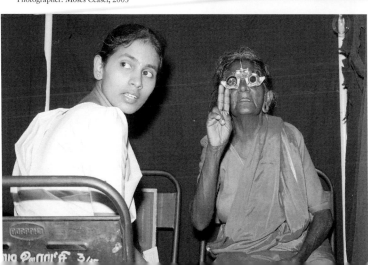

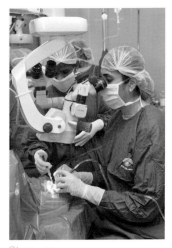

✤ ARAVIND EYE HOSPITAL, MADURAI: This five-story building was painstakingly built over many years. Now Aravind's network of hospitals see 7,500 patients on a daily basis.

Photographer: Raj Kumar, 2011

✤ DR. HARIPRIYA PERFORMING CATARACT SURGERY: Cataract, the clouding of the eye's lens, is the leading cause of blindness in the developing world.

Photographer: Raj Kumar, 2011

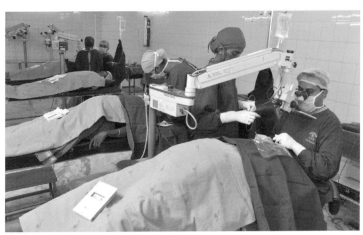

✤ OPERATING ROOM, ARAVIND–MADURAI: Assembly-line procedures and rigorous quality tracking give Aravind's patients outcomes that compare favorably with those in the West. Photographer: Raj Kumar, 2011

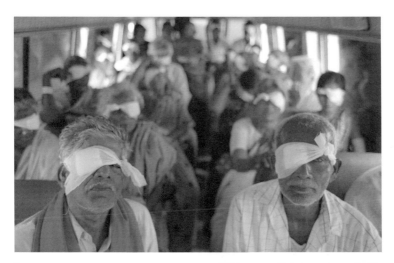

※ AFTER FREE SURGERY: Aravind
eye camps cover the patient's
food, accommodation, surgery,
and transport costs, enabling
thousands to access care.

Photographer: Ryan Pyle, 2011

※ READY FOR THE RIDE HOME: A
pensive post-op cataract patient
looks out the van window, en
route to his village.

Photographer: Ryan Pyle, 2011

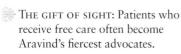

※ THE GIFT OF SIGHT: Patients who
receive free care often become
Aravind's fiercest advocates.

Photographer: Pavithra Mehta, 2011

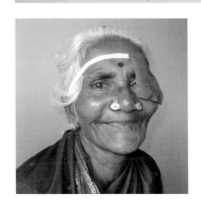

**FROM MICHIGAN TO MADURAI:** Managing Director Dr. Bala Krishnan moved back to India after ten years abroad, to help launch Aurolab, Aravind's manufacturing unit.

Photographer: Raj Kumar, 2011

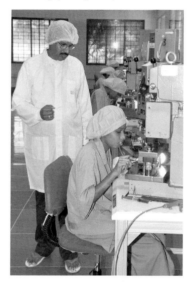

**IOL PRODUCTION FLOOR:** Aurolab brought down the cost of state-of-the-art intraocular lenses from $200 to $5. Director of Operations R. D. Sriram (*left*) oversees the multistage production process.

Photographer: Raj Kumar, 2011

**SUTURE DIVISION:** Today, Aurolab produces a wide range of high-quality, affordable ophthalmic products, exporting them to more than 120 countries worldwide. Photographer: Jacques J. Vekemans, 2009

❊ THE LIONS ARAVIND INSTITUTE OF COMMUNITY OPHTHALMOLOGY (LAICO): Aravind's training and consulting institute runs programs that have helped spread its model worldwide. Photographer: Mike Myers, 2011

❊ LEARNING FROM ARAVIND: After attending a workshop at LAICO, Javier Okhuysen (*left*) and Carlos Orellana launched an Aravind-like effort in Mexico City. Photograph: 2011

*Intelligence and capability are not enough. There must be the joy of doing something beautiful.*
– Dr. G. Venkataswamy

❊ TALKING WITH THE RESIDENTS: Dr. Prajna (*far right*) strives to improve work–life balance for students and employees in the organization. Fifteen percent of all eye doctors in India have undergone some form of training at Aravind. Photographer: Raj Kumar, 2011

🌸 WITH FRIENDS AT SEVA FOUNDATION, 1998:
Founded by an eclectic group of doctors,
activists, and artists, Seva is one of Aravind's
strongest partners in the West. *Left to right:*
seated, Ram Dass, James O' Dea; standing,
D. Nagarajan, Amy Sherts, Dr. Suzanne
Gilbert, Dr. Larry Brilliant, Dr. V, David
Green, Dr. Natchiar, Wavy Gravy.

Photograph courtesy of AECS

🌸 DR. V AND DR. FRED MUNSON, 1990S:
Munson (*right*) and his wife, Mary, have
volunteered with Aravind for over 30 years.
He plays a unique role as confidant and
facilitator for first- and second-generation
leaders at Aravind. Photograph courtesy of AECS

🌸 PARTNERS ACROSS THE
GLOBE: Dr. Christine
Melton visited Aravind
in the 1980s and has
stayed involved ever
since. She is president
of the Aravind Eye
Foundation, USA. *Left
to right:* Dr. Nam, Dr.
Melton, Dr. Ravi.

Photographer: Suzanne Gilbert, 2008

✻ GROWING BEYOND FAMILY: Today the majority of Aravind's doctors are unrelated to Dr. V. Many, like the senior leaders shown here, play an integral role in the organization's continued growth. *Left to right:* Drs. Ilango, Shukla, Das, Shetty, Ravichandar, Krishnadas, Banushree, Rathinam, Pamona, Sharmila, Ravichandran, Mahesh, Rupa.

Photographer: Raj Kumar, 2011

✻ AN OPEN-SOURCE MODEL: Dr. Aravind Srinivasan, the administrator of Aravind–Madurai, addresses a group of young social entrepreneurs. Giving away secrets of its success is part of the organization's DNA.

Photographer: Ashesh Shah, 2010

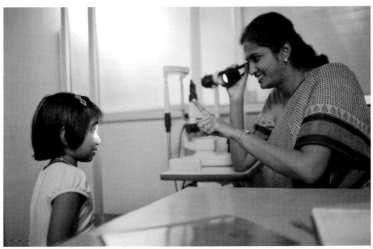

❧ DR. USHA WITH A YOUNG PATIENT: Aravind goes far beyond cataract operations, offering a wide range of specialized eye departments, including pediatrics, cornea, glaucoma, retina, and ocular oncology.

Photographer: Willie Davis, 2011

❧ IN TIMES OF CHANGE: Dr. Ravi Ravilla (*left*), the current head of the Aravind Eye Care System, with his brother Thulsi, the executive director of Aravind's consulting institute, LAICO. India's rapid growth poses new opportunities and challenges for Aravind's leadership. Photographer: Raj Kumar, 2011

LEADERSHIP IN TRANSITION: Still including the founders, Aravind's governing team is now largely composed of second-generation members—nieces and nephews of Dr. V and their spouses. *Left to right:* front row, Thulsi, Dr. Prajna, Kannamma, Dr. Viji, Varalakshmi, Dr. Usha, Dr. Lalitha; middle row, Dr. Natchiar, Dr. Bala, Dr. Ravi, Dr. Kim, Chitra R., Dr. Aravind; back row, Dr. Nam, G. Srinivasan, Dr. MS, Dr. Haripriya. (Not shown: Dr. RK, Sharada, Dr. Kalpana, Dr. Narendran, Vishnu, Chitra P.)

Photographer: Mike Myers, 2011

🌸 THE NEW AGE GROUP, 1994: To strengthen family ties, Dr. V had all the children of the third generation deliver special presentations to their elders every Sunday morning. *Left to right:* front row, Sathya, Vivek R., Dr. V., Deepa; back row, Pavithra, Karthik, Gowtham, Vivek S., R. Duraisamy, Dhivya R., Ramya. Photograph courtesy of AECS

🌸 THIRD GENERATION AT ARAVIND: Thirty-five members of Dr. V's family work at Aravind, a number that continues to grow. The original members of the New Age Group, now in their 20s and 30s, have joined the organization as doctors and managers. *Left to right:* front row, Dhivya R., Sathya, Deepa, Janani, Vivek S.; back row, Vivek R., Sankar, Dhivya K., Karthik, Ashok. Photographer: Raj Kumar, 2011

❧ MORE THAN 35 YEARS LATER:
Members of the founding team
sit on the terrace of the Madurai
hospital with various Aravind
buildings punctuating the skyline
behind them. All of them remain
deeply active in the organization
they created. *Left to right:* Dr.
Nam, Thulsi, Dr. Viji, Dr. MS,
G. Srinivasan, Dr. Natchiar.
Photographer: Raj Kumar, 2011

❧ MEENAKSHI TEMPLE, MADURAI:
This ancient temple in the heart
of Madurai was constructed over
multiple centuries. "Institutions
should be like temples," Dr. V
often said—enduring, timeless,
and built for the benefit of humanity. Photographer: Mike Myers, 2005

**Dr. Govindappa Venkataswamy:** The retired eye surgeon who, with little money, no business plan, and a magnificent vision, lit the eyes of millions. Photographer: Rameshwar Das, 1986

*Include people from other states and countries.* His far-sighted aspirations aligned Aravind's work with a much broader effort, making it one of the strongest links in a global chain of contribution.

❧

PERSISTENCE OF VISION is an ocular phenomenon; the term refers to the eye's ability to retain the impression of an image for a brief period (1/25 second) after the image itself has vanished. In the life of a visionary, the term takes on a whole new richness. People who encountered Dr. V in the early years confess to underestimating the muscular tenacity of his dreams. "I first met Dr. V in 1978," says Seva Foundation's Suzanne Gilbert. "I was at the University of Michigan School of Medicine. Dr. V came to meet me there out of his interest in education and training, and he remarked, 'One day, I would like to have a center like this one.' And at the back of my mind, I was thinking, 'Now wait a minute, he has an 11-bed eye clinic in India, he's coming to the States and walking around this 40,000-square-foot training facility, saying he wants one just like this . . . how is he ever going to do it?'"

As she speaks, it is easy to picture a freshly retired Dr. V, restless with the weight of unfinished work in the field. An improbable visionary with crippled fingers, modest means, and a thick Indian accent. Gilbert shrugs, smiles, and continues, "In a matter of years—in around 14 years—*he had done it.*"

She is referring to the Lions Aravind Institute of Community Ophthalmology, which opened in 1992. Today it goes by the acronym LAICO. Situated kitty-corner from the Aravind Eye Hospital in Madurai, LAICO is a high-domed, pillared building, surrounded by a stone wall edged with vibrant bougainvillea. At the entrance is a life-sized engraving of Mahatma Gandhi. He is poised mid-stride, walking stick in hand, as if about to enter. At LAICO you never really know who the next visitor will be.

Larry Page, cofounder of Google, once flew in on a chartered plane for a visit. MBA students from the Wharton School and the Ross School of Business cycle through annually on class projects. Right now, a Tanzanian hospital's staff is debating outreach strategy in the conference room as a visiting team from China strides through the hallways. LAICO is Aravind's training and consultancy institute. It aims to replicate the Aravind model to build international capacity for eye care, and as of 2011, it has trained more than 6,000 people from 69 countries.[5] LAICO operates as a kind of United Nations for blindness prevention. Its creation was the combined outcome of diligent preparation, skillful alliance, and serendipity.

In the mid-1980s, Aravind collaborated with Seva Foundation on its first replication effort. Aiming to tackle cataract blindness in Nepal, Seva had adopted the Lumbini Eye Institute, a small rural eye hospital near the Buddha's birthplace. *Buddha from Nepal 2,000 years ago spread his compassion all over the world*, wrote Dr. V in his journal. *Lumbini is a sacred place and we must endeavor to create this center to repeat what Buddha did.* Aravind was strapped for resources at the time, struggling with staff retention and sustainability issues at its recently established second hospital, but Dr. V held nothing back from the new partnership. As a result, all of Lumbini's eye surgeons were sent to Aravind for training, and everything at the Nepali hospital, from the architecture of the building to the tiered fee structure, the patient workflow, and the technique of running eye camps, was modeled after Aravind.[6]

The modest hospital steadily grew to become one of the first self-sustaining, high-volume, high-quality eye care service providers outside of India. In 2010, the Lumbini hospital screened about 172,000 patients and performed more than 32,500 surgeries.[7] But when it began, neither Seva nor Aravind knew that this effort to extend Aravind's model was perfectly timed for the next phase of their shared evolution.

In 1990, LIONS International established SightFirst, a global initiative that pledged $215 million for the prevention of curable blindness.[8] In the same year, they approached Aravind with a specific concern: Lions was funding hundreds of eye hospitals across the developing world, a number of which were performing suboptimally. "And yet, there was a constant demand from their hospitals for more money to expand existing facilities," says Thulsi. "The funding agencies were worried that this wasn't the best use of their money." In short, Lions International wanted to know if there was a way to make the hospitals they supported run more like Aravind. This was not an idle request; they were offering to back it with more than $1 million. The opportunity was hard to pass up, not because of the money but because Dr. V's work had aspired to this kind of global confluence all along.

Lions International is the world's largest service club organization (boasting over one million members across 45,000 clubs in 202 nations). An offer from an organization with such deep-rooted local ties around the world presented Aravind with a chance to exponentially amplify its work. That fall, Aravind held intensive brainstorming sessions to determine the best course forward. In attendance were all of its senior leaders, along with Suzanne Gilbert and Ram Dass from Seva Foundation. Ram Dass writes of this formative period, "I find myself less skeptical about the possibility, championed by Dr. Venkataswamy of Aravind . . . that preventable and curable blindness in the world can be turned into a non-problem. Maybe the time is right and the fair winds are blowing."[9] It turned out to be more than fair winds. It was all the ingredients for a perfect storm.

Seeds of Dr. V's vision had germinated across the decades, and in the early 1990s, their shoots began to burst through the ground. It was one of the most fertile periods in the organization's history. Aravind had already scaled to hospitals in three locations across Tamil Nadu and was expanding its base in Madurai. It had launched a formal training platform for ophthalmologists, developed extensive specialty clinics, and begun the groundwork for Aurolab. The Harvard Business School case study was just around the corner, and the Aravind model had already begun to assert its widespread relevance. Lions' support to create Aravind's teaching and consultancy institute would prove to be an important tipping point.

✍

THULSI RAVILLA, LAICO's executive director, sits in a sunlit corner office, his bookshelves bursting with files. His door is open, a signal to staff that he is not traveling—a rarity these days. His deep expertise in hospital systems and large-scale program planning for eye care keeps him in high demand on the international circuit. His itinerary for autumn 2010 includes a talk at Stockholm's Karolinska University Hospital; the International Agency for the Prevention of Blindness annual conference and the WHO First Global Symposium on Health Systems Research in Switzerland; panelist duties at a social entrepreneurship conference at Oxford University; and a lead role consulting with China's He Eye Hospital in Shenyang. None of these duties would have come to pass, but for an early shift in Thulsi's career path.

In 1981, Thulsi was an MBA graduate from one of India's finest business schools and had a well-paying job with British Paints, a company in the metropolis of Kolkata. When his wife's uncle (Dr. V) talked to him pointedly and repeatedly of Aravind's need for an administrator, Thulsi assumed that he was being made an offer. A period of soul-searching ensued: Thulsi had a wife and a one-year-old daughter to support. His corporate salary came with club memberships, housing, and other benefits. The job with Aravind promised a drastic pay cut, severe challenges, and, as Dr. V put it, "an opportunity to develop spiritually." In the end, an inner compulsion combined with an appetite for adventure led Thulsi to write to Dr. V, stating his intention to quit his job and come to Aravind. "I thought he would say at once, 'Yes, come and work here,'" says Thulsi with a grin. "But no, I had to go through the due process."

Seva Foundation's Larry Brilliant continues the story, "Dr. V rang me up in the U.S., and he said, 'I am thinking of hiring an administrator for Aravind, because I need a good manager. I have found this boy and I want you to kindly interview him.' And of course that 'boy' was his nephew by marriage, Thulsi." Brilliant subsequently roped in Sujit Gupta, an old friend and then-director of Tata Industries Ltd. (one of India's largest multinational conglomerates). Thulsi received a call from Gupta asking him to go to the Tata offices for a formal interview. He was given no indication of what the interview was for. In some bewilderment Thulsi showed up. "Sujit called me afterwards," recounts Brilliant. "He said, 'The guy works with a *paint company*. How will he ever be able to manage a hospital? He has no training!' And I said, 'Yes, but Dr. V has a way of looking into people's hearts and knowing who they are.'"

Brilliant did a second round of interviewing and took a strong liking to the young executive. He wholeheartedly recommended Thulsi for the post. When Thulsi joined Aravind, Dr. V dispatched him to the University of Michigan. He was a visiting scholar in hospital administration there for a year and was mentored by Fred Munson. On his return, Thulsi was put in charge of systems design and implementation at Aravind.

It turned out that he came as a package deal. As the eldest of four siblings, Thulsi exerted a Dr. V–like influence of his own. Over the years, his *entire* family trailed after him to Aravind. Thulsi's younger brother Ravi married Thulsi's wife's sister and began ophthalmology training in Madurai, along with Dr. Ramakrishnan (RK, who is married to Thulsi's younger sister, Saradha). Thulsi's father, R. Duraisamy, and youngest brother, Sriram, joined Aurolab's staff. His eldest daughter is now on the faculty at LAICO, while his younger daughter and her husband are both ophthalmologists at Aravind (as are three more of his siblings' children and their spouses). The Ravillas, as they are known within the broader family, are an irrepressible clan now spread throughout the organization and known for their warm humor, outgoing personalities, and infamous tendency to be late to family gatherings.

But Thulsi is responsible for more than a sizable contribution to Aravind personnel. He was one of the most crucial hires in Aravind's history, and his recruitment hinged on Dr. V's prescient conviction that sound business principles and systems could dramatically redefine eye care services. Because of this conviction, Thulsi was heavily involved in refining the Aravind model early on. "Management in eye care was absolutely virgin territory then," says Thulsi. "So whatever little I could do to design and implement systems had a lot of impact and got a lot of recognition, internally and externally." He has, for instance, chaired several international bodies in the field that are typically led by ophthalmologists. Today, as LAICO's executive director, he functions as ambassador and coach. The majority of his work is outward-facing and involves parsing Aravind's vastly detailed and interrelated systems into lessons for dissemination across the globe.

"ESSENTIALLY LAICO PACKAGED what Aravind has learned over the years into broad areas," Thulsi explains. "We figured the fundamental laws of delivering good eye care are fairly simple: you treat a lot of people; you do it with really good quality and in a sustainable manner." It is these fundamentals and the practices accompanying them that LAICO seeks to transfer.

LAICO's initial goal was to help 100 eye hospitals boost their sustainability and productivity to at least 5,000 high-quality surgeries a year. By 2011, it had consulted for 273 eye hospitals across 29 different countries and trained professionals from close to 70 nations. According to its own estimates, LAICO's work adds between 500,000 and 750,000 vision-restoring surgeries to the world's total each year.

"We could try to create dominance with Aravind's level of expertise, but we don't," says Thulsi. "Instead, we try and create training programs around those competitive skills. We see training as a form of sharing." This ethos of formally transferring knowledge and capability outside its walls is why, today, one in ten eye doctors across India has undergone some form of training at Aravind. Currently, LAICO and Aravind's hospitals together offer 31 clinical courses for ophthalmologists and nurses, a dozen nonclinical eye care management courses, and custom-designed workshops ranging from operation-theater management to architectural design for eye hospitals. LAICO regularly invites guest faculty members from eminent international agencies and other institutions to co-chair its sessions. The institute helps Aravind train more than 350 eye care professionals externally each year.

"That's how Aravind's brand recognition happens," claims Thulsi. "Not just through volume growth or the bottom line but through its spirit of sharing. Brand building is a consequence, not a goal, in this process. A lot of good things happen when you focus entirely on just what needs to be done."

THULSI HEADS A team of six dedicated LAICO faculty members. Apart from teaching classes, running workshops, and creating instructional materials, they also offer individualized consulting services to eye hospitals in India and around the world. A typical engagement starts with an initial needs-assessment visit by LAICO faculty. Then a multidisciplinary team from the client hospital makes a visit to Aravind–Madurai (often sponsored by an international funding agency). Six months later, the LAICO faculty member returns to the client hospital to conduct an onsite follow-up visit.

While in Madurai, the visiting team gets to know the Aravind model firsthand and, with LAICO's help, draws up concrete business plans for their specific context. These plans set new targets that almost always call for drastic increases in volume, sustainability, and quality. "If we were doing 10 surgeries, Aravind told us we could do 100. They kept pushing us to do more and showing us, scientifically and systematically, how we could get there," says Dr. Madan Deshpande, from the Desai Hospital in Pune, India. "Before coming to LAICO, we never thought of economic viability," he adds. "Like a child asking for candy, I would just point to the resources I wanted to share with the poor and the community and wait for the money to come from funders."[10] Says a hospital administrator from the state of Andhra Pradesh, "Being at LAICO was like getting a cataract surgery in management."

As of 2011, 78 percent of all the hospitals that LAICO worked with were in India, including dozens based close to Aravind's own hospitals. "People ask us why we spend so much effort on training our competition," says Thulsi, laughing. "By definition, competition would mean a situation where the service supply is greater than the demand. Right now that may be the case, but only because the demand is a small fraction of the *need*."

Approximately 200 million people in India are in need of some form of eye care. From this perspective, competition resembles rivalry over the first piece of pie, heedless of the untouched remainder. "Aravind's focus is making the need manifest itself as demand, through market penetration, awareness building, and outreach," Thulsi says. "The work to be done there is enormous, and when you take that into account, there is no competition. In fact, the more people we can get on this path with us, the better."

"Do you remember how Senegal beat France in the 2002 World Cup?" Dr. V is seated in the LAICO conference room, chuckling and triumphant, while a puzzled group of doctors from Nigeria nod their heads slowly, smiling in spite of themselves. The victory took place the previous year and was pretty unforgettable. Dr. V is a closet sports fan. He follows basketball, soccer, tennis, of course cricket, and even world wrestling championships. The passion, rigor, and teamwork demonstrated by athletes inspire him. He manages to convert their accomplishments into teaching points for the field of eye care. "Can you imagine a little country in Africa beating one of the world's most advanced nations! What does that mean?" There is a pregnant pause in the room before Dr. V slams his hands down on the table in front of him. "It means that if they can do it in football, you can do it with eye care—you can be the best in the world."

IN A WHITEWASHED seminary building atop a green hillside in Kigali, Rwanda, in 2008, a four-person team from Aravind leads a workshop focused on developing a nationwide plan for eye care services. Countrywide planning is not something they have done before, a fact that does not appear to faze them. The team from India is used to encountering far bigger numbers than Rwanda's. The scale of Aravind's hospitals far outstrips not just current eye care activities in Rwanda but also the magnitude of their need. "Planning for any of our own hospitals is like planning for a small country," says Thulsi. "That's why our people can walk into situations like the Rwandan one and feel confident about framing a solution." The estimated accumulated backlog of people with treatable blindness in Rwanda is 65,000, compared with India's 12 million. To successfully tackle the problem, the country must do at least 19,000 operations per year.[11] Compare that with the 300,000 surgeries that Aravind's network of hospitals annually performs. Its hospital in Theni, the smallest with 163 beds, performs roughly 10,700 surgeries a year.[12]

"Look, right now you're doing about 285 surgeries a year at your hospital," Thulsi tells a Rwandan doctor. "With the right systems in place, you can be doing 2,000." Inconceivable as that seems to the Rwandans, in just 48 hours they will have started to redefine possibilities for eye care in their country. And they will have a concrete, comprehensive roadmap for how to get there. But the Aravind team will also have to examine and grapple with the differences in this environment that challenge their model. The principles of self-sustaining, high-volume, high-quality, and affordable eye care at Aravind are backed by a dedicated attention to detail. But replicating the details across vastly different geographies and cultures is not always possible, or even desirable. Socioeconomic conditions, politics, and disease distribution each play a part. Together, Aravind's consulting team and the Rwandan doctors must account for the interplay of these factors and fine-tune Aravind's processes for the local context.

For instance, the Rwandan health ministry taxes nonessential medical equipment and consumables. It classifies intraocular lenses and spectacle frames in this category, which is part of the reason why delivering eye care is more costly in Rwanda than in India. In such scenarios, LAICO's muscle in international policy setting can help. While in Rwanda, Thulsi secures a series of meetings with its ministry of health to discuss the implications of this tax and to consider alternatives. Within days, the ministry requests a revised list of essential eye care items, aiming to reconsider its tax policy to save Rwandan hospitals the burden of taxation.

Alongside such practical matters, there is arguably a bigger task to be tackled: the inertia of the status quo has to be shaken off. The team from Aravind must light, and help keep alive, the flame of possibility. Thulsi and the other consultants are there to deliver an urgent vote of confidence: Gamble the odds. The impossible can be done. Remember how Senegal beat France. If one institution in the developing world can deliver world-class eye care on a shoestring budget with limited human resources, then *so can you.*

It is a brave, uplifting message and one that Dr. V deeply believes in. To him, Aravind is not a one-off success story but a widely replicable miracle.

A JEEP TAKES you from the bustling city of Kolkata, with its 13 million inhabitants, to the small town of Raichak, where you can catch a ferry to the village of Chaitanyapur. The drive to Raichak takes an hour and a half on a long, narrow road that rambles alongside green fields and ramshackle villages. Then, across a wide wash of gray-blue water a factory zone appears. Petrochemicals and oil refineries are the major industries here, and smokestacks and concrete buildings rise above the trees. Fishermen's huts dot the shoreline. The bleak landscape is populated almost entirely by poor farmers, fishermen, and low-wage factory workers. It is hard to believe that in this forsaken nook of West Bengal (one of India's northeastern states), there is a hospital delivering advanced eye surgeries along the lines of the Aravind model.

Swami Biswanathananda is a tall, wiry man dressed in a monk's orange robes. He is the head of the Vivekananda Mission ashram in Chaitanyapur. Besides setting up an eye hospital, he has founded educational facilities that serve more than 5,000 students, a successful community blindness rehabilitation center, and one of the largest Braille libraries in India. The Chaitanyapur hospital serves a population of over six million villagers. Most of the area's inhabitants use local buses as their mode of transport; patients often save bus fare by either walking several miles to the hospital or riding on the carrier seat of a bicycle. Biswanathananda's right-hand man at this hospital is Dr. Asim K. Sil.

Hailing from a little village that borders Bangladesh, Sil was introduced to the world of blindness early on. "My grandfather, who lived with us, lost his sight," he says.[13] "My mother always asked me to sit in his room while I was studying or doing my homework. As a child, I tended to read out loud a lot—so this was her way of making sure he didn't feel lonely. Subconsciously I think it had a big impact on me—it made me want to help people who are blind."

After completing medical school and spending a few years in general practice, Sil applied for specialized programs in ophthalmology. He was accepted by Aravind–Madurai where he quickly developed a special connection with the founding team, perhaps because of the simple upbringing and readiness for hard work that he shares with them. One morning during his time there, Sil was informed that "Chief" (Dr. V) was making a visit to the Aravind hospital in Theni and wanted him to come along.

"When we were driving out of Madurai, Chief said, 'Sil, look outside. Do you see more people walking or driving?' 'There are more people walking, sir,'" Sil says, recalling the conversation. "'How far do you think they can walk?' Dr. V asked me. 'About four or five kilometers, sir; then they need to rest,' I answered.

"'And the people in the cars? How long can they drive?'

"'Sir, they can go much farther.'

"'Right. So remember, if you want to really help the world, you should do something to help the people who are walking.'"

Sil recalls the words with something akin to wonder. "That conversation really stayed in my mind for a long time."

Sil arrived in Chaitanyapur in 1995 after completing residency at Aravind. By the time he reached the ashram gates, it was late evening. There were no streetlights, and the roads were slick with mud from monsoon rains. Just before he entered the ashram, Sil made up his mind: he would not stay here; he was going to go back to Aravind. But after lunch the next day, he chanced upon Biswanathananda's elder brother. On seeing Sil, the man opened his palm, offering him a few fragrant cloves. "While he was giving me the cloves, I looked at him," Sil recalls. "He looked so luminous. He said to me, 'Doctor, I think you will stay here.' And I said, 'Yes.' And right after saying that, I felt so light. Like some heaviness had been taken away."

At Chaitanyapur, it didn't bother Sil that he was earning less than he could have elsewhere. "After training at Madurai, my view of money and everything else was changed!" he says. His biggest challenge was getting the ashram management to understand the principles behind good eye care delivery systems—changes were needed in workflow, community outreach, and hospital design. "I did not have to struggle long," he says, smiling. "Within a few months, we signed up for a workshop at LAICO." Biswanathananda and Sil, along with an administrative officer and ophthalmic assistant from Chaitanyapur, traveled to Madurai for an extended consulting session. In LAICO's experience, working with multidisciplinary teams from client hospitals is vital to the change process. Involving people at every level during the planning stage has proved more effective than top-down enforcement. Teams that visit typically comprise the director of the hospital, chief medical officer, head nurse, and, in some cases, directors of IT and finance.

Over a period of seven days, the Chaitanyapur team was exposed to the best that Aravind had to offer. They worked with top management on both clinical and administrative topics to develop action plans for their specific situation. The workshop accomplished what Sil had been struggling to do alone: convince his hospital's management and senior staff that things had to be done differently, and provide guidance on how these changes could be implemented. The effect on Sil's team was exhilarating. On the train back to West Bengal, he remembers, they all stayed up long into the night, bursting with ideas from the workshop. "Swami Biswanathananda himself made so many sketches on that train ride of how to modify our wards!" he says, laughing.

The desired changes ranged from facility improvements to improved hiring and training of employees. While Sightsavers International helped finance the hospital's remodeling, most of the other changes required not just money but fundamental shifts in strategy. Simply put, the Chaitanyapur hospital needed more doctors, more nurses, and more patients.

Sil was able to rapidly increase patient load by systematically launching Aravind-style eye camps that partnered with local leaders and social-welfare groups. On the nursing front, when Sil began working at Chaitanyapur, the hospital had only one trained nurse: a man with a college degree who left as soon as he landed a job with the government. LAICO pointed to Aravind's model and suggested that Chaitanyapur's leadership stop depending on skilled professionals from the outside and begin to cultivate its own pool of talent. In 1996, under Sil's leadership and with Aravind's assistance for curriculum design, the Chaitanyapur hospital began to recruit and train its own nurses locally.

Doctor retention was a bigger challenge. A year after moving to Chaitanyapur, Sil married his fiancée, Subhra, a pediatric ophthalmologist also trained at Aravind. Like him, she willingly traded in the luxuries of an urban lifestyle for the simplicity of the ashram. But the Chaitanyapur hospital came nowhere close to paying competitive salaries, and doctors like the Sils, intrinsically motivated by service to the poor and willing to work in a village setting, were hard to come by. To improve its recruitment and retention of doctors, the hospital needed to strengthen its financial standing. By introducing a tiered fee system and counseling services, and steadily ramping up cataract surgeries with IOL implants, the hospital increased its paying-patient pool and thus drastically boosted its revenues. Within three years of working with LAICO, Chaitanyapur saw its cost recovery rise to over 150 percent.[14] This strong financial foundation would, over time, allow for specialization and better staff recruitment and retention.

❧

DEEPA KRISHNAN IS a third-generation member of Dr. V's family. A computer engineer with an MBA degree, she joined the management team at LAICO and spent a month at Chaitanyapur studying the hospital's organizational systems and recommending strategies to improve their efficiency and productivity. "One of the things she observed was that the majority of our patients come to us by 8 a.m.," Sil recalls. "She suggested that all our doctors be posted in the outpatient division in the morning and have the operations start later in the day." The suggestion was implemented to good effect. "It's a mini-Aravind there," says Deepa. "Everything is the same—the case sheets they use, the receipts they print. It is the exact same format, with only the name of the hospital changed. Their operating room protocol, prep, and sterilization are the same. The camp set-up is the same too—just on a smaller scale."[15]

Beyond this external transfer of Aravind's systems, the two institutes deeply share a common sense of mission and commitment to serving those who are most in need. Thulsi, who has paid frequent visits to the hospital in Chaitanyapur, says he always comes back from it "feeling inspired."

"Sil and his team really embody what it means to be patient-centric," says Thulsi. "Like when they realized that many patients traveled to them from distant villages, accompanied by relatives who didn't have a place to stay—they straightaway built travelers' dorms. It's not really strategy—it's just really *seeing* and responding to the needs of the people you treat."

Swami Biswanathananda has sprained his back but is still working today because, as he says, smiling, "God does not permit bed rest." He speaks of Aravind with the same enthusiasm as Sil. "I had no knowledge regarding hospital building," he says candidly. "Everyone at LAICO and Aravind was a tremendous help. It cannot be expressed in words."[16] Swami Biswanathananda has been a monk for over 30 years and is given to effusive speeches. With every few sentences he offers "a million *pranams* [bows] to the lotus feet of the Divine." But his angular frame carries the stamp of an unmistakable sincerity and determination. It rings through in his closing words, echoing Dr. V's philosophy: "Humanitarian service is quite difficult if you are not able to love with your whole heart. Love is the most important factor to disseminate anything . . . and then God has his plans."

# FIFTEEN

# ARAVIND IS LIKE KILIMANJARO

The roads that wind around the airport in Moshi, Tanzania, are flanked by fields of maize standing at attention like silent guards in the moonlight. The houses have corrugated metal roofs and lights glowing in the windows. Everything seems a little tucked away, like so many well-kept secrets waiting to be discovered. This town is home to an American family—Dr. Susan Lewallen; her husband, Dr. Paul Courtright; and their two young boys. She is an ophthalmologist and he has a graduate degree in public health. The couple have worked in Africa for over 15 years and first visited Aravind in 2002 for guidance on an ambitious project—they were building a LAICO equivalent in the little town of Moshi.

Lewallen and Courtright are the founders and joint directors of the Kilimanjaro Centre for Community Ophthalmology (KCCO). Started in 2001, this donor-funded center is dedicated to public health ophthalmology in eastern Africa. Its training programs for eye care management and delivery cover 18 countries and a population of 210 million. KCCO is independently funded but works closely with the eye department of the region's largest hospital, the Kilimanjaro Christian Medical Centre (KCMC).[1]

LAICO has worked in many parts of Africa. It has trained doctors and nurses in Malawi, helped with outreach systems and operating room flow at a major eye care facility in Cairo, and consulted for the government of Rwanda. With its support, a brand-new hospital in the

Democratic Republic of Congo was able to go from zero to 1,000 surgeries in its first year, despite rampant civil unrest. An Ethiopian doctor who attended a LAICO course after surgical training at Aravind now runs a gleaming facility that performs 3,000 surgeries a year in his hometown.[2] The numbers might be modest compared with Aravind's massive scale, but they indicate the relevance and successful replication of Aravind's basic tenets, despite the less-than-ideal conditions in these countries.

In 2006, a LAICO team flew into Moshi, Tanzania, for a needs-assessment visit. They were engaged not only to help KCMC's eye department but also to provide guidance to KCCO as a training facility. Only a few months later, evidence of their impact is everywhere. Names are posted on office doors that were anonymous before. It seems like a trivial detail, but this recommendation was included in LAICO's feedback report. Their analysis takes nothing for granted and ranges from the granular to the macro. A variety of LAICO's systemic suggestions have been implemented here with positive results: a shift from paper files to computerized registration at the hospital, the creation of a counseling unit, a revised fee structure for the various classes of patient accommodation, wall dividers in the visual acuity testing unit, and the introduction of ward protocol. An important part of LAICO's role, whether working with a hospital in Bangladesh, Bhutan, or Rwanda, is to emphasize the vital role that systems and codified procedures play in a hospital's efficiency.

Edson Eliah is KCCO's sustainability planner. "I get all my knowledge about management from Aravind," he says with a broad smile. Transferring that knowledge to others is not always smooth sailing. "With the eye department at KCMC, the biggest task was to set up a proper inventory and accounting system to monitor costs; the second was to talk with the managers about sustainability—it is a new concept for a lot of people here," says Eliah.[3] "At Aravind, everyone was passionate about it. But here sometimes people think containing costs is hard and means more work." He states this without impatience, as an observation, not an accusation—and one that applies more broadly than just to this hospital. KCCO's close relationship and experience with KCMC deeply informs its work with other eye care programs in the region that operate in similar conditions.

The eye department at KCMC examines an average of 129 patients and admits roughly 12 inpatients a day. Most of the steps for patient screening and diagnosis are executed in the same order, if not with the same speed, as at Aravind. The head of the nursing staff is inexorably convinced that they do not have enough nurses to manage their patient flow as quickly. Eliah and LAICO are of a different opinion. With comparable staffing, Aravind's smallest hospital (in Theni) sees nearly four times KCMC's patient load per day.

"The main challenge is resistance from the staff who are used to the old way," says one of the Tanzanian managers. "We point out to them that at Aravind, two nurses do what five nurses do here and urge them to try getting to that level. But people's commitment is less here. And to some extent they are less hardworking." There is a leisure to the way things are done in Moshi that is in stark contrast to the brisk efficiency at Aravind. *Pole-pole* is a gentle Swahili phrase that means "slowly, slowly" or "everything in its time." You glimpse it in the way people walk through the hallways of the hospital, the way they stop to talk to each other or to just look around. It is an approach to life (common to much of India as well) that, depending on the context, can be deeply charming or exceedingly frustrating.

Then there is Sister Evangeline—she is in her mid-50s, an age not uncommon among the nurses here but markedly different from the youthfulness of the nursing staff at Aravind, where the average age is the early to mid-20s. This age difference plays into some of the efficiency lag in Moshi, though Evangeline herself makes up in buoyant warmth for anything she might lack in agility. She is a large and large-hearted woman who grew up in a pastor's family and always knew that she wanted to care for other people. "To be healthy is a gift, to wake up and go to work and be able to work hard and help people see is—how do you say it—a blessing? This day, too, is a blessing," says Evangeline with a sunburst smile.

∽

ON A CLEAR DAY, Africa's highest peak can be seen from the hospital premises. It is hard to comprehend something as massive as a mountain being obscured, but today it is completely hidden by cloud cover and its existence seems almost mythical. "Aravind is like Kilimanjaro," says Dr. Anthony Hall. "It has to be seen to be believed." Tall, lean, and sandy-haired, Hall has a good-natured face that often looks preoccupied. Director of KCMC's eye department, he is a deeply respected specialist and has trained several of Africa's vitreo-retinal surgeons. "You hear people talking about Aravind's numbers all the time," he says, "but you can't quite fathom its scope till you get there."

Certain factors make Aravind's scale challenging to replicate in Africa. For one, there is a severe lack of surgical manpower on the continent. Tanzania has only about 30 ophthalmologists for the entire country, roughly 1 per million of its population (India, by comparison, has about 12 ophthalmologists per million and the United States 58 ophthalmologists per million).[4]

Eye diseases also strike differently in Africa and in India. "Cataract starts later here," says Hall. "We see it here mostly in people who are in their 60s and 70s. Elderly people tend to have other health issues, which make their cataracts more complicated to treat—our junior doctors can't always handle them." This slows down surgical productivity. "Conversely, glaucoma is more aggressive in Africa and has an earlier onset than in India," continues Hall. "So we see a lot of those cases, and because we're a referral center, we also see a high proportion of patients with diabetic retinopathy." Unlike treatment for cataract, treatments for glaucoma and diabetic retinopathy require long-term follow-up and are relatively complex and expensive.

KCMC, unlike private hospitals in India, has to work very closely with the government, and the Ministry of Health plays a fairly hands-on role in regulating the dos and don'ts of service delivery. Making changes requires wading through red tape, which often delays or discourages transformation. Aravind's multitiered pricing system, with its self-selecting paid and free options, has not been replicated here. The lack of community networks for eye care and the absence of government subsidies lead to low numbers of people seeking treatment. This creates a vicious circle that makes it necessary for the hospital to charge fees for all its patients. "The hospital has had trouble figuring out here what people should pay," says Courtright. "The Aravind method of pricing for the poor based on their average wage doesn't work in a place where many rural people still barter their crops. We eventually settled on the price of $15 for cataract surgery, and it seems to work OK."

KCMC waives the fees for patients who bring in letters from their village leader attesting to their poverty, but in actual practice very few do this. The hospital has a skilled counselor, but fear of surgery, lack of money, and superstition are strong barriers to eye care here.

Each challenging reality—poverty, bureaucracy, and superstition—lowers the acceptance rate for surgery at KCMC. Of all the patients recommended for a cataract operation, only 60 percent pursue the care they need. The outreach system in this part of the world faces a variety of hurdles. For starters, "rural Tanzania is much more widely dispersed than rural India," says Courtright. "Go up to Kilema, and you'll see how it is."

❧

THE JEEP HEADS up the green slopes of Kilema; it passes rushing streams, tangled banana groves, pine trees, purple wildflowers, coffee plantations, and little dirt paths disappearing into tall fields of ready-to-be-harvested maize. Women with brightly colored scarves around their heads look up from their busy tasks to smile and cry out, "*Habari?*" ("How are you?") They bring to mind the spirit of rural India—a resilient, sparkling spirit that does not seem to know it leads a difficult life. "Hard to access" in these parts can mean simply no roads. The jeep turns sharply and drives up a grassy slope, eventually pulling into a small clearing. Up ahead is the rural health center, a modest cement building. A woman is plowing outside, and the scent of damp earth fills the air. Two boys run past, kicking an empty oilcan between them.

It is well past 9 a.m., and no one, not even the doctor, is onsite. He shows up eventually, only to find the examination lamp missing. Patients straggle in, old men in striped suits with floppy hats, women with brightly colored scarves and wide hoops in their ears. A young nurse conducts the primary visual testing on the wide verandah of the building. She uses an alphabet chart and the finger test, and has to shush the children who crowd around trying to beat the older folks to an answer. Camps here are held in coordination with village harvest dates. Harvest time means that more people have the money to pay for services. It is 5:30 p.m. by the time the last patient is seen. Eighty-two patients have been screened; five were advised to have surgery but only one woman accepted.

It is hard not to compare performance. A small camp at Aravind typically screens 300 patients between 9 a.m. and 3 p.m. Roughly 20 percent of that number are brought back to the Aravind hospital for surgery.[5] Many reasons, in addition to fear, poverty, and the lower prevalence of cataract, account for the differences in volume. In Tanzania, as Courtright pointed out, the rural population is widely scattered and villages are sparsely populated. Transportation connecting villages to cities is poor, and from village to village it is almost nonexistent. All of this contrasts with the large population, high density, and relatively well-established transport systems that feed patients into the Aravind system and allow each of its camps to effectively reach scores of villages. These differences dramatically affect costs. While it typically costs around $5 to bring in a patient for surgery at Aravind, in this part of Africa it costs between $40 and $60.[6]

A scarcity of managers and administrators is another bottleneck in Tanzania. Physicians here tend to be consumed by the medical aspects of their profession, and experienced managers to keep hospital processes and systems running smoothly are in short supply. KCCO attempts to bridge the gaps through a series of year-round training programs, workshops, and course materials for the region's eye care administrators. Notably, its own staff of a dozen (not counting the founders) is composed entirely of East Africans who have been carefully groomed over the years, demonstrating the center's commitment to fostering local talent.

Lewallen has a warm impetuosity; she is driven, anxious, and disarmingly frank about not having all the answers. Courtright is less emotional but just as warm, with a wry sense of humor. He gives difficult people the benefit of the doubt—an optimistic attitude that he calls "a protection measure against a jaded paralysis." The two are complementary forces in this work. They have dedicated their lives to improving eye care service delivery in Africa and view their early relationship with Aravind as the crucial beginning of a long process of transformation. Notwithstanding the challenges, their work is certainly bearing fruit.

In its first six years, KCCO helped raise the number of cataract surgeries in the area by a staggering 300 percent.[7] It has trained over 1,500 doctors in Africa, and works with hospitals and regional eye programs in nine very diverse countries of eastern Africa, including Madagascar, Ethiopia, Burundi, and Zambia. In 2008, Lewallen and Courtright inaugurated a spacious new training facility to accommodate the growing demand for eye care services. In the same year, they were awarded the prestigious International Blindness Prevention Award from the American Academy of Ophthalmology. The first recipient of this award was Dr. V, "a man whose life's work epitomizes the kind of dedication Susan and I strive for every day," says Courtright.

"Today is not the same as tomorrow, and it's different from yesterday," says one of KCMC's matronly nurses, nodding her head sagely. She is right. Despite the uphill battle, a dedicated team is making a difference here, every day.

∽

LAICO-ESQUE INSTITUTES LIKE KCCO are now a growing tribe. By 2010, Swami Biswanathananda's rural facility in Chaitanyapur was consulting for five hospitals located in West Bengal, Orissa, and Bangladesh. And the Lumbini Eye Institute was doing the same with a dozen different programs in Nepal, Thailand, and Cambodia. These centers of excellence in community eye care steadily ripple out lessons learned from Aravind as well as their own experiences across the developing world.

LAICO itself continues to work with programs of all shapes and sizes in a continuum of engagement. It typically coaches small eye care programs toward high-volume, high-quality surgery and financial viability; urges midsized programs toward specialty services and ophthalmic training programs; and gives larger, more established institutions a vision for replication efforts and regional capacity building.

Each of these relationships brings to focus a distinct set of personalities, aspirations, strengths, and inefficiencies. Often the consulting process involves replacing old systems with new. A pricing model at a hospital in Paraguay, for instance, involved social workers' deciding treatment costs for individual patients based on lengthy affordability discussions with them. It was an inefficient system, and the hospital was running at a loss. "We sent one of our own managers there for a whole month to help them design and implement a tiered fee system," says Sashipriya Karumanchi, a passionate faculty member at LAICO. "Now the social workers are able to clearly communicate the fee system to patients and allow them to make their own decisions rather than deciding for them. The uptake of surgery has actually increased; they are now more than breaking even; and their volumes are continuing to grow."[8]

Sashipriya describes the problem of misaligned incentives at a client hospital in China. "They're struggling to create a strong training program for residents," she explains. "But at their hospital, a surgeon's salary is linked to the number of operations he does, so none of the doctors want to share their patients with residents." This significantly limits residents' hands-on practice, weakening the quality of their training. Changing the mindset of an organization's leadership and replacing deeply ingrained practices with new processes is not easy. In the course of attempting this work, LAICO sometimes bumps up against the limits of its own understanding.

An interesting finding came to light in 2000 when LAICO studied three years of data across 40 hospitals that it had worked with. This internal study revealed that in the two years following LAICO's consulting intervention, the collective number of surgeries these hospitals performed had gone up by a stunning 75 percent, compared with their shared total the year before the engagement with LAICO. On the surface, the statistic seemed like a tremendous indicator of success. But it masked wild variations in performance among the individual hospitals. While a select few had managed to double or even triple their surgical productivity and demonstrated a considerable increase in financial stability, most had experienced only incremental improvements. Giving the Aravind model away successfully was apparently much easier in theory than in practice.

The LAICO team reviewed the data, considering the many factors that might account for these differences in exporting Aravind's model. Interestingly, their findings indicated that it was not the macro factors of environment, economy, or culture that determined a hospital's progress. The most powerful keys to improvement were surprisingly within each hospital's control.

LAICO faculty was soon able to flag certain conditions as barriers to effective replication—conditions like frequent changes in leadership, a staff of part-time doctors (who split their time with other institutions), volume-based salary systems, and leadership that was indifferent to performance monitoring or resistant to rigorous financial accountability. Hospitals where executive decisions were made by outside authorities (a structure common among some missionary hospitals, where the chief executive might also be the bishop of a diocese who visited the hospital only a few times a year) were also found to have greater implementation challenges. But subtler aspects influenced the adoption of Aravind's model as well, and these aspects were harder to define.

LAICO's faculty members had built competence in transferring their formal knowledge. They could ensure that LAICO's clients understood the operating-room processes that maximize productivity and how to disaggregate hospital workflow into the most efficient component steps. They could hand over multiple, excruciatingly detailed manuals on how to organize an eye camp or design a patient examination room. But how would they transfer the qualities, discernment, and values that created and sustained these practices and systems within Aravind? You can package and share what you do through workshops and training programs, but how do you systematize and give away what you *are*?

"We found that we could really only give away what we were conscious of—and that's the obvious stuff," says Thulsi. "But in reality, a lot of what makes Aravind work lies at a deeper level. It's in the psyche of the organization, and in that sense it's subconscious. There's a big chunk that's in the unknown." It is a confession and a realization of some significance.

Embodied in Aravind's leadership are principles, commitments, and aspirations that infuse its actions with a certain powerful energy, one that many visitors have sensed. But when it came to replicating its model through LAICO's consulting and training, this essential Aravind mojo is a black box—loosely labeled "values" or "culture"—peripherally referenced during trainings but absent from core lessons and certainly lacking documentation in any manual. Someone was going to call out this missing piece very soon.

# SIXTEEN

# BUSINESS, POLITICS, AND PRAHALAD'S DARE

"How do you define your spirituality?" asked C. K. Prahalad in early 2003. He was in Madurai addressing Aravind's second generation of leaders. The founding team sat at one end of the conference room with the anxious air of parents watching their children being quizzed. From the far wall, a photograph of the Mother smiled down on the group, as if in amused anticipation of their answer.

The late Coimbatore Krishnarao Prahalad was an acclaimed management strategist. His work shone a spotlight on innovative business models that treat the poor not as passive beneficiaries of charity but as customers in an economic marketplace. He deeply admired Aravind's work and in his own words "tap-danced around its success" for years. Through his writing, he helped Aravind to win global recognition and a reputation for serving what he famously termed "the Bottom of the Pyramid." During this meeting, however, he made no attempt at polite praise. He was there to prod, to instigate, and maybe even to inspire a deeper inquiry from Aravind's next-in-line leaders. "The founders of this place relate its success to spirituality. So what is that spirituality—and how are you going to bottle it up and export it to other countries?" he asked again. A blank silence greeted his persistent questions. Spirituality, for Aravind's second generation, seemed to lie outside their work as surgeons and administrators.

Most of the people whom Prahalad was addressing were in their 30s. Almost all were related to Dr. V and had entered Aravind roughly a decade earlier, as postgraduate students in ophthalmology. They had stepped into the system at its takeoff point in history, bypassing the founding years of uncertainty, risk, and financial struggle. Their biggest battle was the threat of anonymity. In an organization with an indelible work code and a broad-shouldered founding team still striding through the corridors, their challenge was to emerge from the cocoon of conformity. To establish an individual identity and to make a unique contribution—all while juggling the demands of their personal lives.

Among the nephews and nieces of Dr. V at the table were Dr. Kim Ramaswamy, the affable chief of retina services whose incurable love of gadgets had embedded him in Aravind's IT projects; his wife Dr. Usha, the tall, striking head of the Oculoplastics Department and supervisor of Aravind's nursing program; the nonchalant Dr. Prajna, who had recently been given charge of the residency program and who was negotiating unprecedented salary revisions for staff doctors. Next to him sat Dr. Aravind, chafing against the confines of routine hospital work, and Dr. Aravind's wife, Dr. Haripriya, a quiet young surgeon focused on building her clinical and surgical skills.

Swept up in their individual preoccupations and responsibilities, this group had no ready answers to how, or if, spirituality affected Aravind's work. Prahalad swiftly transitioned their loss for words to another, more personal, topic: the weight of their legacy. "You are standing on an extraordinary platform!" he thundered. "Are you just going to shuffle along complacently, or are you going to take it to the next level?"

People at Aravind work very hard. The bar is set so high that it is unusual for someone from outside the organization to demand to know if they plan to raise it. But Prahalad asked the question with an avuncular air of authority that was startlingly dismissive of LAICO's achievements. He swept aside mention of the hundreds of hospitals across dozens of countries that had thus far participated in various capacity-building programs at Aravind. He was not denying their growth but questioning the extent of true replication. If the model was really being transferred, then why was there only one institution like Aravind? With the air of the proverbial child pointing out that the emperor had no clothes, Prahalad called out the differences in scale and scope between the Aravind Eye Care System and the array of hospitals that had attempted to transfer its success to their own regions.

Prahalad turned his attention abruptly to Usha. "Would you be willing to pack up and go live in Africa for a few years to set up a hospital there?" he asked bluntly. Usha was taken aback. In addition to her surgical work, she was a faculty member with teaching responsibilities and was also working hard to set up what would be one of India's first ocular oncology units, specializing in treating children with potentially fatal eye cancer. Hospital duties aside, she and Kim had a ten-year-old son and a host of family responsibilities anchoring them in Madurai. The prospect of picking up and moving to Africa seemed a little short of ridiculous, and Usha said so, if not in those exact words.

It was clear from the widespread response around the table that Aravind's new generation was not interested in more hospitals. Construction of Dr. V's dream hospital in Pondicherry was currently under way; it would be Aravind's fifth facility and was viewed as a fitting conclusion to the arc of Aravind's expansion. "We get several requests from hospitals around the country," Dr. Aravind tried explaining, "from people who want us to run their hospitals for them. Our standard response has been, 'We'll teach you what we know, and then you must run it yourself.' We don't want to spread ourselves thin—there's too much work remaining within our own service population." His words were backed by murmurs of agreement from others at the table.

Prahalad, however, remained unconvinced. He sensed latent potential beneath the day-to-day activities of the organization, and he was prodding Aravind's young leaders to discover it. He was gazing into the crystal ball of his expertise in organizational strategy at Aravind's future. And what he saw made it abundantly clear to him that the organization needed to get busy studying its DNA if it really wanted to extend its impact.

Nothing concrete came out of that particular meeting. Yet seeds sown by the professor's unanswered questions quietly took root over the next couple of years. The years that followed brought a period of soul-searching for the Aravind Eye Care System that would lead to dramatic shifts in thinking and action.

ON CHRISTMAS DAY 2000, a few years before Prahalad's anticlimactic visit, an unusual visitor turned up on Aravind's doorstep. Mrs. Priyamvada Birla was a frail woman in her 70s with a sweet face and grandmotherly air. She spent the day touring the hospital facilities in a wheelchair and asking a series of unexpectedly pointed questions about Aravind's expansion plans, various partnerships, and financial health. She smiled, nodded, and observed each detail with interest. Then, to everyone's surprise, she dug in her heels and vowed not to leave the premises until Aravind signed off on a partnership with her company.

The M. P. Birla Group is a multibillion-dollar business conglomerate and one of India's leading family-run enterprises. While its companies run the gamut from telecom and textiles to coal and cement, the Birla Group also has an active philanthropic bent. When Mrs. Birla's husband, the company patriarch, died, most people expected her to break up the company. But the quiet homemaker with no prior business experience astonished everyone by taking over the reins of the corporation with gutsy tenacity—the same tenacity that would catch Aravind off-guard.

In 1995, Rajendra Lodha, a senior auditor for the Birla conglomerate, had been seated on an international flight next to Dr. Carl Kupfer, then director of the National Eye Institute in the United States, and a close friend and partner of Aravind's. Kupfer spent much of the flight educating Lodha on the wonder that was Aravind. Lodha was so impressed by the conversation that he later discussed the model at length with Mrs. Birla, who, it turned out, was surprisingly interested in starting an eye hospital in West Bengal.

The Birlas' contribution to India's economic and social development was undeniable, but Aravind's leadership had long resisted forging alliances with corporate entities to build hospitals. It did not want its integrity to be compromised by other agendas. In the past, when approached by wealthy individuals or companies wanting to partner to this end, Aravind's leaders had always found a diplomatic way to say, "No thanks." But when this deceptively fragile-looking widow refused to leave until she had it in writing that there would be a Birla–Aravind eye hospital in Kolkata, no one knew quite what to do.

She seemed as stubborn as Dr. V, and her age and position commanded respect and a certain amount of deference. Dr. V himself remained strangely silent about the whole dilemma. In some consternation, the rest of the founding team attempted to find a workable compromise, to no avail. In the end, a little before midnight, they signed a memorandum of understanding but withheld permission for the Birla group to use Aravind's name for their project (a decision they would capitulate on a few years later). The joint venture was handed over to Thulsi and Dr. Aravind to plan and implement, the latter having just returned from the University of Michigan with a freshly minted MBA.

◯)

As A TEENAGER, Dr. Aravind found himself drawn to certain recurring themes in his uncle's conversations. "He talked to me a lot about franchising, about groups like the Tatas and Birlas—soaring companies that had really taken on the world. He was so curious about how they worked and what he could learn from them." These excursions into the world of enterprise fascinated Dr. V's nephew—who, like most of his cousins, would toe the family line straight into medical school. The prospect of being a surgeon did not excite him, but the idea of being able to fuse those skills with business acumen to accomplish something audacious, did.

After four years as one of Aravind's fastest cataract surgeons, Dr. Aravind announced to the family that he was going to pursue an MBA degree in the United States. The founding team, including Dr. V, disapproved. "They said, 'We've been doing surgery here for 40 years; what do you mean you're tired already?'" Dr. Aravind grins ruefully. "Maybe I didn't express myself right. Basically, I had a lot of pent-up energy and ideas that I wanted to channel differently." He held his ground, and once it was clear that he intended to pursue his passion, Dr. V dropped his resistance and offered wholehearted support. After two years at the Ross School of Business in Michigan, Dr. Aravind returned to Madurai.

"Coming back, I worked in a bunch of different areas—expanding our outpatient division, overseeing the outreach program, getting involved in human resource management—while also continuing to do surgeries. I started to appreciate how an overarching mission really pulls the different parts of this organization together," says Dr. Aravind.

But he was also itching for the chance to take on something more entrepreneurial. When Thulsi, sensing this, assigned him the lead role on the Birla project, it was like a dream come true. "The early days were interesting. I thought, 'Oh, the Birla Group!' and had all these expectations of grandeur. Then I get to Kolkata and find that the space

allotted for the clinic was a small apartment in a residential building,"
says Dr. Aravind, smiling.

Confronted with this reality, he felt an odd sense of elation. Here
was an opportunity hard to come by in an established organization
like Aravind—a shot at building something big and totally new from
a tiny beginning. He was hooked. "I got our small team very excited
about our first day," he says, laughing. "They had advertised and had
got lots of enquiries—around 500 calls. So I said, 'Just watch—we are
going to get so many patients.' We opened with lots of expectation.
Then we waited and waited. I sat there all day long and only one patient turned up—the whole day!"

After that unpromising beginning, Dr. Aravind rapidly pumped in
more support. He transferred a team of nurses from Aravind–Madurai
to the Birla clinic, arranged for the additional nurses recruited in West
Bengal to be trained onsite in Madurai, and split his own time between
the two facilities to closely mentor the medical team in Kolkata. This
form of in-depth operational involvement with an external hospital
was unprecedented at Aravind—it shifted the focus of its replication
efforts from consulting to implementation.

Core aspects of Aravind's model—for example, the tiered fee
structure that included free treatment as an option, and community
outreach in the form of eye camps—were retained in the Birla partnership. The details, such as staff salaries and pricing for services, were
revised to take into account the local economy and market rates. Dr.
Aravind flew in Thulsi and Dr. Datta (the head of Aravind–Theni) for
a LAICO-style workshop in Kolkata to work through bottlenecks and
communicate the greater vision to the team.

Dr. Aravind's zeal in all of this stemmed partly from a longstanding ambition to apply his medical and managerial expertise toward
building a new operation, but also from his desire to dispel what
he sees to be common myths. The Aravind Eye Care System has a
visionary founder at its helm and the convenience of a family of pro-

fessionals spanning several generations, dedicated to its cause. Those are two conditions hard to replicate. But tying the success of the organization to the mystique of the former and the blood ties of the latter (as some do) is, to him, a severely limited view. "You mean to say a retired individual at the age of 58, with crippling arthritis, had more opportunities and more favorable circumstances than you or I today?" asks Dr. Aravind sharply. Taking charge of the Birla hospital was an attempt to prove (perhaps to himself as much as anyone else) that the core model could be replicated independent of charismatic personalities and close connections—and in a metropolitan city thousands of miles from Madurai, no less, where the organization's brand was unknown.

Four years into its existence, the small Birla clinic was seeing 70 patients a day and performing over 3,500 surgeries a year.[1] In 2006, the team moved from its cramped fourth-floor quarters into the Priyamvada Birla Aravind Eye Hospital, a towering five-story building in the heart of metropolitan Kolkata.

From the Birla hospital experience emerged a more hands-on approach to replication, hinting at the challenge Prahalad had posed to Aravind's young leaders. Though no one was quite ready to move to Africa, the new generation was spreading its wings and investing more time and energy in external partnerships. Until this time, for all of Dr. V's McDonald's analogies, there had never been any concrete plans at Aravind for nationwide expansion or global franchising. But in 2005, the Aravind Eye Care System announced a new goal: expansion to 100 eye hospitals under a new partnership model with the aim of collectively performing one million surgeries a year by 2015.

In this new approach to collaboration, partner hospitals would contribute funding, infrastructure, and local ties. The Aravind Eye Care System would be deeply involved in the planning, training, and running of these new hospitals, and would receive an annual fee. The Birla partnership slowly came to be seen as an accidental pilot for this new goal and growth model. It had already provided some valuable lessons in replication. And another unlikely partnership was just around the corner.

❧

WHEN KANNAMMA RAVINDRAN, a niece of Dr. V's, received a phone call from a man claiming to be calling on behalf of Mr. Rahul Gandhi, she thought it was a prank call and hung up. The second time the phone rang, the man rushed to identify himself as Kanishka Singh, close friend and associate of Rahul Gandhi. Kannamma, though not entirely convinced, gave him the benefit of the doubt and stayed on the line.

What the Kennedys are to the United States, the Gandhis are to India. Rahul Gandhi is a member of Parliament. His great-grandfather, grandmother, and father all served as prime ministers of India. His father's political assassination, his Italian mother's pivotal position in the Congress party, his sister's refusal to enter politics, and his own work to energize grass-roots political participation place him squarely in the public eye. Now, according to Singh, Gandhi was interested in visiting to learn more about the Aravind model and to explore the possibility of replicating it in his constituency of Amethi, in the northern state of Uttar Pradesh (UP).

Aravind's leaders received the news of Gandhi's interest with mixed feelings. They were as hesitant to get involved with politics as they had been to mix with big business. Dr. V was the only one without any reservations. He made it clear that he wanted to support the visit, and was rather delighted at the prospect of it. In the decades when Dr. V was a government physician, Prime Minister Indira Gandhi (Rahul Gandhi's grandmother) had given his pioneering rural eye camp program national impetus. Now this prospective meeting seemed to be bringing things full circle.

A date was set for early 2005, and when it arrived, the entire founding team, along with Dr. Aravind, all took the train from Madurai to meet the young politician at Aravind–Pondicherry. Gandhi showed up sporting a purple T-shirt and jeans. Next to Aravind's senior leadership team, he and Singh looked like misplaced college students.

After taking the visitors on a quick tour of the hospital, Thulsi led the discussion with a detailed presentation on the status of eye care delivery services in UP and, more specifically, Amethi. The Aravind team had clearly done their homework. Thulsi's presentation was peppered with telling statistics. UP's blindness prevalence at 1.15 percent was significantly higher than Tamil Nadu's. Only 57 percent of the cataract surgeries being done in the state were performed using IOLs (compared with 97 percent in Tamil Nadu)—a clear indication of the quality lag. The research revealed that 230,000 people in Amethi needed cataract surgery.

Gandhi and the Aravind leaders discussed this need and the opportunity at hand, and debated the appropriate scale for the new hospital. While the magnitude of need merited a full-blown hospital with specialty departments, there were advantages to starting simple. Gandhi and Singh, ignited by the possibilities, posed a stream of questions regarding recruitment, retention, leadership, and sustainability. In the end, the group decided to start small with an initial focus on cataract surgery and spectacles dispensing, and build service diversity down the line. "You are in a position to make things happen," Dr. V said with unflinching optimism, looking the young politician straight in the eye. "You can do it. And we will help you in the ways we can."

THE VISIT LEFT a strong impression on the two visitors. Kanishka Singh would later say, "We came expecting a superficial meet-and-greet situation at Aravind, but there was really no B.S. involved!"[2] Though the momentum from the meeting carried into swift action, the partnership would have its share of hiccups.

Initial problems with staff discipline escalated into a mass exodus of nurses just a few months into the hospital's opening. In retrospect, it was an accident waiting to happen.

Dr. Usha Kim from Aravind–Madurai had flown in to Amethi to assist with recruiting the new hospital's nursing staff. A preselected pool of candidates was waiting for her. Most of them were English-speaking college graduates from urban areas, in sharp contrast to the young women, fluent primarily in local languages, whom Aravind typically recruits right after high school from small towns and villages.

Armed with higher qualifications, the women in Amethi naturally required higher starting salaries, but they also had difficulty conforming to Aravind norms. During their training period in Madurai, many of them resisted the strict protocols on punctuality, discipline, and dress code that govern all Aravind employees. But the real trouble began when hierarchical treatment toward patients crept in.

In India, the power dynamic of caste still asserts itself throughout society, insidiously influencing relationships and outcomes. Most of the nurses hired to work at the Amethi hospital came from high-caste families. Many of them rebelled against helping poor, and presumably low-caste, patients put on the sterilized socks worn for surgery. They felt it was beneath their dignity to perform a task that involved touching a patient's feet. (In India, this gesture is a sign of respect.)

The work of Aravind's paraprofessional staff includes many small interactions that are rooted in a sense of equality and caring for patients from all backgrounds. They are a fundamental part of the model, and the organization relies heavily on them to render its colossal scale kind and human. The hospital in Amethi would need to find nurses better suited to deliver compassionate, high-touch care. A second round of interviews was held, this time with more attention to each candidate's fit with the hospital's values.

With a new cohort of nurses on board, Aravind's team of trainers also relaxed certain staff rules to accommodate cultural differences and bring the new recruits up to speed. Over time, Amethi's staff settled into a good rhythm and the hospital began to swiftly gain momentum. Less than a year into the partnership, the senior leadership at Aravind received a letter of gratitude from the head doctor at Amethi. "Our hospital's honesty and integrity has won many a heart," he wrote. "We are attracting patients not only from the adjoining districts but also from relatively far off cities." And as for the nurses? "They have matured into a hardworking and dedicated team who are willing to learn. The immense support and advice from everyone at Aravind has been our greatest strength."

All was well in Amethi, but meanwhile, on the Kolkata front, things were in disarray. Mrs. Birla had died and stunned her clan by leaving her entire fortune to her auditor, Mr. Lodha—who was now embroiled in a raging billion-dollar lawsuit. It was the messy brand of controversy that Aravind's founders had always tried to steer clear of. The senior management of the Kolkata hospital was also in flux, and small differences of opinion were creating hairline fissures in the partnership. Aravind's leaders brushed aside these weaknesses, given the pressures at the time. With a 100-hospital vision driving its expansion, they decided it was best to just press forward.

THE ARAVIND EYE CARE SYSTEM'S new approach to growth, via more-involved partnerships, grew slowly in the first decade of the millennium. After the facilities in Kolkata and Amethi, its next partnerships were in Lucknow, Uttar Pradesh (also with Rahul Gandhi); and Amreli, Gujarat (in partnership with a pharmaceuticals company). But as 2009 drew to a close, though the hospitals themselves continued to do well, it seemed that the synergy of the various relationships had either reached a plateau or declined.

Thulsi, Dr. Aravind, and others weighed the value of these partnerships versus Aravind's mission and considered the implications of stepping back from the current mode of involvement. They concluded that the period of pronounced mutual benefit was confined to the initial two to three years of each new venture. Once staff members had been recruited and trained, systems implemented, and all the major bottlenecks ironed out, involvement from Aravind's end became either increasingly redundant or out of sync with the local team's approach. Past a certain stage, Aravind's guidelines and requirements could also be interpreted as uncomfortably restrictive.

Differing views on public relations strategy, for instance, created a degree of tension. As an organization, Aravind maintained a low-profile approach to marketing, relying on word of mouth to build trust and attract new patients over time. It had traditionally steered clear of glossy advertising campaigns and avoided, as Thulsi puts it, "getting sucked into an energy that aims at creating an effect." An approach that often seemed naïve to some of its high-profile partners.

From the Aravind team's vantage point, the new partnerships brought capital funding and local expertise to the table. But funding was not an area of pressing need, as Aravind's own financial returns were strong enough for it to start a new hospital each year, if desired. And though local expertise was appreciated, Aravind's brand was strong enough in South India that it could be leveraged to generate community support far beyond the boundaries of its current locations.

The greater priority of Aravind's leaders was to maintain their core values of patient-centric care, universal access, and a focus on reaching the unreached. Over time, these things proved hard to control in new hospitals, where the local management often had competing concerns and priorities of its own. Given the realities, Aravind leaders made a quiet decision to step down from their ambitious 100-hospitals goal. For Dr. Aravind, who had been the early advocate and impassioned architect of many of the partnerships, it was a particularly wrenching period.

"Initially it was painful," he says. "But in retrospect, the whole process gave me very real execution experience—I got to test the model out in different places and with very different kinds of partners. Even if they didn't work out as long-term collaborations, at the end of the day, through this work, we basically helped create hospitals that now add 50,000 sight-restoring surgeries to India's total each year. That's a pretty amazing feeling."

"One thing I've learned is that we can't get complacent just because we have helped a lot of hospitals," he continues. "Sure, we helped them at one point, but if we want to keep helping, then you have to stay ahead of the learning curve by doing new things, experimenting and improving. We have to stay hungry for change." He grows steadily more animated as he speaks. "We need to treat what Dr. V and his generation did as just a foundation and not the end result."

Something is stirring within Dr. Aravind and others of his generation at Aravind. The upcoming leadership is growing less inclined to remain in maintenance mode with the model. Not long after calling off its 100-hospitals goal in 2010, the Aravind Eye Care System found itself surprisingly open to doing what it had refused to consider seven years earlier, when Prahalad had interrogated them about expansion: it was now open to building more hospitals of its own.

❧

WHILE THE ORGANIZATION slowly ramped down or redefined several of its existing partnerships, LAICO, under Thulsi's leadership, continued consulting for hospitals outside of Aravind's network. When the values were particularly well aligned, Aravind's team would still get involved in an engaged, hands-on manner. One such engagement was with a hospital network initiated by Muhammad Yunus, the Nobel Laureate and founder of Grameen Bank.

In recent years, with key inputs from LAICO and in close partnership with Seva Foundation, Grameen has opened two successful eye hospitals in Bangladesh and has plans for five more. Its doctors spent an entire year training at Aravind; after that, core clinical and managerial staff from Aravind spent three months onsite in Bangladesh helping the new team set up. Grameen is a household name in Bangladesh with a strong brand, thanks to Yunus's work in microfinance. But not all of LAICO's relationships are with such established partners. Every so often, relative rookies come to the attention of its faculty.

In 2005, Carlos Orellana, from El Salvador, and Javier Okhuysen, from Mexico, were working together in Madrid. The two production engineers turned investment bankers had chanced upon C. K. Prahalad's book *The Fortune at the Bottom of the Pyramid*. The section on Aravind excited them. "Why not start something like this in Latin America?" they thought. They were 25 years old at the time, whizzing along on high-powered career tracks. It was hard to hit the brakes—so they ended up going their separate ways.

Five years later, Javier, who was working at a private equity firm in London, got a call from Carlos, who was finishing an MBA and a master's in public health at the University of California, Berkeley. "The Aravind idea we had," he said, "it's time to move on it. I want to start an eye care center in Mexico City this summer. Are you in?" Javier considered the question. He had a great job but no wife or kids, and he had just seen the film *The Social Network*, about the origins of Facebook. He figured that with big ideas, catching the tide was everything. "This was a train I wasn't going to miss," he says. "I'm in," he told Carlos. Within a couple of months, they had flown to Madurai, determined to learn everything they could about starting an eye hospital. (At the time, Javier had never even heard of phacoemulsification).

Javier and Carlos enrolled in a LAICO workshop on eye care management. They took notes furiously during the day and worked late each night. At the end of the workshop, "we both had big bags under our eyes," says Javier, "and the beginnings of a business plan."[3] Over the next two weeks, they tested their ideas on Aravind's leadership in a series of meetings. Thulsi and other staff at LAICO found themselves unexpectedly moved by, as one faculty member put it, "the sheer sincerity of these kids." The smart, suave Latin American duo had real heart behind their ambition, and they were chasing their dream with everything they had, putting their combined life savings on the line. While still in Madurai, they even recruited an outreach coordinator—Javier's mother, who flew to Aravind to undergo the requisite training. "Aravind is about family," says Javier with a grin. "It was the obvious thing to do."

"I tell people that this is the most impressive organization I've ever come across," says Carlos. "And I've seen my fair share of good companies. What they do at Aravind comes together in a really unique way. Their spirit, personality, work ethic, and their willingness to share what they have—it's amazing. And it becomes pretty apparent that these qualities drive what they do."

LAICO knows the value and impact of these qualities, even as it struggles to fully articulate and package them. Principle holds sway over process in this model, and as they transfer practices and protocols, LAICO faculty members attempt to underline the importance of values. But they do so tentatively, knowing that they risk sounding didactic. They are more comfortable demonstrating, for instance, how zero can be a legitimate price point than talking in a vacuum about the importance of compassion and human dignity.

And as for replicating the role of spirituality in the model, "We don't really try going there anymore," says Thulsi openly. "We did experiment with talking about the aspect of being an instrument of service, etc. . . . but we weren't really effective. So now we take a more rational tack." For the most part, LAICO takes responsibility for sharing the pragmatic and leaves the profound to happen more subliminally.

As it turns out, Aravind's transfer of knowledge does not happen only through formal partnerships and consulting. Its spiral of influence is not perfectly traceable, but the far-reaching effects of its inspiration cannot be ignored.

❧

DR. GEOFF TABIN has an unusual résumé. He helped invent bungee jumping, has scaled the seven highest peaks in the world, and also happens to be a distinguished ophthalmologist. The charismatic American eye doctor cites Aravind's work as a key inspiration for many organizations, including a program he cofounded in the mountains of Nepal.

In the early 1990s, Tabin and Dr. Sanduk Ruit (a young Nepali doctor who had spent some time at Aravind) pioneered a similar high-volume, high-quality, and in this case high-altitude approach to tackling needless blindness. Their doctors often perform cataract surgeries in villages that have no running water or electricity and are only reachable by foot. In their outreach model, schools and village halls are converted into temporary operating theaters. Ruit and Tabin have perfected their surgical processes such that cataract surgery performed in these makeshift centers yields results comparable to those in the West. Their work now covers most inhabited regions of the Himalayan range.[4]

The duo also followed Aravind's lead, going beyond direct provision of eye care. They set up a training center for all levels of ophthalmic personnel and a skill-transfer program between Nepal and sub-Saharan·Africa; and in 1994, two years after Aurolab's launch, they opened a Nepali factory for the manufacture of high-quality, affordable IOLs.

Tabin and Ruit's Himalayan Cataract Program, amazing in its own right, drew from the key principles of the Aravind model and Dr. V's inspiration. As Tabin phrased it, Aravind represents "a trendsetter that has lifted the quality of cataract surgery in India and set a new paradigm for delivering high-volume, high-quality surgery to the poor. . . . The founding genius was a spiritual guru for all who now work in international eye care."[5]

Now in its fourth decade, the model Dr. V created has begun to encounter growing interest from one of the wealthiest and most powerful countries on the planet.

# SEVENTEEN

# ARAVIND IN AMERICA

The 2010 annual meeting of the Institute of Medicine of the National Academies, held in the United States, was themed around health care innovations. Dr. Kim Ramaswamy, retinal surgeon and chief medical officer of Aravind–Madurai, was asked to present on the Aravind model. His talk was followed by an animated panel discussion on how Aravind's core principles could be transferred to the West. The panel included senior executives from both the National Health Service (NHS) in the United Kingdom and the United States Department of Health and Human Services.

The last slide in Kim's presentation included a telling graph. It showed Aravind performing roughly 50 percent of the entire NHS's ophthalmic surgical volume, while spending less than 1 percent of the 1.6 billion pounds expended annually by the United Kingdom for eye care delivery. As the audience erupted into thunderous applause, Kim returned to his seat and shot an apologetic smile at the NHS executive sitting next to him. The man leaned over with a grin and whispered, "Hey, it's a good thing you didn't compare your numbers against the U.S.—that computer screen would have blown out!"

SEVERAL MAJOR STUDIES have drawn attention to the United States' massive health care costs and its disproportionate quality outcomes.

In 2009, the country as a whole spent 17 percent of its GDP (a whopping $2.5 trillion) on health care.[1] The United States spends more than twice per capita on health care what any other country in the world spends and yet performs poorly on many major indicators of health.[2] It is also the only wealthy and industrialized nation in the world that does not offer universal coverage.[3]

With health care costs in the United States rapidly outpacing means, some experts in the field are optimistic that the growing crisis will accelerate much-needed reform. "Every cloud has its silver lining," says Regina Herzlinger, a Harvard professor of business administration and one of America's leading advocates for market-driven, consumer-centric health care. "The gross costs we're bearing will force a restructuring of our system along the lines of Aravind," she says. "We absolutely need specialized hospitals that are both highly productive and *very* introspective about how they deliver care so they continuously improve quality. It would be great if they also adopted the charitable aspect of Aravind—but I'm not holding my breath for that day."[4]

When asked if there are relevant applications of the Aravind model in the United States, the renowned cataract surgeon Dr. David Chang sighs ever so slightly. "There are," he says. "But the health care system here is so different. While everybody has a priority for safety, we [in the United States] practice defensive medicine with lots of additional steps, tests, and paperwork because of medico-legal liability." Chang cites the example of U.S. health codes that require many supplies and surgical devices to be discarded after a single use. "But Aravind has shown that with proper sterilization, certain resources can be reused with no compromise in safety and a substantial slash in costs," says Chang. To him, the beauty of the Aravind model resides in the fact that "at Aravind there's no red tape, no bureaucracy. Everything that is done is done for a reason, and it's *got* to be cost-effective and efficient—or more people go blind."

Optimistic about bringing that mindset to the United States and unwilling to accept the status quo, a team based in California has begun the first serious exploration of what it would take to bring Aravind to the West.

❧

DR. SUSAN DAY is a former president of the American Academy of Ophthalmology (the first woman to hold that title) and chair of the Accreditation Council for Graduate Medical Education, the body that governs medical residents across all disciplines in America. In 2007, when she first began to dream of setting up an Aravind-style institute in the United States, she found an impressive ally in the president of the International Council of Ophthalmology, Dr. Bruce Spivey. Spivey does not mince words: "I've heard perfectly rational people say, 'Aravind can't work here,' and I've always thought, that's just uninformed," he says firmly. "Will it work *exactly* the same as in India? Of course not. You can't plop a system into a totally new culture and environment without modifications. But the basic premise is so clear, I believe it should work anywhere."[5] Another person who felt as strongly as Spivey was David Green, who had played a key role in Aurolab's creation and also had experience working with LAICO to transfer the Aravind model to other countries.

Spivey, Day, and Green, three powerhouses in the field of eye care and social entrepreneurship, had banded together. But even so, trying to import ideas and practices from Aravind would not be a simple process. The implications of the tax code, legal requirements, and health care regulations in the United States would have to be carefully studied. It was unclear to the group whether duplicating any of Aravind's high-efficiency techniques and, more fundamentally, whether a combination of for-profit and nonprofit structures was even legal.

Enter David Roe, a lawyer with more than three decades of experience in public interest strategy. Roe was brought on board to conduct a feasibility study for the venture. His role would involve careful research and testing of all the immediate grounds of objection. Going into it, Roe figured the project had about a 15 percent chance of surviving the feasibility study. He was in for a real surprise.

❧

"THE RESEARCH SHOWED it was possible," says Roe. "There was no law we could find that said it couldn't happen."[6] Certain particulars of the Aravind model, of course, were a no-go, given U.S. regulations. For instance, one could not have multiple patients undergoing surgery simultaneously within the same operating room, because U.S. codes mandate only one patient at a time per operating theater. But other aspects could certainly be transferred to the West and in fact had been successfully piloted in parts of Europe.

A consulting firm based in Helsinki had carried out a series of detailed time–motion studies across half a dozen Finnish eye care centers as well as at Aravind. The studies surfaced an array of efficiency techniques that could be transferred from the Indian facility: things like segmenting cases based on complexity, standardizing the use of instrument sets and equipment, and creating structured documentation and checklists.[7] Based on the findings, two hospital centers in Finland and one in Sweden had been able to significantly cut down their waiting lists.

Roe's research proved that on paper there were no immediate barriers to doing what the team in San Francisco had defined as their goal: "To create a permanent source of free medical and surgical care for the uninsured, by top specialists, that supports itself financially without ongoing support from government or charities."[8]

Rather than running a hospital, the team's research favored establishing a specialized, full-service eye institute that included an ambulatory surgical center (ASC)—a type of surgical facility less regulated than a hospital's operating rooms and significantly less expensive to set up and maintain. Not as encumbered by bureaucracy as a hospital, an ASC could potentially increase throughput more easily, offer a tiered pricing system, and be financially self-sustaining like Aravind. "We calculated that we could break even at a pretty conservative case volume while providing 20 percent of the surgeries for free," Roe says. Their plan for staffing was to sign on highly respected eye surgeons with private practices who were also committed to teaching, and to allow them to invest directly in the ASC. "This is a private practice model—and in that sense differs completely from Aravind," says Roe. "But essentially the plan is to take some of the gains from high-efficiency procedures and put them to the service of free care."

In early 2011, the group acquired real estate for the project in downtown San Francisco, but it remains to be seen how long it will take to raise the $60 million in initial capital required. For now, Roe summarizes the ambitious initiative in simple terms. "What this project offers is a conscientious effort to bring not the exact Aravind model, but the Aravind *notion*, to one part of American medicine."

Roe was deeply moved by his visit to Madurai. "At Aravind, I learned it's an attitude, more than just the techniques or the business model," he says pensively. "It's a spirit that needs to pervade everything that we do—a sense that we're all doing this together and will each do whatever needs to be done. I've become convinced that the kind of attitude that Aravind epitomizes is the secret. Set up the environment for it, model it, and let it pervade. The rewards are built-in."

❧

EMBEDDED IN ARAVIND'S work is the mystery of how Dr. V was able to draw inspiration from the golden arches in the West and, with his team, create a powerful network that delivers products far more essential than hamburgers. Today, replication of the Aravind model ranges from close duplication of processes and systems to the transplanting of principles and values that are more abstract but just as vital.

"Dr. V is a saint," says Fred Munson matter-of-factly. "That's two or three levels above any issues of models or anything else. So it doesn't matter what he's doing—his spirituality will infuse that. This is something very, very important and very different. You can't see the model at work without recognizing that it works best, you might even say it only works, if people who care deeply about improving the human condition are the ones who are implementing it. In that sense, spirituality is a part of the model and is part of the foundation on which Aravind's contribution has been built." Though difficult to systematically replicate, this facet of Aravind's work does ripple out. It often happens independent of the business elements of the model, and beyond the realm of eye care and the boundaries of the developing world. It surfaces quietly and without conscious effort— occasionally yielding radical results. Dr. William Stewart can vouch for its impact.

"I first went to Aravind in 1983 as the self-assured surgeon to 'help' the developing country," says Stewart candidly, "and then my mind just got rearranged when I saw the number of patients being treated and the quality of services that was being provided."[9] Stewart was invited to Aravind to build on the hospital's plastic reconstructive ophthalmic work. Over the next 27 years, Stewart saw the department and the organization undergo exponential transformations.

A twist that Stewart had not expected was a change in the direction of his own career. After his initial visit to Aravind, he received a letter from Dr. V that included a few startling lines. "I see your work evolving from a one-to-one practice to being more about consciousness and larger groups of people," it said, and Stewart remembers highlighting those words in his mind. They were part of what would give him the courage to step away from his traditional surgery practice and dedicate his attention to a new calling. "Dr. V and Aravind changed my perspective," says Stewart. "It was at Aravind that I saw that health and healing are not just scientific but also spiritual pursuits."

In 1990, he cofounded California Pacific Medical Center's Institute for Health & Healing (IHH), seeking to ground these insights in his Western medical experience. "Initially I was called 'Dr. Om,'" chuckles Stewart. In his book *Deep Medicine*, he writes of the institute's decades of work. "IHH is recognized as a national leader in evidence-based integrative medicine, combining knowledge bases, skill sets, and practices from other cultures and other times with contemporary medicine."[10] Through its various services, it now touches the lives of over 50,000 people each year.[11]

Aravind shifted the lives of many others in similar if less dramatic ways. Tech whiz Mike Myers first heard of Aravind in 1980 while working for a computer company run by Seva cofounder Larry Brilliant. When Brilliant approached him to help set up Aravind's computer systems for research data analysis, Myers said yes. He had no idea he was embarking on a journey that would change his life. Myers is now in his early 70s and has for many years spent roughly half his time volunteering at Aravind.

"I don't know if my views of Dr. V match those of others," he says humbly. "All I know is how I felt during and after each time we met. Dr. V seemed to me to be a person who wanted to share his dream with others and leave it to them to find a way to make it happen. He didn't pass on a blueprint as someone in the USA would have— instead, he passed on an idea. Between this dream and the capabilities of the people he surrounded himself with, vaporware became reality; and these dreams became functioning parts of everyone's reality, even those who didn't share in the dream but who simply became involved in the emerging reality."[12]

It is a beautiful reflection, and one that summons up the different shades of practical magic that Dr. V's vision and the work of his team inspire in the world. "If you want to build a ship, don't drum up people to collect wood and don't assign them tasks and work, but rather teach them to long for the endless immensity of the sea," wrote the pilot-writer Antoine de Saint-Exupéry.[13]

Dr. V's approach was to do all of the above.

PART V

# How Do You Retire a Saint?

## On Change and Integrity

*How is one to live a moral and compassionate existence*

*. . . when one finds darkness not only in one's culture but*

*within oneself? If there is a stage at which an individual life*

*becomes truly adult, it must be when one grasps the irony in*

*its unfolding and accepts responsibility for a life lived in the*

*midst of such paradox. . . . There are simply no answers to*

*some of the great pressing questions. You continue to*

*live them out, making your life a worthy expression of leaning*

*into the light.*

—Barry Lopez, *Arctic Dreams*

# EIGHTEEN

# SAME SAME BUT DIFFERENT

D r. V is known to pace the corridors of the Madurai hospital, gauging the crowd and monitoring the workflow. Now in his 80s, he has started using a walking stick on these excursions. But he still tires occasionally and has to stop abruptly, putting an arm out to the wall for support. On one such occasion, a concerned nurse rushed up to inquire if something was wrong. "Not at all," said Dr. V. "I'm just holding up the hospital." The quick-witted response was not a total exaggeration.

Without Dr. V, Aravind simply would not exist. "He is its core and driving force," says Fred Munson. "He is the one who turned Aravind from a little made-over nursing home into the largest eye care system in the world." Yet Dr. V knew that a charismatic leader at the center of a visionary organization could quickly become a liability.

In the mid-20th century, a highly reputed ophthalmologist established a flourishing eye hospital that was orbited by a network of 30 satellite clinics in northern India. Dr. V held him and his institution in high regard, often speaking of their work as something to emulate. But when the founder passed away, within the span of a single generation most of the clinics either shut down or fell into severe disrepair. Soon there was little trace of the progressive organization that had led the country in the community eye care movement.

It was a storyline that Dr. V saw repeatedly and warned his team of. He did not want Aravind to join a procession of ill-fated organizations that prospered as long as the influential founder was around and then quietly folded after that leader was gone. The irony was that Dr. V issued these warnings and stressed the importance of decentralization while continuing to monopolize Aravind's reins.

"Every organization has to be able to arrange for succession," says Munson. "But . . . how do you retire a saint?" Planning for the transition was not easy. Dr. V's role went beyond any simple job description. To assume that his was a transferable position seemed almost presumptuous. There was a luminous mystery to Dr. V's methods that the others acknowledged and knew they could not replicate. Layered on top of this were the patriarchal norms of Indian culture. Dr. V was the revered elder brother whose vision and compassion had molded each founding member.

And yet as Aravind entered its third decade, it was clear to the leadership that for the organization to survive in the long run, executive decision-making authority had to be passed on. Others would need a direct share in shaping Aravind's vision. They would need experience in growing the organization guided by their own judgment, and not through wisdom mandated or borrowed from their already-legendary founder.

In early 1997, Munson facilitated a series of sensitive discussions with Aravind's founding members to determine the next in line for the role of leader. He entered the process thinking that Dr. Natchiar, with her leadership skills and strong surgical background, would be the likely choice. But he recalls being pulled aside by GS. "He quickly set me straight about how things worked in this culture," Munson says. "You couldn't pass over a husband and give the post to the wife. It would be unheard of." Despite the fact that 80 percent of Aravind's workforce is female and that women do hold significant leadership posts within the organization, there is a tacit bias here (common to much of the world) that favors men. The Trust's nomination ultimately pointed to Natchiar's husband, Dr. Nam, as Dr. V's successor. Natchiar was accorded joint director status.

Though Nam's nomination was influenced by gender bias, his impressive track record certainly helped clinch the decision. Nam had founded the nation's premier low-vision-aid clinic and was one of India's earliest retina specialists. He trained at Harvard Medical School under Dr. Charles Schepens (recognized as the father of modern retina surgery). Nam's own prowess as a surgeon and teacher had earned him numerous awards, and he had personally trained over 100 ophthalmologists in his specialty.

After the decision, Dr. V took some time to issue the public announcement effecting the transition. Aravind was his life's work; he had suffered, sacrificed, toiled, and dreamed for it against improbable odds. He had always been the keeper of its flame. Stepping away from the helm was perhaps one of the most difficult things he would ever do. He had defined this organization. But the reverse was also true.

In May 1997, a week after formally announcing the change in leadership, Dr. V traveled to Pondicherry for a month's retreat at the Sri Aurobindo Ashram.

ॐ

AN ENTRY FROM Dr. V's journal:

*May 18 1997*

*10:30 am Pondy [Pondicherry]*

*I am alone in the room. If I want I can read. There is no work waiting for me. No meetings to attend, no letters to reply to, no people to meet. No watching the Medical Records at 7:30 am, no statistics of the day's operations. I watch the sea, the horizon, the clouds, the waves, the beggars, people known and unknown moving about. It was full moon yesterday. After 7 pm I could see some lights on the horizon from boats passing. No TV to distract me no local politics or relatives' problems. No magazines, daily papers, emails or faxes from Seva. No decisions to make,*

*no shouting at the telephone operator. No wastepaper to
pick up.*

*How will it be if I am dead and gone away from this scene.*

*I should gradually condition myself to a different routine.
To concentrate on the sadhana of Integral yoga and
reading of Savitri.*

Then almost exactly a month later comes this entry:

*June 17: An idea came to me to have an eye hospital at
Pondy. Goal: Divine Life on Earth.*

Apparently you could take Dr. V out of Aravind, but there was
no taking Aravind out of Dr. V. With Dr. Nam handling operational
leadership as director, the board had made Dr. V chairman. Upon his
return to Madurai, Dr. V kept his office, remained a part of the senior
leadership team, continued to come in to the hospital before 7 each
morning, and still examined patients. But his primary focus shifted to
mentoring the new leadership, drawing in new partnerships, and pushing for a new hospital in Pondicherry. His stream of ideas and aspirations for the organization was unchecked, with the healthy difference
that now others were responsible for driving the vision.

DR. NAM CUTS a distinguished figure, the combined effect of his six-
foot frame, high forehead, leonine features, and steel-rimmed spectacles. Like Dr. V, Nam is the eldest son of his parents and the first doctor
out of his village. As a student, he was hardworking and responsible,
and displayed strong ties to his rural home—qualities that did not go
unnoticed by his first professor of ophthalmology. Nam and Natchiar
were classmates in medical school when Dr. V (their dean, and chair
of the eye department) singled out Nam as a suitable match for his
youngest sister.

Dr. V had mailed their photographs to the ashram in Pondicherry asking the Mother for her verdict (the first and only time a marriage in the family would be decided this way). Nam laughs remembering the long wait—it was several months before a response with her blessings finally came.

His close association with Dr. V, the endurance test of Aravind's founding years, and his professional accomplishments groomed Nam well for the new role. As director, he brought passion and urgency to areas that had long taken a backseat. "We have to change what we are doing now to match the times," he declared repeatedly. "It's the only way to stay true to our vision and mission."

Nam's energy spurred the organization toward the intersection of eye care, information technology, and medical research. He founded Aravind's Virtual Academy in partnership with India's equivalent of NASA, the Indian Space Research Organization. They provided satellite technology that connected Aravind's multiple hospitals, allowing for joint grand rounds, clinical meetings, and the like. Nam wants to evolve this into a global resource center for online ophthalmic education and hospital consulting.

Early in his directorship, Nam decided to make diabetic retinopathy services a priority. India has the second largest diabetic population in the world and is home to approximately 50.8 million (and growing) diabetics.[1] Nearly half of them are estimated to have some degree of diabetic retinopathy (DR), a potentially blinding condition and one of the leading causes of blindness in India.[2] Nam's efforts toward early identification and sustainable treatment of the condition resulted in the establishment of a program housed within Aravind for DR service delivery research, collaboratively funded by Lions International and later by the World Diabetes Foundation. By the time external funding expired, the DR program had proved its worth, and Aravind took over the running and funding of it. The project's findings and systems were also documented and packaged to enable a swift transfer to other eye care programs across the globe.

Nam's defining contribution to Aravind's vision, however, was his dogged conviction that the organization had both the potential and the responsibility to develop a cutting-edge global research center. Medical research is an exorbitant undertaking, with potentially huge gains for patient care in the long run but little direct short-term benefit. For many years, Aravind's limited resources and focus on meeting immediate needs for eye care made advanced research a luxury it could ill afford. But by the time Nam took over, conditions were different.

"For years, big agencies and institutes had been coming to us to use our patient pool for their research," says Nam. "We collaborated, but not as equal partners—we were just handing over our data. But as we evolved, there was really no excuse for us not to be initiating some of these advanced clinical studies instead of responding to requests from others. We needed to do this to remain at the leading edge of eye care."

Nam hauled Aravind's research potential into the limelight and paved the road to a multimillion-dollar global research institute. Today the Dr. G. Venkataswamy Eye Research Institute's chrome-and-glass-fronted building stands next door to LAICO and across the street from the Aravind hospital in Madurai. It boasts state-of-the art research laboratories and is closely affiliated with half a dozen international organizations, including the National Eye Institute in the United States and the United Kingdom's International Centre for Eye Health.

The institute is a recognized center for postgraduate research in genetics, immunology, and ophthalmology. It investigates genetic factors responsible for major eye diseases and seeks to engineer against gene mutations that lead to vision loss. This research building—from where you can see the ancient towers of the Meenakshi Amman temple—even houses advanced projects in proteomics and stem cell research. Meanwhile, Nam is also looking ahead to the sweeping possibilities of nanotechnology and genetic counseling for eye diseases.

The advancements on the research front rippled into a steady surge in Aravind's publications. Dr. Prajna (Nam's son) shares that in 2009, Aravind doctors published close to 100 papers in peer-reviewed journals, the highest number from any single eye care institute in the country. "Research helps grow our reputation in a different professional realm," says Prajna.[3] "Otherwise, we would easily get written off as a good community eye care provider. Now we're really in demand. All the big eye care equipment companies want to work with us. Collaborating with them helps us stay ahead of the curve. It's a powerful, indirect contribution to our mission of delivering the best to our patients."

Under Nam, Aravind passed its first succession test. He pushed the organization to innovate and respond to the needs of the community in radically different ways than Dr. V had, but what remained was an unbroken thread of common values and purpose. As the saying in India goes, the two leaders were "same same, but different."

When Nam is asked about Aravind's potential for medical tourism, for instance, the corners of his mouth turn down. "I'm not for it," he says frankly. "Paying patients are important, but we need to balance our priorities. We want to be a hospital for everyone, but we don't want to start chasing the super-wealthy. If we start directing a lot of time and resources trying to cater to small numbers of extremely rich patients from abroad, then we lose our focus on the people badly in need. The energy of the work starts to change and get diluted. We don't want that to happen—ever."

# NINETEEN

# ALL WILL PASS FROM THE EARTH

Though Aravind does not project itself as a family-run organization, the leading role that Dr. V's kin play is impossible to ignore. Today, over 35 members across three generations of his family work in the Aravind Eye Care System. Several are employed in nonmedical areas of LAICO and Aurolab, while a few of his nieces are full-time volunteers heading divisions such as publishing, hospitality, and catering. By 2011, more than 20 people from Dr. V's family were senior surgeons or student doctors at Aravind. An additional four were in medical school.

A potent blend of custom, trust, caring, and respect molded members of Dr. V's family to be guardians and implementers of his legacy. Children of the founding team grew up in strict households. Sleeping in on weekends was frowned on, going to the movies was discouraged, and school vacations were spent "volunteering" at the patient-registration desk in the hospital or at eye camps. It was taken for granted that these children (and their children, in turn) would one day join Aravind. That none of them permanently rebelled against this expectation was extraordinary. Even the few who chose to work outside the organization eventually did return to contribute to Dr. V's vision. Natchiar and Nam's younger son, Vishnu Prasad, for instance, studied and worked abroad for well over a decade. He and his wife, Chitra, now live in Madurai, where Vishnu is Aurolab's international marketing manager and Chitra works in the Finance Department at LAICO.

Dr. V often attached designations to members of the younger generation when introducing them to visitors. "This is Sathya, our future pediatric chief," he announced at a time when his grandniece, Sathya, was all of seven years old. Today, Sathya Ravilla is a surgeon at Aravind–Madurai and is considering specializing in pediatric ophthalmology. Her husband is also an eye doctor here.

The odds of finding so many ophthalmologists in a single clan were considerably aided by the Indian custom of arranged marriages. Dr. V and his siblings had a knack for discovering eligible young doctors who could join the fold. This matchmaking trend did meet with some initial resistance. Three of Dr. V's nephews, Kim, Aravind, and Prajna, each announced an unwillingness to marry a doctor. Knowing firsthand what it was like to be a child of two surgeons at Aravind, they did not wish that on their future offspring. A running joke in the family is that they offered to pool money and pay for more ophthalmologists just to avoid betrothal to women in white coats. But when presented with the family's selection (the prospective bride was always a doctor), they each buckled. Today, all three are happily married to partners who are not just ophthalmologists but department heads at Aravind.

Visitors are often struck by the commitment of the second generation. Dr. Pulin Shah, a visiting resident from the United States, got to know Dr. Aravind; his wife, Dr. Haripriya; and their children quite well during the course of his stay. The tenor of their daily lives made a deep impression on him. "They have two small kids, and they still work six days a week!" says Shah. "It's a Saturday and they're operating. They start very early, and then they'll teach and then they'll do rounds and go on camps and—when I see their daily lives . . ." He falls silent for a moment, searching for the right words. "Part of my purpose in coming to Aravind was to try and experience that atmosphere of service to the community, and to get that—that *flame* inside of me. It was very tangible there," he says quietly.

The second generation is certainly called to work hard, though on a different scale from what the founders experienced. "They have worked much, much harder than we have," says GS's daughter, Dr. Kalpana, referring to the older generation. "I know they never got Sundays off to relax. Their mindset was so different. We could never do what they did."[1]

Nor do any of them necessarily wish to. For the founding team, work-life balance was a foreign concept. Their children, by circumstance and choice, are now doing things differently. The financial success of the organization has allowed for pay scales that put Aravind's next leadership in the upper income bracket of society. Their lives hold none of the harsh privations or tradeoffs of the founding years. They are a savvy generation that has embraced the privileges of modernity, with two cars to a family, homes fitted with modern amenities, and vacations abroad penciled into their calendars. They are less daunting as leaders, more available as parents, and more worldly in their lifestyles than Aravind's founders ever were.

"I work smart and don't really believe in working hard. I have never had a role model in the family who does *not* work hard—that is the problem," says Prajna with a twinkle. His wife, Lalitha (also an eye surgeon), heads Aravind's microbiology department, and the couple has two children. Prajna is clear that family comes first for him and working at Aravind represents only one part of his life. "I don't get emotionally involved. This has helped me identify my priorities. You can view it as an indifferent attitude, but it's not. Actually, it's very healthy for the long-term sustainability of the institution. I don't feel like I've sacrificed my life at the hospital. You don't need to."

Prajna's words border on blasphemy for some members of the family. But while Aravind was certainly not built on this attitude, his determined push for balance plays an important role in the organization today. The exacting demands that Dr. V placed on the founding team are inspiring as anecdotes but set an anachronistic standard. As the organization has grown, the single-minded fervor required of the founders has had to be redefined for a mélange of professionals with diverse ambitions.

"There's a fine line between a culture of hard work and one that feels like exploitation," says Prajna. He is now one of the organization's most determined advocates for fixed working hours, sponsored department dinners, pay raises, mandatory vacations, and shorter shift options for doctors with young children. "My job is to make this a more likable organization for the people who work here," he says. Along with several of his cousins, Prajna has implemented various initiatives over the last five years that have significantly decreased, if not halted, the threat of high turnover among Aravind's doctors.

According to Fred Munson, retention is a problem that is never entirely going to go away at Aravind. "The better you train them, the more they can make outside," he declares. "The larger scale you do it at, the more visible you become to other organizations." Munson also points to the elephant in the room: the family-versus-nonfamily dynamic at Aravind. Today, nonfamily members head the majority of Aravind's specialty departments. But the organization's governing trust and executive leadership are almost exclusively composed of Dr. V's kin.

Nonfamily staff members have divergent perspectives on how this balance of power plays out. "It alienates some doctors," says Aravind's outspoken retinal surgeon, Dr. Shukla. "It can create a bit of an 'us and them' mentality. To be frank, I initially felt it, too. Now I'm doing exactly what I want to do, but I know some nonfamily members don't end up staying because they feel there's some sort of glass ceiling." Others, like Dr. Krishnadas, dismiss the idea of nepotism. He points out that in the span of his career at Aravind, he has been promoted over Dr. V's family members into the positions of chief of glaucoma services, chief medical officer, and director of human resources (his current title).

In partial agreement with him is Dr. George Thomas, Aravind–Madurai's current glaucoma head. "Being nonfamily doesn't really affect your career growth," says Thomas. "In surgery, the systems are so strong, there is no question of preferential treatment creeping in."[2] Then he adds, "But I've been here 13 years and know from experience that outside of my core job, it's difficult to get some things done, being nonfamily. For instance, if I need the medical records unit to transfer a file or the audiovisual department to edit a surgical video, it takes time to get their attention. But if I copy a family member on the e-mail request, then it gets done the very next day."

Thomas shrugs off this invisible layer of authority that some find unacceptable. "I have to say, I've been treated really well by this family," he says. "Recently I was hospitalized with acute fever, and everyone from Dr. Natchiar to Kim and Prajna and the others came trooping in to see me. When it comes down to it, the care they show is pretty unbelievable." Thomas's wife is also an ophthalmologist at Aravind who only recently returned to work after an extended maternity leave. "She was a bit nervous coming in, because she wanted to ask Prajna for a short-shift option and wasn't sure what he would say. He basically told her, 'You're an asset to the institution and we don't want to lose you—we'll work something out.' That kind of flexibility and openness makes a huge difference," declares Thomas.

Among the Aravind Eye Care System's 3,000-plus staff there are more than 50 people unrelated to Dr. V who have been with the organization for more than 20 years and nearly 200 others who have crossed the ten-year mark.[3] As the organization grows, it is clear to the leadership that the presence and involvement of such people will need to be nurtured and grown.

THE HUB OF the Aravind Eye Care System is unequivocally in Madurai. All the founding members (and 19 of the 21 ophthalmologists in Dr. V's family) are stationed here. Aravind–Madurai is the flagship of the organization, and its biggest patient facility and postgraduate and paraprofessional training center. Clustered here too are the large-scale initiatives outside direct patient care: the manufacturing plant Aurolab, the consulting arm LAICO, and the Dr. G. Venkataswamy Eye Research Institute. All this combines to create a unique vibrancy in the work culture. There is, however, a flip side to it. Madurai is also the Aravind locale where the stifling effect of too many bosses is felt most keenly. And though all key innovations of the organization arose from here, this center, ironically, is not necessarily the most conducive environment for experimentation.

Like Dr. V, his siblings habitually mentor and assign people to senior roles. But they also have his tendency to impose decisions at will, in a way that sometimes undercuts the younger leaders' authority. In the past this has led to demoralizing situations, where a department head might discover (after the fact) that staff members from his division had been transferred to another hospital or that a significant change had been implemented in the training program he was running. And often this control from Madurai extended to Aravind hospitals in other cities.

Dr. Kalpana (Dr. V's niece), along with her husband, Dr. Narendran, runs Aravind's hospital in the city of Coimbatore. She remembers walking out of surgery one afternoon to discover that the tops of all the trees on the hospital grounds had been lopped off. When she questioned the gardening staff, she was told that "Madam" from Madurai (Dr. Natchiar) had called and issued the orders. "I didn't know whether to laugh or to cry!" she says. It was a feeling all too familiar at Aravind—regardless of whether or not you were family. The founding team members had a maddening way of assuming that they knew best (and the fact that they often did was no comfort).

◯

"DR. V USED TO say to us, 'Give me your son, I will mold him,'" says ophthalmologist Richard Litwin, chuckling. "It's not a very Western viewpoint, to imply that you have the power, duty, and authority to mold someone's son—but he certainly molded us!" (Litwin's son did spend time in Madurai, as did the children of many other Aravind partners and well-wishers from the West.) Mentoring and coaching people was part of Dr. V's repertoire.

In laying out a succession plan, Dr. V worked far ahead of the curve, not stopping with his own or the second generation but extending his attention to the third. *I must spend more time developing the children mentally and physically*, he states firmly in an early 1990s journal entry. He put these intentions to immediate action by starting a children's forum for the third generation of the family. He dubbed it the New Age Group, and as an induction token, he gifted each child (there were roughly a dozen in all) a brand new notebook.

The New Age Group convened at 8 a.m. every Sunday over a period of five years. All the children, with their parents in tow, congregated at one of the family homes. Prior to a potluck breakfast, each child made a short presentation in front of what was, in essence, the entire senior leadership team of Aravind. Dr. V assigned the topics for these meetings, and they ranged from presentations on polar bears, planets, world religions, and freedom fighters to poetry recitations, quizzes, and dramatized performances of India's old epics. Since participants ranged in age from 2 to 17, nursery rhymes were also on the agenda.

The meetings of the New Age Group were lighthearted, laughter-filled events that charmed many Aravind visitors who were invited to sit in over the years. The spirit of the gatherings exemplified the inclusiveness and deep solidarity of this family. It was a living room tradition where the personal dimensions of their lives were braided together, connecting three generations. Systems thinker that he was, Dr.

V created the New Age Group as a mechanism through which roughly 40 people came together week after week to applaud each other's children, share a meal, and create memories of caring that would long outlast his lifetime.

❧

IN THE LATE 1980s and 1990s, Dr. V had several strong premonitions of death. *A feeling that all men come like a maize crop and all will pass from the earth in the course of time and new people will come*, he writes in a journal entry. *Death is around the corner. How to prepare for death.* These entries often read as self-interrogations: *What was the purpose of life and what did I do to achieve it.*

Another entry: *Soul eternal. With birth and death as different doors.*

❧

IT IS SPRING 2006. A room on the second floor of Aravind–Madurai has been occupied for over a month, and here, lying in a hospital bed and fighting for each breath, is Dr. V.

At 88, he is thin and extremely weak, with a serious infection of the lungs. Natchiar is ten pillars of strength rolled into one. She fights a grim battle every single day to keep him alive and is steeled by a love born of gratitude that others can only begin to fathom. Dr. V has been brother and father, teacher and friend. He has been her strength, just as now she is his. He often asks for her, and she is always only a few steps away. Even on days of acute pain, it is not uncommon for him to turn to her suddenly and ask, "How many patients today?"

His nephew Prajna flies to Singapore to receive an award on Dr. V's behalf. Before leaving, he says to a cousin, "I think Uncle is pulling on physically, but it's getting harder for him mentally." Then he adds, "But I may have to eat my words. We thought that a few months ago, too. Then he got better and marched into LAICO and addressed a gathering of a couple hundred people!"

GS visits the room often to give his brother updates on various land possibilities for building future hospitals. "Very good, very good," says Dr. V. A well-worn phrase, and familiar to the family, it is Dr. V's sweet response to much that is placed in front of him: the annual increase in patient numbers, a nephew or niece's upcoming conference schedule, details of a screening camp, each child's presentation during the New Age Group meetings, news of winning prestigious awards, or a staff member's marriage. He is not a man given to elaborate praise, so this short phrase stands in for a stamp of approval. He manages to pack both warmth and caring into it.

Two calendars with pictures of Sri Aurobindo and the Mother have been pinned to the curtain in his room. The Mother's palms are folded in a gesture of blessing. Sri Aurobindo's picture is sterner, more aloof. "One soul's ambition lifted up the race," reads the quote underneath his photograph. During the day, Natchiar and Dr. V's nieces and grandnieces read to him writings from the teachers he loves so dearly. He often asks to hear one of his favorite passages from *Savitri*, the closing lines of which seem to wash over the room and his being with a special force each time.

> He made great dreams a mould for coming things
> And cast his deeds like bronze to front the years.
> His walk through Time outstripped the human stride.
> Lonely his days and splendid like the sun's.

There is a television in the room, and one evening Dr. V smiles faintly as he watches a steely-eyed Maria Sharapova slam a tennis ball with expert grace across the court. Turning to a grandniece sitting by his side, he says, "Do you see that woman? You too must be strong like that."

OVER THE NEXT few months, visitors come trickling in to see him, some from great distances. They have all been touched and, in some way, transformed by him. His family feels the quiet drama of all the dispersed elements of his life drawing together: boyhood friends from his village, colleagues, students, staff members, patients, community leaders, and international partners come to Aravind to pay their respects. They keep coming—long past the time he is able to receive them with his full attention and far beyond the stage when he is capable of conversation.

He is transferred briefly to a specialty hospital. But on the afternoon of July 7, 2006, the attending staff doctor tells Natchiar quietly that there is nothing more they can do for him. It is time for the final farewell. A calm surrender fills the incongruous brightness of the day.

Back at Aravind, Natchiar is in the room that Dr. V will be brought to, sitting with her head bowed and her hands clasped like a little girl's. She is crying softly. The nurses around her have quietly taken charge. They are freshening up the room, sweeping and mopping the floor and clearing space for the crowd that will come. Incense is lit and spirals of fragrant smoke rise and disappear into the air. A hospital van pulls in through the front gates, and for one last time Dr. V enters Aravind.

Slowly, wordlessly, the room fills with people. Almost all of his nieces and nephews are present. Dr. Usha, still in her surgeon's blue cap and gown; Kim and his sisters, Vara, Chitra, and Kannamma; Prajna; Haripriya with her eight-month-old son, Arya Venkat (named after Dr. V); Aravind and his sister, Kalpana, from Coimbatore. Lalitha (GS's wife) is there, too, her eyes filled with tears. She silently took care of Dr. V for all the years he lived in their home. At the foot of the bed are Dr. V's grandnieces; at the head is Natchiar, with Dr. Nam and GS close by. "I know you can hear me, Brother," Natchiar says, her voice breaking. "We are all here, and we will work hard to keep your vision strong."

There are nearly 40 people in the room, and they seem to exist as one collective being, bound tightly in life before the imminence of death. Dr. V's breathing is labored. It quickens suddenly, as if he is about to say something. Instead, the room fills with the heightened presence of departure. There is a hush, a moment cradled in stillness, and then Nam reaches over and, in quiet grief, gently closes for the last time those deep-visioned eyes.

OUTSIDE, IN THE busy corridors, nothing comes to a standstill. Patients, rich and poor, old and young, continue to stream through this system of care. A hospital cannot afford to be paralyzed by grief. But the news of Dr. V's passing runs swiftly through the nervous system of the organization. It reaches surgeons looking up between operations, receptionists printing admission cards, and nurses administering drops and retying bandages. It reaches the gray-haired security man at the gate and the medical teams unloading equipment after a camp; it reaches LAICO's classrooms full of international trainees and the factory floor of Aurolab. It leaps from one hospital in Madurai to all the others. From one heart to the next, it soon reaches across the globe.

The messages come pouring in from friends, partners, and even strangers. A young doctor from the United States writes, "He will always be that example of how to approach medicine, how to be human. And this is how I feel without ever interacting with him." Writes another, "It is amazing to think that, all across the world, Dr. V is once again causing people to marvel at how great a life can be." Before the cremation, there will be phone calls from the president of India offering brotherly condolences to the founding team; there will be house visits from vegetable sellers, university professors, CEOs, and rickshaw drivers coming to pay last respects. There will be prayer vigils held through the night by Aravind's nurses.

"I wrote about that day in my diary," says senior Aravind nurse A. Sundari. "How our hearts were so heavy when we first heard the news. But we couldn't stop to cry—we knew his work had to continue."

# TWENTY

# THE BOTTOM IS MOVING UP

Typically, in the lives of countries and organizations, after the fertile dreams and flux of the founding years come the halcyon days of stability. A period of security wrapped in routine lasts only so long before tumult and possibility move in to force new change. That feverish time has now descended on Aravind and India.

Indifferent to the initial tug of globalization, Madurai has long been more of a vibrant, overgrown village than a slick, modern-day metropolis. But a decade into the 21st century, progress has whetted a new ambition in this ancient city and brought a novel prosperity within reach. It is on the cusp of change, and the evidence is everywhere. Hay-stacked bullock carts halt at traffic lights with digital displays, and first-time escalator riders wander barefoot through the city's brand new mall. Domino's Pizza delivers where hawkers still carry vegetable baskets on their heads; and at the doorsteps of coffee bars serving frothy cappuccinos, coconut-water vendors split their hard green fruit with scythes.

After decades of a closed economy and slow growth, India underwent dramatic economic reforms in 1991. In the 20 years since, a heady sense of progress has swept across the nation. The unprecedented growth rate has brought about drastic upgrades to India's infrastructure. New highways are being laid, colleges are being built, and widespread health insurance and a social security net for the rural poor are emerging. The needs of the poor, typically left to charities and nonprofits, are starting to be addressed by market-based solutions. Companies seeking to build hybrid business models that "do well by doing good" are on the rise. In this shifting environment, Aravind has continued to evolve.

Four years after Dr. V's passing, the organization he founded shows no signs of slowing down. Every few months, new vision centers spreading permanent eye care access into rural India are being launched. Aurolab has transitioned from its former cramped quarters to a sprawling, state-of the-art facility. The massive Dr. G. Venkataswamy Eye Research Institute has been inaugurated next door to LAICO. On the same street, construction of a brand-new seven-story building for Aravind's inpatients is under way (when completed, it will nearly double the hospital's square footage). And in the midst of all this relentless activity, new and conflicting models of expansion and growth are being debated.

❧

It is a Monday morning in spring 2010. The temperature in Madurai is just over 100 degrees, and Aravind's registration area is packed. Patients spill over to the narrow porch outside, waiting their turn. Steel snack boxes are opened; a child plays with marbles on the floor; his mother pulls the loose end of her sari over her head, stretches out, and promptly falls asleep. The scene brims with casual, unhurried Indian charm.

The hospital's administrator, Dr. Aravind, is not beguiled by any of this. "This large-scale model just isn't sustainable," he says. "The way we work now, our high volume is becoming a bit of a drawback. A lot of people don't want to deal with the heat, the wait, and the crowd. We're turning into a hospital for the masses."

His words and vehemence are startling. High volume is a pivotal aspect of the Aravind model. Without this cornerstone, the organization's financial viability, mission reach, training capacities, and so many other elements of its success would falter. A hospital for the masses is what Dr. V designed this place to be—not a plush boutique for eye care.

Dr. Aravind presses on, "We need to start building hospitals in midsized towns and are also looking to open one in Chennai, on a small scale but with upgraded facilities." Chennai is the capital of the state of Tamil Nadu, home to several well-known eye hospitals and not the most obvious choice for a new Aravind center. "We can set up there as a paying facility without the free-hospital concept," he says. "Then maybe do eye camps as the charity side of things."

Maybe? This new vision sounds dangerously like a violation of founding principles and a dramatic shift in focus away from the poor. The organization's model evolved directly out of a focus on serving the underserved. That spirit of service is not an add-on feature to the model; it was the front and center of Dr. V's work. But Dr. Aravind knows all this better than most—he grew up under the same roof as Dr. V and has absorbed much of his uncle's ethos.

"For years, we've talked about increasing our outpatient numbers," he says. "Now for the first time we need to talk about decreasing those numbers in individual facilities but increasing them overall through the creation of more hospitals." The economic changes in the country have had an impact on the organization, and Dr. Aravind is itching to respond to them. "Look, five years ago, 90 percent of our patients used to opt for treatment at the lower end of the scale," he says. "Now, only 60 percent make that choice. A dollar a day isn't the standard anymore. Many housemaids earn much more than that. Brand consciousness is picking up. More people have cars, go to the cinema, "need" air conditioning . . . are we responding to these changes in society?"

"The financial incapacity of the majority is what made our free and subsidized care relevant," he goes on to say. "Now the government is bringing in health insurance schemes. Once insurance for the poor kicks in, an individual's poverty won't have the same bearing. In that case, do we need to be charitable to insurance companies? We have to keep our ear to the ground—it hasn't shifted in 30 years, but it's shifting now. Yes, we still want to cover the bottom of the pyramid, *but the bottom of the pyramid is moving up.*"

Dr. Aravind's impassioned words hook the imagination; they carry a sense of positive upheaval, rich with the promise of a better life for the marginalized. "If as an organization we don't change our approach in this environment, we'll cease to be relevant," he says emphatically. "We won't die—we're too big for that—we'll end up kind of toddling along." He interrupts himself here with a quick, rueful smile. "But maybe I'm just in this mode today because of the crowd outside."

Other realities are prompting change. The rising economy has affected Aravind's recruitment pool. Government schemes offering a free college education, the boom in the retail industry, and the mush-rooming of call centers in South India have all created an array of new and attractive opportunities for young women armed with high school degrees. As a result, Aravind's hospitals have seen a drop in applicant volume for their paraprofessional training. At the same time, they are encountering changed expectations around pay scale, workload, and on-the-job skills enhancement.

Adding to the pressure is the fact that "eye care is big business in India right now," as Prajna puts it. A slew of private companies have entered the field of medical care and are rapidly expanding across the country. Aravind often loses doctors and nurses to competitors offer-ing corporate-size pay packages along with attractive perks. The chal-lenges for the organization in this period extend well beyond staffing for its hospitals.

The ophthalmic-products industry in India is exploding. Multi-nationals as well as domestic players are jostling at the doorstep of a multibillion-dollar opportunity, with slashed prices, rampant product development, and aggressive marketing. In this new scenario, Aurolab must re-stake its territory and figure out a long-term strategy for growth.

LAICO, meanwhile, is grappling with questions of sustainability. The institute currently just about breaks even, even though there is a clear and growing demand for its services in the eye care community. Its challenge is that many small eye hospitals do not have the internal funds or international donor backing to pay for consulting. Adding to the difficulty is the fact that several of LAICO's highly trained consultants have migrated to the big cities for jobs with international eye care foundations. As many of its second generation leaders point out, if the Aravind Eye Care System does not respond, its relevance will be displaced.

Prajna echoes Dr. Aravind's thinking. "We can't just sit around telling stories of how hard the older generation worked," says Prajna. "We have to do something new. People want more high-end options now. Maybe we will try following the airlines model: we'll market services as either Aravind Business Class or Aravind Economy Class." He pauses for a moment. "I know the older generation is a bit unnerved by the pace of growth all around us," he says—and then, with a conspiratorial grin, he adds, "but the truth is, we're ready to take on the world."

Meanwhile, Nam (Prajna's father) is looking through the patient suggestion book in the hospital's lobby. He carefully reads each handwritten entry and writes in a few comments, assigning items for follow-up to the human resources department. Talking about the current situation, he takes a different tack than Dr. Aravind or Prajna. "We have to be really aware of how the changing demands can change us," he says. "Insurance, for instance—if we start thinking, 'Why do outreach camps? Let's just wait for people to get insurance and come to us. They get free treatment, and we still get our money.' But that kind of thinking is exactly what could dilute our approach." His argument is that Aravind needs to use the situation to look for other underserved eye care needs in the community.

Nam, just shy of 70, is headed this week to an eye camp north of Madurai, where he will spend a day in the blistering heat helping to screen over a thousand patients. The founding team members still regularly participate in Aravind's community work. As they prepare to step back from day-to-day leadership activities, they are keen to set strong precedents for their successors.

The center stage at Aravind is clearing for the next act, in which the nephews and nieces of Dr. V will play lead roles. Nam has announced his decision to step down from directorship of Aravind in 2010. Natchiar and others from the founding team are discussing delegation of their roles as well. A new structure of governance is forming, in which Prajna, Dr. Aravind, and their peers will shape the future of the organization.

"The younger generation has been groomed," says Nam. "There won't be any problems. The basic principles and philosophy of the institute will be maintained." His words belie the nervousness the founding team feels at the imminence of this turning point. It is the organization's first intergenerational transition at the highest level of leadership.

❧

GETTING INTO THE CAR, GS notices a bag with two bottles of fruit juice on the floor. "Are we going on a picnic?" he asks with a half-scowl, half-smile. "Who put those in here?" From the back, his sister Natchiar pleads innocent. He turns to Subramaniam, the timid chauffeur who has been with the hospital for 30 years and is hard of hearing. "Did you put these in here?" GS demands. Natchiar starts to laugh and says, "Of course he didn't—let's go." GS, ever the resource manager, cannot help himself. "Shall we return one of the bottles to the cafeteria?" he asks. "No," says Natchiar, still laughing. "If no one wants it, we'll bring it back." "There's a cushion for you behind the seat," her brother says gruffly in reply.

These siblings have an easy camaraderie. They begin to discuss an unusual donation that Aravind has just received: a mansion in a small town called Udamalpet, gifted to the organization by a wealthy mill owner. There are plans to convert it into a mini-hospital that will focus primarily on cataract surgery. "We should send an e-mail to Dr. V to let him know," says Natchiar, only half-joking. "Do you think he's arranging all of this from wherever he is?" GS's response is terse: "If people have that kind of faith here, that would be a good thing—instead of all the 'I did this, I did that' talk going around." Sore spot. Natchiar winks and says stoutly, "Who says that? Let's give them a piece of our mind!"

Subramaniam drives them up to Aurofarm, situated about 15 minutes away from the hospital and on the same property as Aurolab. Natchiar visits it every day after long hours of work. Twenty different varieties of frangipani trees have been planted close to the entrance. To the right is a garden planted with roses and jasmine. At the far end is a wide lake with stone benches scattered around it. A riot of silk cotton trees, hibiscus bushes, pink bottlebrush trees, waterlilies, bougainvillea, impatiens, and canna lilies dot the landscape. "I love this place because it was designed and executed by amateurs—more than 100 people worked to create this," says Natchiar.

In 2002, in a return to her family's farming roots, she asked her siblings for a piece of earth to cultivate. They laughed her off, but she persisted and was eventually given a few acres on the barren 80-acre property that would house Aurolab's new facility. Under Natchiar's hands-on leadership, Aurofarm blossomed into being. In her typical fashion, she ensured collective participation. All the senior nurses, doctors, and various department heads at Aravind have planted a sapling on this property. Natchiar pauses by the young banyan tree that Dr. V placed in the ground. "He used to come and monitor its progress each evening," she says, smiling. "Why did you pick a banyan tree for me?" Dr. V had asked his sister. "I told him, 'Because even after you and I are gone, the trees that come after us must still be standing strong,'" says Natchiar.

This particular tree is still a scraggly adolescent, but it belongs to a magnificent species. A banyan's outstretched branches eventually drop down tough aerial roots that anchor themselves in the soil over a wide expanse. With time, these woody pillars thicken into a ring of multiple trunks that are nearly identical to the original. In this way, the lifespan of a banyan can outlast centuries.

Natchiar looks across the wide fields of paddy where golden stalks of rice are bent almost to the ground, heavy with grain. "The poets always compared wise men to rice ready for harvest," she murmurs. "The wise, too, carry their gifts with humility." She is very excited about the crop this season. "We will harvest 200 sacks of rice this week. It's a record yield—and all organic!" she says proudly.

Yesterday, Aravind's leadership learned that the organization had won the prestigious Hilton Humanitarian Prize for 2010. At $1.5 million in award money, it is the largest cash prize for social work in the world. Natchiar is certainly pleased with the high honor, but in the week ahead, she will tell far more people about Aurofarm's bumper rice crop.

❧

IN THE PAST few years, the Aravind Eye Care System's visibility has steadily increased. In addition to the Gates Award for Global Health and recognition from the Clinton Global Initiative, Aravind has ties with the World Economic Forum, the Schwab Foundation for Social Entrepreneurship, Skoll Foundation, Acumen Fund, Google.org, and scores of other influential players in the social sector. In 2010, Dr. Nam was featured in *Time* magazine's list of the 100 most influential people in the world. All of this has brought an unaccustomed degree of celebrity to the organization.

The days of obscurity, low salaries, and painfully stretched resources have long been left behind. But Aravind's founders see the changed circumstances as a double-edged sword. They are uncertain about the effects that this era of relative prosperity will have on organizational culture.

"It was our duty to take care of each of Dr. V's visions—one after the other. It gave us such powerful energy," says Natchiar. "The present generation should find new energies, new challenges . . . the only problem is that they don't have financial difficulties." She sighs, smiles, and continues, "From our perspective, we used to have ten meetings to figure out whether or not we could afford to buy a fan. So sometimes we're scared that our conservative approach will be lost, now that we have money."

Thulsi is matter-of-fact in his view of the matter. "It could work both ways. We could become more adventurous; do things with more financial risks. But it's also easy to become extravagant." He pauses and then continues, "For the immediate future, however, I don't see the next generation of leadership becoming wasteful."

But waste is a relative concept. In the summer of 2010, doctors at Aravind asked that vehicles used for rural eye camps be air-conditioned. Not an unreasonable request, given summer temperatures that regularly exceed 104 degrees Fahrenheit. They were successful in their petitioning, but the request set off an alarm among the founders. Dr. Viji talks about the situation with some consternation: "What to do? My word of caution to the young people is that you can't put comfort first. You have to put our values first."

Viji's life had changed dramatically at 18. One morning she was working in the fields alongside her mother when she looked up and saw her brother Nam striding toward her, waving a piece of paper like a flag. It was an application form for medical college that Dr. V had helped procure for her. In that brief instant, a whole new vista of possibility opened up. But like the other founding team members,

Viji never forgot her rural roots or the values of simplicity and thrift that they engendered in her. "This is why we tell our children to keep visiting the villages. You need that experience; otherwise, you live in an artificial world," she says.

To the founders, the good of the institution is inextricably bound up in the welfare of the poorest of those it serves. They don't need to think about it or articulate it; it is bred in their bones. "We need to understand the situation of the common person. This work is about restoring dignity, not just vision. It is important to have that base—if the family doesn't do it, you can't expect others to follow. It's not easy to teach this," says Natchiar. "People used to do things differently when Dr. V was around," observes Viji wistfully. "In Tamil there is a saying: 'like tethered donkeys let loose.' We are like that now. There's a lot of growth now, but that same 'check,' or supervision, isn't there anymore." Her generation harbors an inevitable nostalgia, but it is not the heavy, damaging sort. Viji laughs and adds sincerely, "There are definitely a lot of good things happening, too."

The members of the founding generation know that they carry certain implicit aspects of the model in every fiber of their being, in a way that their children do not. "Sometimes when certain ideas come up, we know very clearly that following them is not the Aravind way. But when the younger generation asks why, I don't have the words to explain it—*I just know*. So it's a bit difficult," admits Natchiar. And yet she and the others are also aware of their own limitations, and the fact that, increasingly, their way of doing things may no longer be in Aravind's best interest. "Things change. Right now we're transitioning. And we're a bit scared about how to hand things over in the right way. To hand over the right amount, at the right time. And of course," says Natchiar, flashing a mischievous grin, "we still need to stick our noses into everything."

Dr. Usha is matter-of-fact about the founding team's rights. "This is their baby, their tree," she says firmly. "They can trim it the way they want. Yes, there will be some differences of opinion. They came up through all these hardships, so for them there is always a fear of extravagance. We were brought up in relative abundance, so for us the mentality is 'When you have it, why not spend it?' We, the next generation, need to make our mistakes while the older generation is around to support us. They should give us a little freedom, and we should pay attention to their advice. Both sides need to give a little."

❧

MEANWHILE, THE ORIGINAL members of the New Age Group, the third generation of Dr. V's family, have just entered the scene. Many are in their 20s and 30s. Half a dozen of them are doctors at various stages of their careers. They struggle to refine their surgical techniques and stay on top of the rigors of postgraduate residency at Aravind, all the while battling the inevitable comparisons with their parents and grandparents. A few have already picked an area of specialization and are working to carve their own niche. Two of the nondoctors, armed with MBAs, have taken on consulting and operations management roles within the organization.

This generation convenes annual retreats to share experiences, concerns, and aspirations, and to collectively explore what it means for them to deepen the values that shaped Aravind. "I remember hearing in the early days, the founding team would bring back fruit, whenever they visited their villages, to share with all the nurses," says Thulsi's daughter (and Aravind surgeon) Dr. Sathya Ravilla at the first retreat of this kind. "They were really close to the whole team. Now that kind of thing doesn't happen because the team is so huge. Now I don't even *know* all the nurses here, let alone connect with them."[1]

Dr. Divya Karthik, a young resident who married into the family, explains how she makes an effort to eat lunch at least once a week with the nurses that support her in the operating room. "If each person makes efforts like that, it will make a difference," she says. Drs. Vivek

Ramakrishnan and Sankar Ravilla, Thulsi's nephews (whose fathers are both deeply respected surgeons at Aravind), are also ophthalmology residents at Aravind. They wish they had more space in which to make mistakes and pick themselves up without attracting such severe censure. Dr. Karthik Srinivasan (Viji and M. Srinivasan's son, who is technically second generation but young enough to be part of the third) laughs and tells them that it is all part of the drill, but to hang in there because "it does get better once you have proved yourself."

The fourth generation of the family also attends monthly meetings of the new New Age Group, now run by Thulsi's eldest daughter, Dhivya Ramasamy. Participation has been broadened to include the children of Aravind staff outside of Dr. V's family as well—a move illustrative of a broadening inner circle. There is an affectionate rapport among all the younger generations, but the truth is, none of them get together nearly as often as the founding team of Aravind did. The increased complexities and pace of modern life, the hectic juggling of work and personal schedules, make it difficult for this large and growing family to congregate on a regular basis.

From the Institute of Family Business in the United States comes a thought-provoking statistic: "Less than one-third of the family businesses will continue to the second generation and less than one-half of those will make it to the third."[2]

Will internal politics weaken family ties, three generations removed from the era of Dr. V? What does it take for a family-run organization to hold together under the multiple pressures of expansion, succession, competition, and changing management trends?

Will scale dilute the values and culture? Will the emphasis subtly switch from the greater good to self-interest? Will financial resources negatively impact decision making? Will the strong sense of connection to the rural communities be lost?

For the future, these and other disconcerting questions hang in the air. Things that were once black and white at Aravind are dissolving into many shades of gray. In this period, everything from Aravind's leadership structure, organizational model, and priority areas to its guiding principles and core beliefs is being thrown in the balance. The organization will need to decide what parts to retain, what to refashion, and what to jettison entirely.

It has never been more imperative for Aravind's leaders to attempt a deeper exploration of Dr. V's compassionate vision.

# TWENTY ONE

# A PLACE TO PRACTICE TRUTH

As Dr. Nam and the other founders announced plans to step back from active leadership, it became obvious that a new executive head for the Aravind Eye Care System had to be named and a new structure designed for upper management. But there was no clear plan for how to do so.

Dr. Kim Ramaswamy is the eldest doctor in the second generation of the family. As the question of succession moved to the fore, he had a discomfiting sense that if an answer was not found soon, Aravind would fall into a period of gradual indifference and disintegration. So in 2009, he wrote to the one person he was confident could help: Fred Munson, Aravind's longtime friend and advisor. He requested Munson to make a special trip to Madurai to facilitate the family's transition plan. Kim knew this transition would be a major inflection point for the organization, and he wanted the process to inform the family's shared understanding and to reinforce its sense of collective stewardship.

"Are you sure you want me to come?" Munson asked, unsure if his facilitation at such a sensitive period would be useful. "Yes, we absolutely do," Kim responded.[1] "The founding team and all of the second generation are in unanimous agreement." The Munsons are in their 80s. The long transatlantic flight that they had made with ease so many times over the decades had become increasingly taxing. "We're getting business-class tickets for you and Mary," Kim said. "You can't do that for both of us," Munson objected. "In that case, we're just fly-ing Mary over," came Kim's response. Munson chuckled and eventu-ally gave in. Sometimes you just do not argue with family.

THE MUNSONS FLEW to Madurai in early 2010. Their daughter, Meg, also a longtime Aravind volunteer, accompanied them. When they ran into the founding team in Aravind's corridors the next day, the hugs and teasing were immediate. Dr. Natchiar said gleefully, "Fred, I know you're here to make me retire—well, I beat you to it! I've already an-nounced I'm doing that!" The hallway rang with laughter so loud that Dr. Aravind stepped out of his office to see what the commotion was about. A few minutes later, GS stuck his head around the corner to say with a mock scowl, "Shhh!" adding, "Fred, don't think you can make *me* leave."

It is a longstanding joke between them. Ever since Munson medi-ated the transition that effectively "retired the saint," Aravind's found-ing team has playfully accused him of being on a mission to "get rid of all the old folk." He enjoys this banter as much as they do.

Supported by Meg, Fred conducted a series of in-depth personal interviews with the leaders across all five of Aravind's hospitals, as well as LAICO and Aurolab. He moderated separate group discus-sions with the two generations that brought to the surface their most pressing concerns. The founding team's great fear was that the next generation would not be able to work together as a strongly united force. The second generation was chiefly wary of being handed only figurehead leadership.

Munson moderated a nomination process for the chief executive post with the second generation. After candid discussions of the pit-falls and possibilities of this era in the organization's lifespan, it was evident that whoever was selected for the chief executive role would be inheriting Aravind at perhaps the most complex and precarious point in its history. Nobody was falling over his or her feet for the responsibility.

What followed was a round of "Not I." "Kim, Prajna, Aravind, Ramakrishnan, and Narendran all said they didn't want it or couldn't do it," says Munson, reeling off a list of senior doctors in the family. They each felt that they were too young or temperamentally unsuited or weighed down by current responsibilities. None of the second-generation women had been considered (or considered themselves) as serious candidates. Thulsi, who had always played a bridge role between the founders and the second generation, voluntarily dropped off the ballot as well, in deference to some people's preference to have the role filled (as it historically always had been) by an ophthalmologist.

It was a process of self-elimination, which according to Munson was carried out not in the spirit of ducking responsibility but rather with genuine openness, mutual respect for each other's individual strengths, and a growing sense of solidarity. After several lengthy rounds of discussion, the buck finally and decisively stopped with one of Thulsi's younger brothers: Dr. R. D. Ravindran.

IN SOME WAYS, Ravi (as he is called) was the dark horse candidate in this nonrace. He was not one of the most visible faces or established brand ambassadors of the Aravind model, and he had certainly never sought out the spotlight. But he was the man who had without protest uprooted his life and that of his family every single time Aravind built a new hospital. As its in-house start-up specialist and a brilliant doctor, he has vast hands-on experience in the art and science of building and replicating hospitals. In a 1989 journal entry, Dr. V (who had never been one to praise his own or his family's gifts) had written prophetically, *Dr. Ravi has a great potential for growth to International Heights.*

Over a span of 30 years, Ravi's work took him from Madurai into the rural locale of Theni, then to the bustling town of Tirunelveli, followed by the industrial city of Coimbatore and later the cultural melting pot of Pondicherry. As a result, Ravi came to know, better than anyone else, the neural network of each Aravind hospital. He developed relationships with staff across all of them and quietly proved his strength as a leader in each diverse location. And now he was being summoned to headquarters, back to Madurai, where it had all begun. Only the previous day, he had shaken his head and told Munson that he just could not see himself taking on the directorship of Aravind.

But something in the democratic process, the honest conversations, and the unanimous chorus of voices in the room that supported his nomination changed his mind. It was clear that whatever the challenges ahead, he would face them with the larger family firmly united behind him. "The founding team, too, was delighted with Ravi's nomination as Nam's successor," says Munson. "He has qualities they really trust. So he had their support from the get-go." Another facet of this process was especially important to the founding team: "They were so pleased that the youngsters had demonstrated they could think things through collectively," Munson says.

Follow-up discussions between the two generations also made clear the need for a more decentralized and democratic management structure. New positions were created and second-generation leaders were nominated to drive system-wide functions in the areas of education, finance, information technology, quality, operations, human resources, new projects, and expansion. A central senior management team was instituted that comprised all hospital heads across the Aravind Eye Care System. These changes aspired to move beyond a Madurai-centric mode to equal representation from across the system. The discussions also yielded a more clearly defined decision-making process and a move to include more nonfamily members in influential roles.

"We are building on the earlier foundation," says Prajna (who in the new scheme of things has taken on directorship of Aravind's education programs as well as its finances). "We want more people contributing and feeling a part of Aravind—not just three or four core members of the family. This requires a lot of letting go," he says. And then, with a smile that delights in his own irreverence, Prajna makes a fervent declaration: "I love letting go."

☙

"Our major challenge, if you ask me, is the fact that the decibel level outside is a lot higher than it was 30 years ago when Dr. V started this organization," says Dr. Aravind thoughtfully. With the management restructuring, he is now the organization's director of new projects and expansion. "When you have a lot of external noise, focus becomes that much harder."

Rampant activity in commercial eye care is part of the "noise" he is referring to. In the last few years, Vasan Eye Care, a private specialty hospital group in India, has expanded to more than 60 strategically placed eye care facilities across India. Catering solely to paying patients, and backed by Sequoia Capital and other global investors, it announced, in early 2011, plans to raise $100 million in private equity funding to expand its network to an additional 50 centers spread across India, as well as a dozen overseas locations. Eye-Q, another Indian company, made a parallel announcement of its own meteoric plans to open 100 eye hospitals in India within the next five years.[2] The market that Aravind helped create is filling up with corporate players.

These new enterprises not only are competitive employers but are also zeroing in on the paying end of the spectrum, which fuels Aravind's cross-subsidies. While alert to the threat, Aravind's leaders are not frenzied by it. "It feels like we're running in a race right now," says Dr. Aravind, "but we have to remember that once upon a time, this organization helped shape *the entire ecosystem* for this race."

The frustration that edged his voice a little less than a year ago is no longer there. He is still as energetic and full of ideas as ever, but a subtle shift has taken place that puts the emphasis not on speed but on direction. "Right now, we can't just run. We need to think of how we can shape the ecosystem further."

❧

RAVI AND HIS TEAM would distill the organization's expansion philosophy, and by the dawn of 2011, the internal clash with the founders over approaches to growth was not nearly as pronounced as it had been just a year ago. They decided that serving the poor and the not-so-poor in a way that creates synergistic value is an integral, nonnegotiable part of the model. There is no longer talk of targeting metropolitan cities for expansion or splitting up free and paying facilities. Ravi is crystal-clear about the latter. "Serving a broad economic spectrum is what drives our success," he says. "Everyone feels like they can come here. Aravind is a hospital for the community. We have to retain that spirit."

Two hundred million people in India require some form of eye care. While access to cataract treatment has rapidly increased, tens of millions of people still suffer from glaucoma, diabetic retinopathy (DR), acute low vision, and simple refractive errors. These fields have not matured across the low end of the market in the way that cataract has and are not the focus of existing care providers. Ravi sums up Aravind's priorities succinctly: "We need to be where the real need is." Thulsi echoes this idea: "We have to use our financial independence to enter underserved areas that are less attractive to other players in the field." With this mindset of continuing to focus on the work that remains to be done, the organization has launched hundreds of targeted screening programs in schools and factories. In an effort to boost public awareness, it also runs specialized programs focused exclusively on leading eye diseases like glaucoma and DR.

The Aravind Eye Care System is now working to build a series of eye care hubs that will vary in size and scope, depending on the needs of different localities. These hubs will cover a wide spectrum of care, from modest vision centers all the way to full-blown teaching eye hospitals offering multiple specialties.

The organization is targeting regions where it has large, existing patient bases. "For instance, we found that more than 10 percent of our outpatient load in Madurai was traveling to us from a small town called Dindigul about an hour away," says Thulsi. "So we decided to construct a facility there."

Under this growth model, a 50-bed Aravind hospital in Dindigul was opened in 2010, and within months another one of similar size was opened in a town called Tirupur. Both of these hospitals are in Aravind's home state of Tamil Nadu. By 2011, following a similar vetting process, plans were on for opening two more full-scale tertiary eye hospitals as well as two more surgical centers. "Local access" is the new catch-phrase at Aravind. The organization now operates centers of varying sizes across 50 different locations, all in the state of Tamil Nadu.

A surprising number of patients from neighboring states choose to make the long trek to Aravind for cataract treatment. Notable among them is a man who in 1995 brought both of his nearly blind parents to Aravind. They traveled over 300 miles from their home in the southern state of Andhra Pradesh just to get to Aravind. Both parents regained their sight after successful cataract operations. Their son, Rangasamy, was so moved by the care they received that he began to organize weekly train trips to Aravind for different sets of poor cataract patients from his region. On all these trips, he or one of his ten handpicked volunteers personally escorted the groups to Aravind and back.

"Over 15 years, his efforts directly mobilized over 150,000 patient visits from across the state of Andhra Pradesh," says Thulsi.

Thousands more from Andhra Pradesh showed up as the word spread. "Now we're actively looking to acquire land to build a hospital in that state and save these communities travel time and cost," Thulsi says, but admits he does not know how quickly this will happen.

"Our pace of growth is pretty sedate when compared to our corporate counterparts," says Dr. Aravind. "That's the reality of our model right now. We're only moving at the rate at which we can still retain our value system." As the organization fans out across a multitude of small towns, the speed of growth is checked by the Aravind leadership's self-imposed constraints around human resources.

"As a rule, 80 percent of the employees that staff our new centers are transferred from existing positions in our older hospitals," says Dr. Aravind. "We don't just recruit a fresh bunch of people." This insistence on an inculcation period and in-house experience is a clear indicator of where the organization places the most emphasis. "Our model hinges on a value-driven approach," says Ravi, "and it takes time to create a workforce that is tuned to that."

The leadership also recognizes that it might be making excuses for itself. "People ask us all the time why we don't expand faster," says Thulsi. "Money isn't a real bottleneck. We have resources of our own and could also raise capital. The bigger part of it really is a mindset issue. For us, expanding in this mode is a comfortable, fail-safe approach."

Ravi makes a similar confession. "Right now, we lack confidence to step outside what we know," he says. "We feel like we haven't cracked how to draw in the right kind of people and train them faster than what we already are doing." And as Natchiar is quick to point out, "It's not about merely increasing the number of trainees we recruit. We don't want to have too many people hanging around just because we need them for a hospital sometime down the line. Our work culture doesn't operate like that."

The founders' insistence on high productivity and low tolerance for slack yields cost-saving and efficiency benefits, but on the flip side, it also contributes to burnout and the sense that working at Aravind takes over one's life. Aware of this tendency, leaders in the second generation are ramping up their efforts to create a more vibrant and balanced environment for employees. What Prajna is attempting to do for doctors, Dr. Usha is driving for other core staff. She leads proactive initiatives for Aravind's nurses and other paraprofessionals. The organization has raised their salaries to be more competitive with the market; has designed more explicit career tracks for them; and also provides them with opportunities for ancillary training in computer applications, spoken English, and communications.

USHA'S OWN PARTICULAR area of passion is ocular oncology—cancer of the eye. Though India has one of the world's highest incidences of retinoblastoma (the most common ocular cancer), it is not a high-volume specialty area. She sees fewer than 100 new cases of this each year, most of them young children and the vast majority from poor families. Awareness of eye tumors is rare in the community, and pediatric checkups are nonexistent among the poor in India. Many patients are brought to her at an advanced stage when their tumors are already life threatening. The parents of these children are often daily wage laborers who are initially disbelieving, later heartbroken, when they hear the seriousness of the condition. Usha and her team quickly become their refuge.

Cancer of the eye lacks the elegant solution of cataract. More times than Usha cares to remember, her patients' eyes have been removed in order to protect their lives. "Initially we didn't have the facilities to administer chemotherapy in-house," she says. "I had to ask repeated favors of oncologists in the community." Being so dependent on external resources did not sit well with her. In 2004, Usha decided to build these capabilities within Aravind. To support the effort, the organization launched the Ring of Hope Fund, inviting donations toward this cause. In the case of Usha's cancer patients, Aravind covers the cost of surgical treatment, medical staff, accommodation, and food, while money from the Ring of Hope fund covers the cost of chemotherapy and radiation treatment.

Hundreds of children and adults have received treatment and had not just their eyes but also, in many cases, their lives saved through this initiative. Though this work does not neatly fit into Aravind's high-volume, high-quality, low-cost model, in the view of Usha and many others, it is a vital and important part of Aravind's mission of providing compassionate and comprehensive eye care to those in need.

THE NEW LEADERSHIP soon discovered that in light of the organization's potential, Aravind's traditional stance on self-reliance could often feel pointlessly restrictive. "They were torn between their legacy of independence and self-sustainability and the enormous possibilities posed by the breadth of their work," says ophthalmologist Christine Melton.

Christine has volunteered with Aravind ever since her 1983 visit to its hospital in Madurai as a short-term resident. Her passionate resonance with Dr. V's vision led her to take charge of the Aravind Eye Foundation (AEF), a U.S.-based nonprofit that serves as the organization's link to resources, training, and partnerships in the United States. As president of AEF, Christine experienced Aravind's deep ambivalence toward external funding firsthand. It restricted the scope, sometimes to a frustrating degree, of what was possible for AEF. "A lot was being done, but the sheer unrealized potential of our platform was huge," she says.

Even though the founding team had engaged in several projects with external support, they had always exhibited a deep reluctance to explicitly enter the domain of fund-raising. To them, the word itself carried uncomfortable connotations. In 2011, leaders from Aravind and AEF held a series of discussions tackling the issues of donated funds head-on.

"Basically, everyone agreed that for core operations and all our new hospital growth, we needed to stay entirely self-funded," says Thulsi. Patient revenue was to be protected for these purposes. But for pilot initiatives, advocacy efforts in the field of blindness prevention, and collaborations in product development at Aurolab, Aravind's leadership was much more comfortable with the idea of inviting donations. It was agreed that AEF would focus on raising funds for important but experimental projects that pushed the boundaries of the model or more indirectly contributed to Aravind's mission.

Today, AEF actively raises seed money for new vision centers and for honing new service delivery models (in areas like diabetic retinopathy). It also looks to fund scholarships for researchers in eye care and to help scale LAICO's consulting services to more developing-world hospitals. While doing all of this, in deference to Aravind's founding spirit, it continues to steer clear of fund-raising through the traditional modes of charitable benefit events, mass media advertising, and untargeted solicitations.

The new leadership has articulated management policies around many other matters that the founding team dealt with intuitively. But even so, not everything in the system has clear edges and tidy definitions. The leadership's inner discernment still has a role to play. "There is no magic law to the way we do things here," says Natchiar briskly. "Some of it's traditional; some of it's modern. Some of it's independent; some of it's collaboration. Some of it's conservative; some of it is risky. We are cautious and conscious and a lot of different things mixed together." And as for pace? "It's really not about what you see," she says. "Sometimes we move fast; sometimes we move slowly. The wisdom of that depends on what's in the heart and mind."

◯

A YOUNG PUBLIC HEALTH expert accustomed to number crunching once asked Dr. V's mentor Sir John Wilson how many blind people there were in the world. As the story goes, Wilson turned the full intensity of his sightless blue gaze on the questioner and let a few moments elapse. Then he said gently, "My friend, people go blind one at a time." One. At. A. Time."

It is a Friday evening, and Ravi, as Aravind's new director, is addressing a group of 400 of its nurses, refractionists, counselors, and other paraprofessionals. He makes a point of facilitating interaction between the organization's leadership and the core of Aravind's workforce. Today he shares the story of a recent patient.

"Shailaja, like most of you, is a young woman in her 20s from a nearby village," he says.[3] "Her parents were killed in a road accident when she was just a baby. Now she's a brick laborer who lives with her grandmother." Ravi goes on to describe a recent construction site accident that left Shailaja blind in both eyes. "Obviously, she could no longer work. The loss of income meant that she and her grandmother had no money for food. They were literally starving." In a few poignant sentences, Ravi describes how the helplessness of their situation drove the two women to seriously contemplate suicide.

"The very next day, a rickshaw blaring announcements rolled through their village," he says. "It was announcing one of our upcoming eye camps." The room is in deep silence as he speaks. At the Aravind camp, the examining doctor discovered trauma-induced cataract in both of Shailaja's eyes. She was taken to the base hospital with a busload of other patients. In less than a week, both of her eyes were successfully operated on. "Now imagine what that meant to her," he says. "She and her grandmother could not stop thanking the doctors and nurses for what they had done—for what *all* of you do."

Aravind's hospitals see thousands of patients every day. It is easy to get lost in the day-to-day work of testing people's vision, administering eyedrops, reciting fee structures, recording case sheets, and so on. It is easy to forget that in each of these actions lies a powerful contribution. "We shouldn't lose touch with the difference that our collective everyday efforts make," says Ravi.

Part of the beauty of Dr. V's approach was his deep recognition that as central as the tenets of high volume, sustainability, and affordability are to this model, eliminating curable blindness is not just about numbers. "It is about reaching people," says Natchiar, "in a *human* way."

RAVI ACCEPTED NEWS of his nomination to Aravind's highest post with few illusions. He was aware of the complexities of the position and the immense responsibilities that accompanied it. But when he speaks of the work that lies ahead and of what values must be held central, he speaks without hesitation. His perspective is clear and surprising in its emphasis on spiritual underpinnings.

"Dr V's goodwill wasn't just for his family and his staff—it extended to the whole society. His spirit created a shield around us and the organization. How long will that shield be there?" he asks. "Probably for a little while, and then it will start to disappear—unless we do something. In the next ten years, we're entering a time when the materialistic part of India will peak. Our challenge is: how do we be modern and still retain inner simplicity? We have to learn to balance. As leaders, we have to be simple, and a few of us must practice at this level. The material support that we give people shouldn't be our focus. At a policy level, yes, we have to implement certain changes:

raise salaries, strengthen retention, give people intellectual opportunities for research, and that kind of thing, but the focus should be on the inner aspiration."

At Aravind–Madurai, the light is on in Dr. V's old office and the door is open. The room has remained untouched for the five years since his passing. All the familiar landmarks are still there—the bursting bookshelves, the world map on the wall, the special backrest on his office chair. On his desk are the paperweights he used to anchor the wide pages of *Savitri* as he read from Sri Aurobindo's epic. Fresh flowers have been placed on the low shelf in front of the poised gray stone statue of the Buddha. There is also a picture of Dr. V taken in this very room, his arms resting wide on the desk, a radiant smile lighting his face.

The room holds a stillness and presence that are palpable, but it is not destined to become a shrine. At Natchiar's insistence (and to Ravi's initial dismay), it has been decided that the new director will occupy Dr. V's office on the ground floor of Aravind–Madurai. Ravi will soon move in.

Though they each carry a part of his legacy, not everyone in the second and third generations at Aravind has inherited Dr. V's strong conviction about the importance of internal transformation and its links to the work they do. And yet together they have selected as the organization's next leader a person who sees this connection as an essential part of Aravind's purpose.

"People who come here to write business studies get fascinated by the numbers—millions of patients, hundreds of thousands of surgeries, financial sustainability, and all that. But what matters is the human touch," says Ravi. "Our patients feel this. I don't know how. But when we talk to them, we don't have that mentality of, 'How do we get more money from this person?' There's some vibration to that kind of interaction," he says thoughtfully. "See, the problem of blindness is going to be eliminated. It's just a matter of time. At Aravind, unless we practice certain things, people won't see what differentiates us from the rest. Through Dr. V's work, Aravind has emerged as a place where you can practice the truth. Through Aravind, he created an external manifestation for an inner aspiration. He ensured that there is a soul behind the systems and procedures.

"New leadership should not just look at Aravind's work as the elimination of needless blindness," he adds. "That is the outer goal. But there is an inner goal. We must not do the outer work at the cost of that inner goal. We have to maintain Aravind as a place where people can express their true nature. We shouldn't forget this." Ravi's words, delivered in his unassuming way, shine like a beacon. In this moment, he sounds very much like Dr. V.

# DEATH'S QUESTION

It was an early morning in the summer of 2004. As had been our custom for many years, I was reading aloud from Sri Aurobindo's *Savitri* to Dr. V—or Dr. Thatha, as we in the third generation always called him. *Thatha* is Tamil for "grandfather." The day's passage was a conversation between Yama, the God of Death, and the princess Savitri. The long, flowing lines were dense with imagery, and I unconsciously began to read a little faster, not waiting for my mind to catch up to the meaning of the words. "Wait, wait, Pavithra," said Dr. V—who reminded me on more than one occasion that *Savitri* was meant to be read as if there were a *laddoo* (a round Indian sweet) in your mouth. He bent his head to the page before him and repeated with gentle deliberation a line that I had rushed through: "Wilt thou claim immortality, O heart?" And then, in a moment I will never forget, he looked up and said with his signature chuckle:

"Yes!"

IT HAS NOW been seven years since that reading. Dr. Aravind is scheduled to operate today and cannot be late. He is walking while he talks. "Dr. V started all this at 58," he says, shaking his head. "In his own lifetime, this man did a little over 100,000 surgeries. And now his organization does 300,000 operations a year. Think about that. With every passing year, Dr. V's direct contribution is multiplied three times over because of the seeds he planted. Then there's Aurolab, producing two million lenses a year, and LAICO, that has trained thousands of health professionals across the globe." He stops short at the entrance to the operating room. "The way I look at it, this one man's work probably touches 40 percent of eye care in the developing world today."

Madurai is famed as the city of temples. Scattered through the maze of its local streets and along the city's outskirts are many ancient sites of worship. Dr. V loved these temples. He was fond of pointing out that the most celebrated among them, the Meenakshi Amman temple, whose proud towers stud the skyline of this city, was not the work of a single ruler. It was a creation of dedication, ingenuity, and selflessness that spanned multiple generations. And the result is a transcendent gift to the world. According to Dr. V, it could be the same with institutions. This was part of his aspiration for Aravind, and because of it, he held himself and his team to a set of powerful, unwritten directives.

*Stay rooted in compassion.* In many ways, the ingenuity of Aravind's model traces back to this deceptively simple commitment. Skillfully channeled, compassion can drive and dictate inclusion, equality, efficiency, excellence, and scale. It can do this in such a way that each of these elements reinforces the others and strengthens the whole. When combined, it creates a finely tuned system that benefits all.

*Serve and deserve.* The austere constraint of self-reliance that Dr. V imposed on Aravind unleashed hidden reserves. When the core of your energy and attention is focused on serving unconditionally, the boundaries of your perception shift. You discover value and relevance in unexpected places. The work acquires a magnetic, generative force. It builds trust and goodwill. It sustains and aligns resources with the mission in ways that money alone cannot.

*Create a movement, not dominance.* Early on, Aravind recognized the wisdom of training the competition. Hoarding expertise limits impact. Sharing your strengths amplifies the effect of the work many-fold. It inspires higher standards, broad participation, and vibrant cross-learning. It extends your reach to new shores. You build a resilient brand based on relationships and mutual respect that has little to do with an advertising budget. In this way, you tap into collective possibilities that far surpass proprietary efforts.

*Practice for perfect vision.* This in essence was what Dr. V always returned to. He believed that the evolution of an organization ultimately hinges on the evolution of the individuals within it. And that clarity in thought and action requires a discipline of mind and heart. He believed that when you sharpen in self-awareness and commit to pushing the boundaries of your compassion, you tap into a deeper wisdom that informs and transforms your work. You become a more conscious instrument of your highest calling.

"Sometimes powerful, higher forces act on your life. At these times you must try and be still, because otherwise they cannot stay," said Dr. V in a reflective moment. "You must step back and stay calm . . . and you must take time to see the sky."

OUTWARDLY, VERY LITTLE has remained still at Aravind. The broader contextual shifts in India are matched by the surging energy and aspirations of the organization's new generation of leaders. With a series of global awards, growing international responsibilities in policymaking, and increasing attention from national health care systems around the world seeking to learn from its work, Aravind is poised on the crest of a powerful wave.

Over the decades, it has shown the world what is possible when we join the best knowledge and tools of our age with timeless principles, or as Aravind's founder put it, if "we can combine modern technology and management with spiritual practice." To Dr. V, that combination paved the way for a much deeper goal, one that left nothing and no one out.

"*When we grow in spiritual consciousness,*" said Dr. V, "*we identify with all that is in the world. And there is no exploitation. It is ourselves we are helping. It is ourselves we are healing.*"

THAT SINGULAR VOICE has long since fallen silent. On this particular day, dusk drifts softly into Madurai. The lingering light slants across rooftops, gilding windowpanes and illuminating preoccupied faces on the streets. Behind Aravind a silver cloud stretches its fingers, each edged in bright gold, over the hospital—a radiant sign that seems in this moment both a blessing, and a promise.

# RESOURCES

◇◇◇◇◇◇◇◇◇◇◇◇◇◇◇◇◇◇◇

## OVERVIEW OF THE ARAVIND EYE CARE SYSTEM

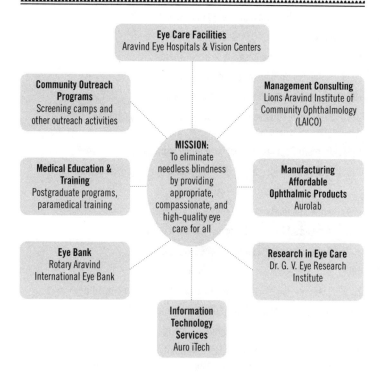

## A DAY IN THE LIFE OF ARAVIND . . .

- ❧ 7,500 total outpatient visits
- ❧ 850–1,000 surgeries performed
- ❧ 5–6 outreach camps conducted
    - ❧ 1,500 patients examined
    - ❧ 300 patients transported to base hospitals for surgery
- ❧ 500–600 telemedicine consultations conducted
- ❧ 7,000 intraocular lenses produced
- ❧ Classes held for 100 doctors, 300 paraprofessionals, and administrators

## ARAVIND EYE CARE SYSTEM MILESTONES

1918: Dr. V is born October 1 in Vadamalapuram, Tamil Nadu, India.

1976: Dr. V retires after over 20 years in government service, and Aravind starts as an 11-bed clinic in a rented house in Madurai.

1981: Aravind reaches 10,000 surgeries a year.

1985: Aravind's second hospital opens in Theni.

1988: Aravind's third hospital opens in Tirunelveli.

1991: Aravind reaches 50,000 surgeries a year.

1992: Aurolab is founded to manufacture high-quality ophthalmic products at affordable prices.

1993: Harvard Business School case study published.

1996: LAICO is founded as an international training and consulting institute.

1996: Aravind reaches 100,000 surgeries a year.

1997: Aravind's fourth hospital opens in Coimbatore.

2003: Aravind's fifth hospital opens in Pondicherry.

2003: Aravind reaches 200,000 surgeries a year.

2006: Dr. V passes away at Aravind–Madurai on July 7.

2008: Inauguration of Dr. G. Venkataswamy Eye Research Institute.

2009: Aravind reaches 300,000 surgeries a year.

2010: Aravind opens surgery centers in Dindigul and Tirupur, Tamil Nadu.

2011: The Dr. G. Venkataswamy Memorial Building is inaugurated as a retreat center, and Aravind's sixth hospital is scheduled to open in Salem, Tamil Nadu.

### RECENT AWARDS

2007: Aravind receives the Antonio Champalimaud Vision Award.

2008: Aravind receives the Gates Award for Global Health.

2010: Aravind's Dr. Namperumalsamy named one of *Time*'s 100 Most Influential People.

2010: Aravind receives the Conrad N. Hilton Humanitarian Prize.

# ARAVIND FEE STRUCTURE AND PATIENT BREAKDOWN*

## CONSULTATION FEE** FOR PAYING PATIENTS:

- Rs. 50 (~$1)
- Valid for 3 months or 3 visits, whichever occurs first

### CATARACT SURGERY PRICING

| Surgery Type | Rates ($) |
|---|---|
| Free | – |
| Minimal Payment | 11–17 |
| Regular | 111–178 |
| Premium | 204–1,044 |

### PATIENT % BY FEE TYPE

| | |
|---|---|
| Free | 27% |
| Minimal Payment | 26% |
| Regular & Premium | 47% |

*Surgery rates include accommodation costs. Difference between regular and premium lies in choice of lens implant and choice of accommodation. Source: Aravind Eye Care System. All data from 2010.

**No consultation fee for free and minimal payment patients.

## ARAVIND OUTPATIENT VOLUME

Aravind now sees more than 2.5 million patients a year.
Total outpatient visits as of May 2011: 32,838,879.

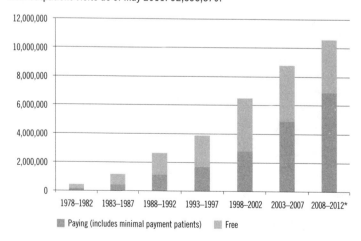

Paying (includes minimal payment patients)    Free

Note: In recent years, Aravind has been seeing an increase in patients electing paid instead of free services.
Source: Aravind Eye Care System.
*2012 data projected.

## ARAVIND SURGICAL VOLUME

Aravind now performs more than 300,000 surgeries per year.
Total surgeries as of May 2011: 4,035,582.

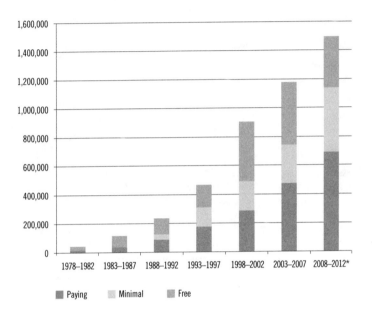

Source: Aravind Eye Care System.
*2012 data projected.

## SURGEON PRODUCTIVITY: A U.S.–INDIA COMPARISON

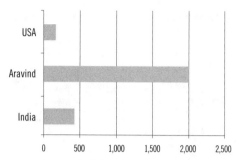

Average number of cataract surgeries per eye surgeon per year

Source: India and Aravind: Naazneen Karmali, "Aravind Eye Care's Vision for India," *Forbes Asia* (March 2010).
USA: U.S. Census Bureau, 2011 Statistical Abstract of the United States: Number of ophthalmologists,
/www.census.gov/compendia/statab/cats/health_nutrition.html,
www.cdc.gov/nchs/pressroom/09newsreleases/outpatientsurgeries.htm.

## ARAVIND'S REVENUES AND EXPENSES (1980–2010)

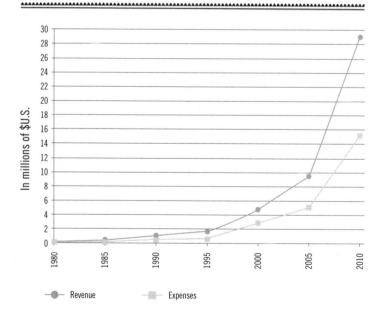

Source: Aravind Eye Care System.

## SURGICAL QUALITY: ARAVIND VS. UNITED KINGDOM

▲▲▲▲▲▲▲▲▲▲▲▲▲▲▲▲▲▲▲▲▲▲▲▲▲▲▲▲▲▲▲▲▲▲▲▲▲▲▲▲▲▲▲▲▲▲▲▲▲▲▲▲▲▲▲▲▲▲▲▲▲▲▲▲▲▲▲▲▲▲▲▲▲▲▲▲▲▲

A comparative study showed that in the majority of complications, Aravind's rates were lower than the UK's.

### ADVERSE EVENTS DURING SURGERY

| Event | Aravind–Coimbatore N = 22,912 | UK National Survey N = 18,472 |
|---|---|---|
| Capsule rupture and vitreous loss | 2.00% | 4.40% |
| Wounds | 0.30% | 0.25% |
| Vitreous to section | 0.10% | 0.30% |
| Incomplete cortical cleanup | 0.75% | 1.00% |
| Iris trauma | 0.30% | 0.70% |
| Persistent iris prolapse | 0.01% | 0.07% |
| Anterior chamber collapse | 0.30% | 0.50% |
| Endophthalmitis | 0.05% | 0.03% |
| Corneal edema | 8.00% | 9.00% |
| Loss of nuclear fragment into vitreous | 0.20% | 0.30% |
| Uveitis more than expected | 5.00% | 5.60% |
| Hypopyon | 0.04% | 0.02% |
| Choroidal hemorrhage | — | 0.07% |
| Loss of intraocular lens into vitreous | 0.01% | 0.16% |
| Periocular bruising and edema more than expected | 1.00% | 1.40% |
| Weak leak/rupture | 0.67% | 1.20% |
| Hyphema | 0.90% | 1.10% |
| Retained lens material | 0.87% | 1.10% |
| Other* | 0.70% | 1.50% |

*Other includes iris abnormality, intraocular lens dislocation, choroiditis, optic neuropathy, and capsule opacity.

Source: Aravind Eye Care System. The data provided by Aravind came to public notice by its inclusion in C. K. Prahalad, *The Fortune at the Bottom of the Pyramid.*

# TRANSFERRING THE ARAVIND MODEL AROUND THE WORLD

LAICO has consulted for 60 hospitals in 29 countries and 213 hospitals in India.

**GLOBAL REACH**

| Countries Covered | |
|---|---|
| Bangladesh | Kenya |
| Bulgaria | Malawi |
| Bolivia | Maldives |
| Botswana | Mexico |
| Cambodia | Nepal |
| Cameroon | Nigeria |
| China | Paraguay |
| Congo | Rwanda |
| Egypt | South Africa |
| El Salvador | Sri Lanka |
| Eritrea | Tanzania |
| Ethiopia | Tibet |
| Finland | Zambia |
| Guatemala | Zimbabwe |
| Indonesia | |

**REACH WITHIN INDIA**

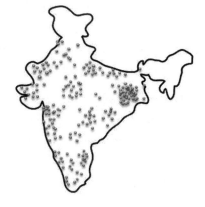

Source: LAICO, Aravind Eye Care System.

# Meet the Family

## First Generation

GOVINDAPPA VENKATASWAMY (DR. V)—Founder, Aravind Eye Care System. He started Aravind as a post-retirement project with no money, business plan, or safety net. His dream: to rid the world of curable blindness.

NALLAKRISHNAN AND MEENAKSHI—Nallakrishnan is Dr. V's brother and an engineer-turned-businessman. He and his wife were founding members (along with all of Dr. V's other siblings and their spouses) of the trust that runs Aravind. Children: Geetha, Ravi N., Murali.

JANAKY AND RAMASWAMY—Janaky, Dr. V's sister, was the maternal force that nurtured the whole family through the intensity of Aravind's founding years. Her quiet, kindly husband was also a pillar of support. Children: Varalakshmi, Chitra R., Kannamma, Kim.

G. SRINIVASAN (GS) AND LALITHA S.—G. Srinivasan is Dr. V's brother and was Aravind's director of buildings and finance for over 30 years. He is known for his stern, no-nonsense approach and astounding ability to control costs. His wife, Lalitha S., helped care for Dr. V through the many decades that he lived with them. Children: Kalpana, Aravind S.

G. NATCHIAR AND NAMPERUMALSAMY (NAM)—Natchiar is Dr. V's younger sister. She is a neuro-ophthalmologist with formidable organizational awareness, beloved for her tidal generosity. Her husband, Nam, one of India's leading retinal surgeons, is the visionary who drove Aravind's foray into research and technology for eye care. Children: Prajna, Vishnu.

P. VIJAYALAKSHMI (VIJI) AND M. SRINIVASAN (MS)—Viji is Nam's sister and the gentle chief of pediatric services at Aravind. She was the first doctor to join Dr. V full time. Her husband, MS, is the straight-shooting director of Aravind's cornea services, deeply admired for his teaching and surgical prowess. Children: Vivek S., Karthik.

R. DURAISAMY AND CHELLAMMA—R. Duraisamy was Aurolab's one-man marketing team for years and helped build the early network of distributors for its high-quality, affordable ophthalmic products. Neither he nor Chellamma is a sibling of the founding team, but their four children all joined Aravind. Children: Thulsi, Ravi, Sriram, and Saradha.

## Second Generation

BALA AND VARALAKSHMI—Bala is a founding member and the managing director of Aurolab, Aravind's manufacturing plant that radically shifted what was possible for eye care delivery in the developing world. Varalakshmi, Dr. V's niece, is the head of Aravind's Catering and Hospitality Department. Children: Pavithra, Deepa.

THULSI AND CHITRA R.—Thulsi was a pivotal early architect of the Aravind model and is now the executive director of LAICO, Aravind's global consulting institute. Chitra R., Dr. V's niece, is the head of Aravind's publishing division. Children: Dhivya R., Sathya.

R. D. RAVINDRAN (RAVI) AND KANNAMMA—Thulsi's brother Ravi is an eye surgeon, the current head of AECS, and famed as Aravind's start-up specialist. Every time a new hospital was built, he and Kannamma, Dr. V's niece, were transferred there to help run and stabilize it. Children: Sankar, Ram Sudharshan.

R. RAMAKRISHNAN (RK) AND SARADHA—RK was the reluctant administrator, mentored far beyond his own aspirations by Dr. V. He is a glaucoma specialist and the director of Aravind–Tirunelveli, where Saradha, Thulsi's sister, assists with administration. Children: Vivek R., Vignesh.

SRIRAM AND MAHALAKSHMI—Sriram is Thulsi's youngest brother and the even-tempered director of operations at Aurolab. Mahalakshmi works with the Artificial Eye Center at Aravind. Children: Prabhu Krishna, Subhashree.

KIM AND USHA—Kim, Dr. V's nephew, is chief of retinal services and chief medical officer of Aravind–Madurai. Usha heads the Orbit and Oculoplasty Department and oversees Aravind's massive paraprofessional program. Children: Gowtham.

ARAVIND AND HARIPRIYA—Aravind, Dr. V's nephew, is the energetic administrator of the hospital he shares a name with and its only surgeon-MBA. Haripriya is chief of cataract services. Her department handles close to 70 percent of the hospital's surgical volume. Children: Nethra, Arya Venkat.

NARENDRAN AND KALPANA—Narendran is a retinal surgeon and the affable director of Aravind–Coimbatore, where Kalpana, Dr. V's niece, is chief of pediatric services. She and her brother, Aravind S., grew up in the same home as Dr. V. Children: Siddharth, Rahul.

PRAJNA AND LALITHA P.—Prajna, Dr. V's nephew, is chief of cornea services and director of academic training. His nonconformist views help balance aspects of Aravind's work culture. Lalitha P. is chief of microbiology. Children: Aravind P., Meera.

VISHNU AND CHITRA P.—Vishnu, Dr. V's nephew, is the international marketing manager at Aurolab. Chitra P. works with the finance division at LAICO. They left well-established careers in the West to return to the Aravind fold. Children: Anjani.

VIVEK S. AND SANGAMITRA—Vivek S. is a senior employee of Aravind's Instruments Maintenance Department. Sangamitra is a former staff member. Children: Hariprasad.

Karthik and Divya K.—Karthik is a retina specialist, and Divya is currently in residency training at Aravind. They and the couple listed above are actually closer in age to Aravind's third generation than its second. Children: Jyotsna.

## Third Generation

As of 2011, this generation numbers over 25 people ranging in age from under a year to 33 years old. Those listed below are all the grandnieces and grandnephews of Dr. V, and their spouses, who are currently working/studying at the organization or en route to it via medical school.

Employed at Aravind—Dhivya R. (faculty, LAICO), Deepa (senior manager of operations), Sathya (medical officer), Ashok (medical officer).

In ophthalmology residency programs at Aravind—Vivek R., Sankar, Janani.

In medical school—Siddharth, Ram Sudharshan, Vignesh, Gowtham.

*Meanwhile, the fourth generation has arrived,*
*and the Aravind family continues to grow . . .*

# NOTES
◇◇◇◇◇◇◇◇◇◇◇◇

### Introduction: The Power and Paradox of Aravind

1. Data supplied by Aravind Eye Care System, 2011.
2. See "Surgical Quality: Aravind vs. United Kingdom," in "Resources."
3. See "Surgeon Productivity: A U.S.–India Comparison," in "Resources."
4. R. D. Ravindran, R. D. Thulasiraj, "Aravind Eye Care System: Developing Sustainable Eyecare," *Cataract & Refractive Surgery* (March 2006), http://bmctoday.net/crstoday/2006/03/article.asp?f=CRST0306_09.php.
5. Data supplied by LAICO, Aravind Eye Care System, 2011.
6. Justin Huggler interview with Dr. V, Aravind–Madurai, 2005.

### Part I: The 5-Minute, $15 Cure: On Efficiency and Compassion
### Chapter 1: Of Burgers and Blindness

1. World Health Organization, "Visual impairment and blindness," Fact Sheet No. 282, April 2011, www.who.int/mediacentre/factsheets/fs282/en/.
2. Vision 2020: The Right to Sight India, *The Vision 2020 Handbook on Equipping a Secondary Eye Hospital*, Vision 2020, January 2008, www.vision2020india.org/Equip_second_manual.pdf.
3. Aravind Eye Care System, *Annual Report*, Aravind Eye Care System, 2009–2010.
4. Comments from Dr. Aravind Srinivasan are drawn from interviews and informal conversations conducted at Aravind–Madurai between 2003 and 2011.
5. Comments from Dr. V are drawn from interviews, informal conversations, e-mail correspondence, and other interactions that took place at various locations of the Aravind Eye Care System, and at his and other family members' homes, primarily between 2002 and 2006.
6. In 2008–2009, the NHS performed 567,629 eye surgeries (National Health Service, UK, www.hesonline.nhs.uk/Ease/servlet/ContentServer?siteID=1937&categoryID=204). In the same year, Aravind performed 269,577 (Aravind Eye Care System, *Annual Report*, 2008–2009).
7. Howard Larkin, "Managing Eye Care Resources, a Different Approach: What Can Be Learned from the Developing World?" *EuroTimes* 15, issue 10 (2010), www.eurotimes.org/10October/managingeyecare.pdf.
8. Comments from Thulsi Ravilla are drawn from interviews, informal conversations, e-mail correspondence, and other interactions between 2003 and 2011.
9. Original source unknown. Quote taken from *Thingal Udhayam*, Aravind's internal newsletter, Aravind Eye Care System Communications Department, 2004.
10. Regina Herzlinger, *Market-Driven Health Care: Who Wins, Who Loses in the Transformation of America's Largest Service Industry* (New York: Perseus Books Group, 1997).
11. Aravind informally refers to the paraprofessionals who work in its operating rooms and patient wards as "nurses." Technically, they are termed "mid-level ophthalmic personnel." For readability, the informal terminology is used in this book.
12. R. Jose, "Present status of the national programme for control of blindness in India," *Community Eye Health Journal Indian Supplement* 21, no. 65 (2008), www.cehjournal.org/indian/journal/21/jceh_21_65_s103.html.

13. Journal entries of Dr. V's included in this book have occasionally been lightly edited; shorthand forms have been expanded and grammar corrected to preserve meaning.
14. Joe Tidd et al., *Aravind Eye Clinics*, Managing Innovation, 2005, www.managing innovation.com/case_studies/Aravind%20Eye%20Clinics.pdf.
15. Monitor Group, Inclusive Markets Team, *Aravind Eye Care Case Study*, 2008.
16. Larkin, "Managing Eye Care Resources, a Different Approach."
17. Comments from Dr. Haripriya Aravind are drawn from interviews at Aravind–Madurai and observation visits to the operating room conducted between 2003 and 2011.
18. Data supplied by Cataract Services Department, Aravind Eye Care System, 2010.
19. Comments from Dr. David Chang are drawn from a telephone interview conducted in September 2007.
20. The video *High Volume, High Quality, Cost Effective Cataract Surgery for the Developing World—MSICS* shows Dr. Venkatesh performing two back-to-back 3.5-minute cataract surgeries in real time. This video won an award from the American Academy of Ophthalmology, 2004.
21. David Chang, "A 5-Minute, $15 Cure for Blindness," *Cataract & Refractive Surgery Today* (October 2005), http://crstoday.com/PDF%20Articles/1005/CRST1005_Sf_Chang.pdf.
22. Data supplied by Cataract Services Department, Aravind Eye Care System, 2010.
23. D. Yorston, "High-volume surgery in developing countries," *Nature* 19 (2005), www .nature.com/eye/journal/v19/n10/full/6701966a.html.

## Chapter 2: When Free Is Not Enough

1. Jacqueline Novogratz, "Dr. Venkataswamy: A rare life remembered," Acumen Fund, August 7, 2006, http://blog.acumenfund.org/2006/08/07/dr-venkataswamy-a-rare-life-remembered/.
2. Mark Wevill, "Epidemiology, Pathophysiology, Causes, Morphology, and Visual Effects of Cataract," in Myron Yanoff and Jay S. Duker, eds., *Ophthalmology* (London: Mosby Elsevier, 2008).
3. Garry Brian and Hugh Taylor, "Cataract blindness—challenges for the 21st century," *Bulletin of the World Health Organization* 79, no. 3 (2001), www.who.int/bulletin/archives/79(3)249.pdf.
4. Barbara Boughton, "WHO Cares: Ophthalmology Struggles to Meet Global Need," *EyeNet Magazine*, American Academy of Ophthalmology, November–December 2008, www.aao.org/publications/eyenet/200811/ feature.cfm.
5. Interview with Dr. Larry Brilliant, 2003.
6. *Harvard Business Review*, "Aravind Eye Hospital, Madurai, India: In Service for Sight," Harvard Business School, 1993, http://hbr.org/product/aravind-eye-hospital-madurai-india-in-service-for-/an/593098-PDF-ENG.
7. India 2001 Census data, http://censusindia.gov.in/Census_Data_2001/India_at_glance/rural.aspx.
8. Dr. Allen Foster, president, CBM, first used a similar slide to illustrate this idea.
9. Comments from Dr. Fred Munson are primarily drawn from a series of interviews and informal conversations that took place primarily at Aravind–Madurai and his home in Manchester, Michigan, between 2003 and 2011.
10. Data supplied by Outreach Services Department, Aravind Eye Care System, 2011.
11. Data supplied by LAICO, Aravind Eye Care System, 2011.
12. Data supplied by R. Meenakshi Sundaram, director of Outreach Services, Aravind Eye Care System, 2011.

13. G. Venkataswamy and Girija Brilliant, "Social and Economic Barriers to Cataract Surgery in Rural South India: A Preliminary Report," Vision 2020 E-resource, 1981, http://laico.org/v2020resource/files/social_economical_barriers.htm.

14. Sankara Nethralaya performed 15,672 free surgeries in 2009–2010. Sankara Nethralaya, *Annual Report*, 2009–2010.

15. Aravind Eye Care System, *Annual Report*, 2009–2010.

16. Data supplied by Outreach Services Department, Aravind Eye Care System, 2011.

17. Ibid.

18. Comments from Dr. G. Natchiar are drawn from interviews, informal conversations, e-mail correspondence, and other interactions that took place at various locations of the Aravind Eye Care System and at her and other family members' homes, primarily between 2002 and 2011.

19. J. C. Javitt et al., eds., *Disease Control Priorities in Developing Countries* (New York: Oxford University Press for the World Bank, 1993).

20. Comments from R. Meenakshi Sundaram are drawn from interviews and observations of various camp meetings that occurred between 2003 and 2011.

21. The camp meeting proceedings as well as the eye camp described earlier took place in March 2010.

22. V. Ponni and Thenmozhi, interview at Aravind–Madurai, December 2010.

23. Sightsavers International, *Strengthening Eye Health—a Focus for Health Systems*, Sightsavers Policy Briefing, 2010, www.sightsavers.org/in_depth/policy_and_research/health/13064_Strengthening%20eye%20health%20-%20a%20focus%20for%20health%20systems.pdf.

24. P. Sambalingam, interview at Aravind–Madurai, March 2003.

25. Nirmalya Kumar, Lisa Scheer, and Philip Kotler, "From market-driven to market driving," *European Management Journal* 18, issue 2 (April 2000).

## Chapter 3: This Case Won't Fly

1. Aravind–Madurai is the exception. Unanticipated growth and a lack of adjacent land availability meant that it is the only one of its hospitals that houses free and paid services in separate though neighboring buildings.

2. All comments from Dr. P. Namperumalsamy are drawn from interviews and informal conversations conducted between the years 2003 and 2011.

3. Chaim M. Bell et al., "Surgeon Volumes and Selected Patient Outcomes in Cataract Surgery: A Population-Based Analysis," *Ophthalmology* 114, issue 3 (March 2007).

4. C. K. Prahalad, *The Fortune at the Bottom of the Pyramid* (Upper Saddle River, NJ: Wharton School Publishing, 2005).

5. Ibid.

6. Philip B. Crosby, *Quality Is Free: The Art of Making Quality Certain* (New York: McGraw Hill, 1979).

7. Michael E. Porter and Elizabeth Olmsted Teisberg, *Redefining Health Care: Creating Value-Based Competition on Results* (Boston: Harvard Business School Press, 2006).

8. Charles Kenney, "Prescriptions for Health Reform," podcast interview, Blue Cross Blue Shield of Massachusetts Foundation, February 2010, http://bluecrossfoundation.org/Multimedia/Podcasts/Prescriptions.aspx?episode=Kenney.

9. Data supplied by Cataract Services Department, Aravind Eye Care System, 2010.

10. Charles Kenney, *The Best Practice: How the New Quality Movement Is Transforming Medicine* (New York: PublicAffairs, 2008).

11. Data supplied by Cataract Services Department, Aravind Eye Care System, 2010.

12. Aravind Eye Care System Outpatient Procedures, www.aravind.org/generalInfo/eyeexamination.aspx.

13. These data points and all comments from Dr. V. Kasturi Rangan are sourced from interviews with him conducted at the Harvard Business School, Cambridge, Massachusetts, April 2006, July 2007.

14. C. K. Prahalad and Allen Hammond, "Serving the World Profitably—the Payoff for Investing in Poor Countries," *Working Knowledge*, Harvard Business School, November 18, 2002, http://hbswk.hbs.edu/archive/3180.html.

**Part II: Do the Work and Money Will Follow: On Sustainability and Selflessness**

**Chapter 4: An Eye Doctor by Sheer Accident**

1. Govindappa Venkataswamy, *Illuminated Spirit*, the Wit Lectures, Harvard University Divinity School (Mahwah, NJ; Paulist Press, 1994).

2. National Program for Control of Blindness, *Rapid Assessment of Avoidable Blindness—INDIA, Report*, Ministry of Health and Family Welfare, Government of India, 2006–2007, www.vision2020india.org/downloads/RAAB_Report_2007.pdf.

3. Lady Jean Wilson, interview conducted in Brighton, UK, July 2006.

4. Susy Stewart, letter to the founders of Aravind Eye Care System, 1983.

**Chapter 5: Get Less, Do More**

1. Comments by Dr. Viji Srinivasan and Dr. M. Srinivasan are drawn from interviews and informal conversations conducted between 2003 and 2011.

2. Comments by G. Srinivasan are drawn from interviews and informal conversations conducted at Aravind–Madurai between 2003 and 2011.

**Chapter 6: The Power of Creative Constraints**

1. Tim Brown, interview at the IDEO offices in Palo Alto, California, December 2007.

2. Data supplied by Finance Department, Aravind Eye Care System, 2010.

3. Naazneen Karmali, "Aravind Eye Care's Vision for India," *Forbes Asia* (March 15, 2010), www.forbes.com/global/2010/0315/companies-india-madurai-blindness-nam-familys-vision.html.

4. Aravind Eye Care System, "A Debate on Funding Eye Care Fee for Service—Yes or No?" PowerPoint presentation, November 2008.

5. Ibid.

6. Dr. B. Swain, "The Forgotten Tribe—Persons with Disability," PowerPoint presentation, Aakar Asha, 2010.

7. The remainder of the income comes from such sources as interest and dividends; tuition fees for its courses; and sales of its books, manuals, and various applications. Based on Income Statement, Aravind Eye Care System, 2009–2010.

8. This story was related by Brother James Kimpton of Reaching the Unreached in an interview at his organization in Kallupatti, Tamil Nadu, April 2002.

9. Dr. Jack Whitcher, interview at Harmony, the Aravind–Madurai guesthouse, 2003.

10. "The Mother Answers on Money," Light Endless Light, www.lightendlesslight.org/Money/Ma%20_answers_on_money_I_page1.htm.

11. V. Kasturi Rangan, *In Service for Sight*, Harvard Business School case study, 1993.

12. Ravindran and Thulasiraj, "Aravind Eye Care System: Developing Sustainable Eye Care."

13. Regional Committee for the Eastern Mediterranean, "The role of medical devices and equipment in contemporary health care systems and services," World Health Organization, June 2006, http://gis.emro.who.int/HealthSystemObservatory/PDF/TechnicalandDiscussionPapers/The%20role%20of%20medical%20devices%20and%20equipment%20in.pdf.

14. Comments from Dr. Usha Kim are drawn from interviews, informal conversations, and other interactions between 2003 and 2011.

## Chapter 7: You Don't Find People, You Build Them

1. Radha Bai, interview at Aravind–Madurai, 2003.
2. Aravind Eye Care System, 2011.
3. Aravind Eye Care System, 2010.
4. Parveen Banu, interview conducted at Aravind–Pondicherry, 2005.
5. Comments by A. R. Jeeva and R. Sundari are drawn from interviews conducted at Aravind–Madurai in January 2011.
6. Lynne Twist, *The Soul of Money: Transforming Your Relationship with Money and Life* (New York: W. W. Norton & Co., 2003).
7. All India Ophthalmological Society, www.aios.org.
8. U.S. Census Bureau, "Statistical Abstract of the United States: 2011, Section 3, Health and Nutrition," www.census.gov/prod/2011pubs/11statab/health.pdf.
9. Dr. S. R. Krishnadas, interview conducted at Aravind–Madurai, 2003, 2005.
10. Dr. R. Ramakrishnan, interview conducted at Aravind–Tirunelveli, 2005.

## Chapter 8: The Question of the Greedy Doctor

1. LAICO, Aravind Eye Care System. The calculation is based on the number of eye doctors of a particular nationality trained (where training is defined as a course for a duration of one month or longer) at Aravind, and the estimated number of doctors in their country.
2. Bill & Melinda Gates Foundation, "Pioneering Eye Surgery Network Receives 2008 Gates Award for Global Health," www.gatesfoundation.org/press-releases/Pages/india-aravind-eye-care-award-080521.aspx.
3. Comments by Dr. Christine Melton are drawn from interviews and informal conversations in New York City between 2006 and 2011.
4. Dr. Pulin Shah, interview at Harmony, the Aravind–Madurai guesthouse, 2005.
5. Dr. Dhananjay Shukla, interview at LAICO offices, January 2011.
6. Dr. Carl Kupfer, phone interview, November 2007.
7. Dr. Rathinam Sivakumar, interview at Aravind–Madurai, 2003.

## Part III: A Vast Surrender: On Innovation and Inner Transformation
## Chapter 9: Humankind Is a Work in Progress

1. Sri Aurobindo, *Savitri*, Sri Aurobindo Ashram Trust, 1950.
2. Craig Hamilton, "Why Sri Aurobindo Is Cool," *EnlightenNext* (Spring–Summer 2002), www.enlightennext.org/magazine/j21/aurobindo.asp.
3. Venkataswamy, *Illuminated Spirit*.
4. Dr. William Stewart, introductory comments made at the Pioneers in Health and Healing award ceremony at the Institute for Health & Healing, February 2005.
5. Comments from Vijay Poddar are drawn from an interview at his home office in Pondicherry, 2003.

## Chapter 10: Dr. V's Practice of Perfect Vision

1. Dr. Ramachandra Pararajasegaram, interview at Harmony, the Aravind–Madurai guesthouse, April 2010.
2. Comments from Dr. Larry Brilliant are drawn from an interview at the Seva Foundation offices in Berkeley, California, July 2003.
3. Comments from Ram Dass are drawn from an interview conducted at Open Secret bookstore, San Rafael, California, 2003.

## Chapter 11: Manufacturing a Revolution

1. Myron Yanoff and Jay S. Duker, eds., *Ophthalmology* (London: Mosby Elsevier, 2008).

2. David J. Apple, "A pioneer in the quest to eradicate world blindness," Bulletin of the World Health Organization 81, no. 10 (2003), www.who.int/bulletin/volumes/81/10/756-757%20(03816).pdf.

3. Buddy D. Ratner et al., eds., *Biomaterials Science: An Introduction to Materials in Medicine* (London: Elsevier Academic Press, 2004).

4. Apple, "A pioneer in the quest to eradicate world blindness."

5. Comments by Dr. Richard Litwin and Judith Litwin are drawn from interviews conducted in Madurai in 2003, and at their home as well as the Seva Foundation offices in Berkeley, California, September 2007 and November 2010, respectively.

6. Richard Kratz, "From von Graefe to Kelman: A timeline of ophthalmic advances in the 20th century," *Cataract & Refractive Surgery Today* 3 (March 2004), http://bmctoday.net/crstoday/pdfs/crst0304_f2_kratz.pdf.

7. Ibid.

8. V. Kasturi Rangan, *Aurolab: Bringing First-World Technology to the Third-World Blind*, Harvard Business School case study, 2007.

9. Ibid.

10. Comments from Dr. Suzanne Gilbert drawn from interviews and conversations conducted at Aravind–Madurai, 2003; in Lumbini, Nepal, 2005; and at the Seva offices in Berkeley, California, between 2006 and 2010.

11. Ibrahim et al., "Making Sight Affordable (Part I): Aurolab Pioneers Production of Low-Cost Technology for Cataract Surgery," MIT Press Journals, *Innovations* 1, no. 3 (Summer 2006).

12. Ibid.

13. Ibid.

14. Jaspal Sandhu et al., "Appropriate Design of Medical Technologies for Emerging Regions: The Case of Aurolab," 2005 Proceedings of IMECE: International Mechanical Engineering Conference and Exposition, November 2005, http://best.berkeley.edu/pubs/05_1101_P.pdf.

15. Data supplied by Aurolab; total sales for 1992–2010 were 11,849,699.

## Chapter 12: Maximize Service, Not Profit

1. Kris Herbst, "Business with Humanitarian Goals," *India Together* (February 2003), www.indiatogether.org/2003/feb/hlt-lwcstman.htm.

2. Ibid.

3. Ibrahim et al., "Making Sight Affordable."

4. Data supplied by Aurolab, 2010.

5. Comments from Dr. Bala Krishnan are drawn from interviews and informal conversations conducted at Aurolab between 2003 and 2011.

6. Susan Lewallen and R. D. Thulasiraj, "Eliminating cataract blindness: How do we apply lessons from Asia to sub-Saharan Africa?" *Global Public Health* 5, issue 6 (2010).

7. Buoyed by the program's success, the Indian government continued the funding even after the World Bank project finished. This arrangement is still in effect today, and the subsidy payments from the government, now roughly $16 per patient, are more regular than they used to be.

8. Data supplied by Aravind Eye Care System.

9. Data supplied by Aravind Eye Care System. Two percent of the patients have conditions too complicated for impants and so get the aphakic surgery.

10. Data supplied by Aravind Eye Care System.

11. Comments from Sriram Ravilla are drawn from interviews conducted at Aurolab between 2003 and 2011.

12. WHO Informal Consultation, "Guidelines for the Manufacture of Intraocular Lenses by Cooperating Organizations in Developing Countries," World Health Organization, 1994, http://whqlibdoc.who.int/hq/1994/WHO_PBL_94.39.pdf.

13. David J. Apple, "Letters to Editor," *Ophthalmology* 6, no. 6 (June 1995).

14. Confirmed by R. D. Sriram, director of operations, and Mr. Sivanand, marketing manager, Aurolab, 2011.

15. Rangan, *Aurolab: Bringing First-World Technology to the Third-World Blind.*

16. Ibid.

17. Ibid.

18. Ibid.

19. Data supplied by Aurolab. Patient demand for imported brands leads Aravind to buy from other suppliers as well.

### Chapter 13: The Flip Side of a Visionary

1. Sri Aurobindo, *Essays in Philosphy and Yoga, Shorter Works 1910–1950* (Pondicherry, India: Sri Aurobindo Ashram Trust, 1998), www.aurobindo.ru/workings/sa/16/essays_in_philosophy_and_yoga_13b_e.pdf.

2. Astrid E. Fletcher et al., "Low Uptake of Eye Services in Rural India," *Archives of Ophthalmology* 117 (October 1999), http://archopht.ama-assn.org/cgi/content/full/117/10/1393.

3. Intel Corporation, *Enabling Eye Care in Rural India, Research at Intel*, 2006, http://blogs.intel.com/research/eyecareindia_%20Final.pdf.

4. Cisco, *Aravind Eye Hospital: Eye on Hope*, www.cisco.com/web/IN/thehumannetwork/assets/pdf/Aravind-Eye-Hospital.pdf.

5. The Swedish Program for ICT in Developing Regions, *E-Health Brings Vision to Blind in India*, www.spidercenter.org/news/e-health-brings-vision-blind-india.

6. Data supplied by Aravind Eye Care System.

7. Comments from Sonesh Surana are drawn from informal conversations at Aravind–Madurai, 2005, and in Belmont, California, November 2010.

### Part IV: Training Your Competition: On Replication and Self-Awareness

### Chapter 14: If We Can Do It, So Can You

1. World Sight Day, Key Message, Vision 2020, October 11, 2007 (Vision 2020 is a joint program between the World Health Organization and the International Agency for the Prevention of Blindness).

2. World Health Organization, *Visual impairment and blindness*, Fact Sheet No. 282, updated April 2011.

3. Prajwal Ciryam, "The Tragedy of Easy Problems," Gresham College lecture, March 2, 2011, www.gresham.ac.uk/lectures-and-events/the-tragedy-of-easy-problems.

4. World Health Organization, "Medium-term strategic plan 2008–2013: Progress report," May 11, 2006, http://apps.who.int/gb/pbac/pdf_files/fourth/PBAC4_4-en.pdf.

5. Data supplied by LAICO, Aravind Eye Care System, 2011.

6. Seva Foundation in Nepal, www.seva.ca/sevainnepal.htm.

7. Data supplied by Lumbini Eye Institute, Nepal.

8. Geneva Mission Lions Club, Lions History, www.genevamissionlions.com/international/international/history.html.

9. Ram Dass, in an internal letter circulated among the Seva Foundation leadership, 1990.

10. Dr. Madan Deshpande, interview at the H. V. Desai Eye Hospital in Pune, Maharashtra, April 2006.

11. Ministry of Health, Republic of Rwanda, "National Plan for the Fight Against Blindness," 2002.
12. Aravind Eye Care System, *Annual Report*, 2009–2010.
13. Comments by Dr. Asim K. Sil drawn from interviews conducted in Chaitanyapur, West Bengal, April 2006.
14. A. K. Sivakumar, *Counselling—A success story*, LAICO White Paper, Vision 2020 Resource, 1998, http://laico.org/v2020resource/files/Counselling%20-%20A%20 success%20story.pdf.
15. Deepa Krishnan, interview in Chaitanyapur, West Bengal, April 2006.
16. Swami Biswanathananda, interview in Chaitanyapur, West Bengal, April 2006.

### Chapter 15: Aravind Is Like Kilimanjaro

1. Kilimanjaro Centre for Community Ophthalmology, www.kcco.net/orgstrinance.html.
2. Data supplied by LAICO, Aravind Eye Care System, 2011.
3. All the comments by Kilimanjaro Centre for Community Ophthalmology staff were drawn from interviews conducted onsite in Moshi, August 2006.
4. Tanzania: IAPB News, "Report on Human Resources Development for middle level eye-care workers in Eastern Africa," July 2005, http://laico.org/v2020resource/files/eastern_africa.htm. India: Ravi Thomas et al., "Public Health and the Eye," *Survey of Ophthalmology* 50, no. 1 (January–February 2005). The United States: U.S. Census Bureau, Statistical Abstract of the United States: 2011, www.census.gov/compendia/statab/cats/health_nutrition.html.
5. R. Meenakshi Sundaram, *Aravind's Model of Community Outreach*, white paper, Vision 2020 resource, http://laico.org/v2020resource/files/aravindmodel_communityoutreach.pdf.
6. Susan Lewallen and R. D. Thulasiraj, "Eliminating cataract blindness: How do we apply lessons from Asia to sub-Saharan Africa?" *Global Public Health* 5, issue 6 (2010).
7. Seva Foundation, "Building a Bridge to Eye Care," www.seva.org/site/PageServer?pagename=News_KCCO_Africa.
8. Sashipriya Karumanchi, interview at the LAICO offices, January 2011.

### Chapter 16: Business, Politics, and Prahalad's Dare

1. Data supplied by LAICO, Aravind Eye Care System, 2010.
2. Kanishka Singh, interview in New Delhi, July 2006.
3. Comments by Javier Okhuysen and Carlos Orellana are drawn from an interview via Skype, March 2011.
4. Himalayan Cataract Project, "HCP's Eye Care Model," www.cureblindness.org/what/hcp-eye-care-model/.
5. Geoffrey Tabin, "The Cataract Blindness Challenge: Innovations Case Discussion: Aravind Eye Care System," MIT Press Journals, *Innovations* 2, no. 4 (Fall 2007), www.mitpressjournals.org/toc/itgg/2/4.

### Chapter 17: Aravind in America

1. U.S. Department of Health and Human Services, Centers for Medicare and Medicaid Services, www.cms.gov/NationalHealthExpendData/25_NHE_Fact_Sheet.asp.
2. Physicians for a National Health Program, "Single-Payer National Health Insurance," www.pnhp.org/facts/single-payer-resources.
3. HealthPAC Online, "Health Care Statistics in the United States," www.healthpaconline.net/health-care-statistics-in-the-united-states.htm.
4. Regina Herzlinger, phone interview, December 2010.

5. Dr. Bruce Spivey, interview in San Francisco, California, September 2010.
6. David Roe, interview in Oakland, California, October 2010.
7. Larkin, "Managing Eye Care Resources, a Different Approach."
8. Quote supplied by David Roe, October 2010.
9. Dr. William Stewart, interview in Muir Beach, California, October 2010.
10. William Stewart, M.D., *Deep Medicine: Harnessing the Source of Your Healing Power* (Oakland, CA: New Harbinger Publications, 2009).
11. Institute for Health & Healing, www.cpmc.org/services/ihh/about/.
12. Mike Myers, in a letter to Dr. V's family, July 2006.
13. Antoine de Saint-Exupéry (1900–1944).

**Part V: How Do You Retire a Saint? On Change and Integrity**

**Chapter 18: Same Same but Different**

1. World Diabetes Foundation, "Diabetes facts," www.worlddiabetesfoundation.org/composite-35.htm.
2. Mayo Clinic, "Treatment of Diabetic Retinopathy," www.mayoclinic.org/retinal-diseases/diabetic-retinopathy.html.
3. Comments from Dr. Prajna Venkatesh are drawn from interviews and informal conversations conducted at Aravind–Madurai between 2003 and 2011.

**Chapter 19: All Will Pass from the Earth**

1. Dr. Kalpana, interview at Aravind–Coimbatore, July 2005.
2. Dr. George Thomas, interview at Aravind–Madurai, January 2011.
3. Data supplied by Publishing Division, Aravind Eye Care System, 2011.

**Chapter 20: The Bottom Is Moving Up**

1. Comments from the third generation of Aravind's family are drawn from conversations at an informal retreat they conducted at Thekkady, Kerala, May 2010.
2. Baylor University, Institute for Family Business, "Seminar Focuses on Survival of Family Businesses," September 4, 1998, www.baylor.edu/pr/news.php? action=story &story=2304.

**Chapter 21: A Place to Practice Truth**

1. Comments by Dr. Kim Ramaswamy are drawn from interviews and informal conversations conducted in 2010 and 2011.
2. Khomba Singh, "Vasan Eyecare, Eye Q in talks for PE funding," *Economic Times*, March 31, 2011, http://articles.economictimes.indiatimes.com/2011-03-31/news/29366068_1_eyecare-centres-venture-capital-pe.
3. Name changed to respect patient's privacy.

# ACKNOWLEDGMENTS

*Everything is held together with stories.*

*That is all that is holding us together, stories and compassion.*

—Barry Lopez, *Winter Count*

First the back story: In 2002, Pavithra Mehta (then Krishnan) sent a formal e-mail request to her granduncle, Dr. V, asking if she could come in each morning to interview him in his office at Aravind–Madurai. She doesn't fully know why she did this. But it changed her life irrevocably. "You can come every day," he replied, "including Sunday." So she did. In those mornings of questions and answers that later flowed into their daily readings from *Savitri*, she first began *listening* to a story she had heard for much of her life. It turned out to be one of the most incandescent, healing, and alive stories that she had ever come across. She wanted very much to be a part of it. Since she doesn't do eye surgery, she began to gather up little bits of the story instead—the way a squirrel gathers acorns for winter. This is not the most efficient way to write a book. (Thankfully, this book knew how it needed to be written and made its own arrangements.) In 2003, she made a film called *Infinite Vision*. Two years later, a young woman named Suchitra Shenoy arrived in Madurai. And because they trusted serendipity, these two strangers decided to collaborate on the project of a lifetime. And really that is the best explanation they have for the blessing of volunteering together on this book.

These thank-yous are from both of them.

THE CORE OF this story is Dr. V, his magnificent vision, his humanity and love. We miss him greatly. But if we listen hard, we can hear him saying, *"Very good, very good."* He is still with us in many ways, perhaps most vividly in the founding team he groomed. Drs. Natchiar, Nam, and Viji, and both of the Srinivasans, opened their lives to us. They continue to blow us away with their searing dedication, wisdom, and compassion. If we captured even a fraction of their spirit here, we are content.

Steve Piersanti recognized this story immediately. He gave us a unique platform that allowed us to tell it with integrity. He, Jeevan Sivasubramaniam, Dianne Platner, and the passionate team at Berrett-Koehler were an honor to work with. The talent of Linda Jupiter, Elissa Rabellino, and Laura Lind touched every page. Our official early reviewers, Dr. David Kerns, Joshua O'Conner, and Ellyn Kerr, shaped this effort with their feedback. Katherine Armstrong did too. She gave us the gift of hearing so clearly the beating heart of the story. Our friends Somik Raha, Anne Que, Ragunath Padmanabhan, Devika Mahadevan, Gaurav Jaswal, and Rahul Brown read the raw draft. Their comments forced us to dive deeper. So did Mark Jacobs, who is responsible for more of the spirituality in this book than he will ever publicly own up to. Seva Foundation's Suzanne Gilbert and Girija Brilliant read the manuscript and provided support when they could not possibly have had the time. Thulsi Ravilla read it late at night and aboard many different flights. He helped us be accurate. J. P. Singh was an early supporter. Kirsten Sandberg was the first person in publishing to believe in this book. Her steady encouragement and warm advice were invaluable.

The friendship and goodwill of a bright circle of individuals involved with Aravind's work brought this book to life. Larry Brilliant, Tim Brown, David Chang, Ram Dass, Suzanne Gilbert, Regina Herzlinger, Richard and Judith Litwin, Jacqueline Novogratz, Vijay Poddar, Kasturi Rangan, David Roe, and Bruce Spivey, among many others, gave generously of their time, stories, and insight into Aravind. So did Asim Sil and Swamiji, who welcomed us to Chaitanyapur, and gracious hosts Susan Lewallen and Paul Courtright in Moshi. Raj Kumar and Mike Myers took beautiful photos especially for us. A handful of other wonderful photographers—Moses Ceaser, Rameshwar Das, Willie Davis, David Heiden, Murugan, Ryan Pyle, Ashesh Shah, and Jacques J. Vekemens—also contributed their work. More than 350 people helped us choose the title that Sonesh Surana dreamt up. There isn't room to include *all* of the remarkable people at Aravind whose daily actions make this a real-life story. But without you there would be no *Infinite Vision*. You made us think, wonder, laugh, cry, and grow. This is your book, written for the generations past, present, and future (especially future). A bow of gratitude to each one of you. And to healers of the world everywhere.

*Pavithra adds:* Suchi came to this project with a sister's heart and such grace. Her intuitive understanding of Aravind and deep respect for its story were a gift to our partnership. She poured effort, insight, and incredible energy into six months that turned into six years. There is no turning back. She is family now. My partner on the *Infinite Vision* film, the gifted and lovely Ayla Gustafson, helped build a foundation for this book. Amanda Greco's keen ear and beautiful heart made epic contributions to multiple drafts. To share a street, this story, and much else with her is incredibly special. Amulya Gopalakrishnan's words were a talisman. Same for the poet-doctor Sriram Shamasunder. Betsy Beaumon and Nicole Gnutzman gave me flexibility when I most needed it. Maria Thomas bravely helped create a tree from a forest. I cherish the time spent with Lady Jean Wilson and Claire Hicks in Brighton. I met Sir John Wilson only once, but he was everything I imagined a knight to be. "Keep writing," he told me. "It keeps you civilized." And he was right. It was an honor to meet and interview C. K. Prahalad and Carl Kupfer while they were with us. Their contributions live on. The love and unconditional support of Fred and Mary

Munson, Christine Melton, Meg and Dick Lueker, and Bill and Susy Stewart are woven into the pages of my life and this book. My assorted aunts, uncles, and cousins at Aravind have let me shadow them for years. They answered an inordinate number of questions and continue to humble me with their intelligence, candor, and affection. Chitra Ravilla, Dhivya Ramasamy, and Deepa Krishnan are three women too good to belong to the same family. But they do, and we could not have done without their ability to send us whatever was needed. Justlikethat. Deepa also happens to be my sister and one of my heroes. She was the first person in the family to read the early draft. I will never forget what she said. My parents, Varalakshmi and Bala Krishnan, gave me more than they will ever know. I am so grateful to be their daughter. Nipun and Guri Mehta are notes of tremendous grace in my life; they and the CharityFocus community kept me close to what this journey is about. My parents-in-love, Harshida and Dinesh Mehta, nourished me along the way. Viral Mehta, your love and wisdom inspire me. Thank you for being in all my best stories, and reminding me to look beyond them.

*Suchitra adds:* It is rare to find oneself in the presence of a legend. Dr. V and his legacy have shaped my life in many ways. For that I am deeply grateful. The depth of my involvement in his story and the Aravind family would not have been possible without Pavi. We experienced being told to comb our hair and straighten our saris; meteor showers in rural Tamil Nadu; the thrill of finding new material; and much, much else as sisters-in-arms.

For all of you who have loved and supported me on this journey and at every way station before—you know who you are—*thank you.*

—Pavithra K. Mehta, Belmont, California
—Suchitra Shenoy, Hyderabad, India
July 2011

# NAME INDEX

# ABOUT THE AUTHORS

## PAVITHRA MEHTA

Photographer: Viral Mehta

Pavithra K. Mehta is a writer-filmmaker, in a family of 21 (and still counting) eye surgeons. This might explain her fondness for stories that help people see. Her award-winning documentary *Infinite Vision* followed the life and work of Dr. V, who is her granduncle. He once created a nine-item To-Do List for her that she has yet to complete. (Item #4 reads: Quality Care For All.) Pavithra is drawn to the space where service and storytelling meet. She started Aravind's story archive in 2002, while freelancing on film and writing projects for nonprofits in India. Later she headed the volunteer program at Benetech, an innovative nonprofit in Silicon Valley, which runs the world's largest digital library of accessible books for people who are blind. She is currently on the boards of the Aravind Eye Foundation and Service Space, an organization rooted in inner change, that designs and runs experiments in generosity. She co-leads its inspiring news portal, DailyGood, as well as its pay-it-forward restaurant, Karma Kitchen, and is working on her next book. Pavithra studied English literature and broadcast journalism. She lives in the Bay Area with her husband and travels back to Madurai each year. Rumi, hillsides, and other noble friends help her write.

## Suchitra Shenoy

Suchitra Shenoy grew up on bedtime stories steeped in science and a vivid moral imagination. The robots were *always* good. Intermittently, she was whisked to Indian villages. There, the stories were quite different. Not surprisingly, she was drawn to work in the social sector. In little over a decade her work has encompassed health care, housing, education, agriculture, and financial services. She is currently working on addressing inclusive finance, as the co-founder of a start-up dedicated to financial services for the poor. As a founding member of the Inclusive Markets team at the Monitor Group, an international consulting firm, she examined market-based solutions to poverty, especially business models that serve the poor as customers and as producers. She is on the advisory board of the Youth 4 Jobs Foundation, which works closely with companies to give impoverished young people the skills they need for meaningful employment. Suchitra enjoys sharing good ideas, especially inspiring ones. She has done so at Deloitte Research, Columbia University Business School, Stanford University's d.school, and the Bangladesh Rural Advancement Committee (BRAC). She holds degrees from Brandeis University and the London School of Economics. She is moved by words, music, and photography.

Photographer: Shreedhar Kanetkar

# CONNECTING TO
# ARAVIND'S WORK

◇◇◇◇◇◇◇◇◇◇◇◇◇◇◇◇◇◇◇◇◇◇◇◇◇◇◇◇◇◇

One hundred percent of the authors' royalties for *Infinite Vision* are being gifted to the Aravind Eye Care System. By purchasing this book, you have made a contribution to its crucial sight-restoring work. On behalf of the extended Aravind community, thank you.

To learn more about the people, business practices, and guiding principles in *Infinite Vision*, visit the book's website:

### www.infinitevisionaries.com

This site offers a window into Aravind through bonus interviews, links to in-depth articles, a photo gallery, and more. It also hosts the film Infinite Vision, a moving 35-minute documentary directed by one of the authors, which brings Aravind's work vividly to life and includes interviews with Dr. V and other founding members.

To learn about volunteer opportunities at Aravind and other ways of contributing to its inspiring mission, visit the Aravind Eye Foundation (AEF) website:

### www.aravindeyefoundation.org

AEF is a nonprofit organization in the United States that leverages various forms of support for the Aravind Eye Care System.

## Berrett–Koehler
Publishers

**Berrett-Koehler** is an independent publisher dedicated to an ambitious mission: *Creating a World That Works for All.*

We believe that to truly create a better world, action is needed at all levels—individual, organizational, and societal. At the individual level, our publications help people align their lives with their values and with their aspirations for a better world. At the organizational level, our publications promote progressive leadership and management practices, socially responsible approaches to business, and humane and effective organizations. At the societal level, our publications advance social and economic justice, shared prosperity, sustainability, and new solutions to national and global issues.

A major theme of our publications is "Opening Up New Space." Berrett-Koehler titles challenge conventional thinking, introduce new ideas, and foster positive change. Their common quest is changing the underlying beliefs, mindsets, institutions, and structures that keep generating the same cycles of problems, no matter who our leaders are or what improvement programs we adopt.

We strive to practice what we preach—to operate our publishing company in line with the ideas in our books. At the core of our approach is stewardship, which we define as a deep sense of responsibility to administer the company for the benefit of all of our "stakeholder" groups: authors, customers, employees, investors, service providers, and the communities and environment around us.

We are grateful to the thousands of readers, authors, and other friends of the company who consider themselves to be part of the "BK Community." We hope that you, too, will join us in our mission.

### A BK Business Book

This book is part of our BK Business series. BK Business titles pioneer new and progressive leadership and management practices in all types of public, private, and nonprofit organizations. They promote socially responsible approaches to business, innovative organizational change methods, and more humane and effective organizations.

# Berrett–Koehler
# Publishers

A community dedicated to creating
a world that works for all

### Visit Our Website: www.bkconnection.com

Read book excerpts, see author videos and Internet movies, read
our authors' blogs, join discussion groups, download book apps, find
out about the BK Affiliate Network, browse subject-area libraries of
books, get special discounts, and more!

### Subscribe to Our Free E-Newsletter, the *BK Communiqué*

Be the first to hear about new publications, special discount offers,
exclusive articles, news about bestsellers, and more! Get on the list
for our free e-newsletter by going to **www.bkconnection.com**.

### Get Quantity Discounts

Berrett-Koehler books are available at quantity discounts for orders
of ten or more copies. Please call us toll-free at (800) 929-2929 or
email us at **bkp.orders@aidcvt.com**.

### Join the BK Community

BKcommunity.com is a virtual meeting place where people from
around the world can engage with kindred spirits to create a world
that works for all. BKcommunity.com members may create their own
profiles, blog, start and participate in forums and discussion groups,
post photos and videos, answer surveys, announce and register for
upcoming events, and chat with others online in real time. Please join
the conversation!